The Wilt
Cotswolds

Exploring Historic Wiltshire 3

Ken Watts

Hobnob Press

First published in the United Kingdom in 2007 by The Hobnob Press,
PO Box 1838, East Knoyle, Salisbury SP3 6FA.

British Library Cataloguing in Publication Data
A catalogue record for this book is available from the British Library.

ISBN 978-0-946418-65-7

Typeset in Octavian and Zurich Black
Typesetting and origination by John Chandler
Printed in Great Britain by Salisbury Printing Company Ltd, Salisbury

This book is a sequel to the same author's two earlier volumes, both published by Ex Libris Press:

Exploring Historic Wiltshire, volume 1: North, 1997 (reprinted 2001)
Exploring Historic Wiltshire, volume 2: South, 1998 (reprinted 2002)

The illustration on the title page is of Colerne on its hill from the south
(see page 168).

Contents

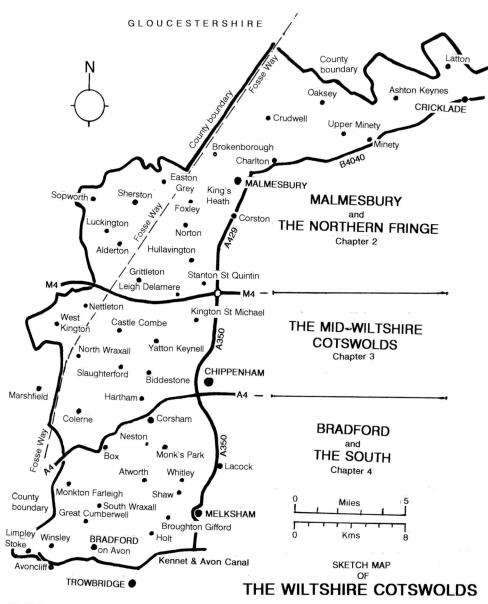

GLOUCESTERSHIRE

N

County
boundary

Latton

Oaksey

Ashton Keynes

Crudwell

Upper Minety

CRICKLADE

Minety

Fosse Way

County boundary

Brokenborough

Charlton

B4040

Easton
Grey

King's
Heath

MALMESBURY

Sopworth

Sherston

Foxley

MALMESBURY
and
THE NORTHERN FRINGE
Chapter 2

Corston

Luckington

Fosse Way

Norton

A429

Alderton

Hullavington

Grittleton

Stanton St Quintin

Leigh Delamere

M4

M4

Nettleton

Kington St Michael

West
Kington

Castle Combe

THE MID-WILTSHIRE
COTSWOLDS
Chapter 3

North Wraxall

Yatton Keynell

A350

Slaughterford

Biddestone

CHIPPENHAM

Marshfield

Hartham

A4

Colerne

Corsham

BRADFORD
and
THE SOUTH
Chapter 4

Neston

A350

Box

Monk's Park

Fosse Way

Atworth

Whitley

Lacock

A4

Monkton Farleigh

Shaw

0   Miles   5

County
boundary

South Wraxall

Great Cumberwell

MELKSHAM

0   Kms   8

Limpley
Stoke

Winsley

BRADFORD
on Avon

Broughton Gifford

Holt

Avoncliff

Kennet & Avon Canal

SKETCH MAP
OF
THE WILTSHIRE COTSWOLDS

TROWBRIDGE

KW 2006

General Introduction

THE GLOUCESTERSHIRE COTSWOLDS with their stone-wall divided wolds and their buildings built almost entirely of their indigenous honey-coloured limestone are justifiably recognised to be one of the most beautiful districts of England. Wiltshire, with its extensive areas of smoothly rounded undulating chalk hills, has tended to be characterised as a rather bleak sparsely uninhabited downland county, although around its north-western and northern fringes adjoining Gloucestershire there exists a region of limestone uplands whose topographical and architectural characteristics so closely resemble those of the Gloucestershire Cotswolds that this district is in places indistinguishable from them.

This part of Wiltshire has often been virtually ignored by the topographers and I as had many writers before me, when choosing the areas to be included in my *Exploring Historic Wiltshire: Volume 1, North*, neglected this district with which I was then less familiar, and devoted that book generally to the north Wiltshire chalk downlands. When subsequently commissioned by North Wiltshire District Council to write a walks publication for the area of Wiltshire that they administered I acquired the knowledge of this district which, augmented by more intensive study and exploration of the area, has enabled me to write this Volume 3 *of Exploring Historic Wiltshire* under the title *The Wiltshire Cotswolds*.

Any attempt to define boundaries for the Wiltshire Cotswolds is likely to be regarded as arbitrary. For the purposes of this book it has been assumed to consist of two areas, the first being the northern fringe of Wiltshire adjoining Gloucestershire to its north and bordered by the B4040 road to its south and by the A429 to its west. The other district included in this book is the limestone area of north-west Wiltshire that is bordered by Gloucestershire to its west and north, the A429 and the A350 to its east, and the Kennet and Avon canal to its south. These areas are delineated on the map opposite.

In *The Making of the English Landscape* (1955) Professor W. G. Hoskins wrote :

> The English landscape itself, to those who know how to read it aright, is the richest historical record we possess. There are discoveries to be made in it

for which no written documents exist, or ever have existed. There is no part of England, however unpromising it may appear at first sight, that is not full of questions for those who have a sense of the past.

With this in mind I have attempted to humanise this book by including, in addition to descriptions of its visible topography and architecture, some of the history that lies hidden in the landscape. Short biographies of relevant historic persons are also included, as are some anecdotes and folklore associated with the region, and accounts of interesting episodes including historic crimes and society scandals. Many of the subjects are listed in the list of contents on pages iii-v.

Few of the many books that have been published on the Cotswolds have recognised that they extend beyond Gloucestershire into this region of north Wiltshire, that was in 1949 described by the prolific Wiltshire-born writer Ralph Whitlock (in his *Wiltshire* volume of Elek's 'Vision of England' series) as 'The fortunate North-West', and as 'the most favoured region of Wiltshire' that was a 'fine stone country . . . containing some of the best building stone in England'.

Parts of this region have now been included in The Cotswold Area of Outstanding Natural Beauty that contain in the words of Mr Whitlock 'stately stone houses, sturdy stone cottages, impressive stone town halls, lovely stone bridges, and other evidences of loving care, supreme craftsmanship and plenty of money being lavished on some of the most responsive material in the world'. This emphasis on the supreme quality of the architecture of this area explains why this book differs in both format and content from my previous volumes of *Exploring Historic Wiltshire* which generally described the essentially rural topography of the chalk downlands of Wiltshire. This book devotes more attention than did its predecessors to architecture and towns, although it is however consistent with those earlier volumes in being written for people who appreciate that knowledge of its history heightens enjoyment of landscape, and I was therefore pleased when a reviewer suggested that the first two volumes 'read as if a good friend is walking beside you, pointing out views, passing on anecdotes, and with the modesty of true scholarship sharing a depth of knowledge that comes from a lifelong, heartfelt enthusiasm'.

Undertaking the research, exploring the terrain, and obtaining the photographs for this book, has provided me with much enjoyment and I earnestly hope that readers of this book will derive similar pleasure from exploring the countryside, towns, and villages of this region. The Gloucestershire poet Ivor Gurney (1890-1937), who loved the Cotswolds, sang (for he set his poem to music) 'Only the wanderer, Knows England's graces, Or can anew see clear, Familiar faces', and I hope that this book will help its readers to 'anew see clear' some of the finer aspects of the

Wiltshire Cotswolds, like Gurney 'come across the strangest things in walks', and perhaps discover some of those small and often unconsidered pleasures that all of us sometimes fail to notice.

Recognising that many people like to plan their own walks I have generally left readers to devise their own routes incorporating the features in which they are interested, but for those who like to be offered planned walks at the end of each of the three topographical chapters (Chapters 2, 3 and 4) I have suggested a number of walks that I have enjoyed. These walks include directions and sketch maps, but I must emphasise that although they follow public rights-of-way the description in this book of a place or building does not necessarily imply any current right of public access. A single sheet of the 1:50,000 Ordnance Survey Landranger maps (Number 173 Swindon & Devizes) covers the entire area described in this book, apart from a few very small areas in the extreme north of Wiltshire and the promontory of Wiltshire that extends west of Winsley to Midford, and shows the current rights-of-way.

In the interests of accuracy and in order to avoid the necessity for long descriptions of location in rural areas where landmarks are often lacking I have included within round brackets in the text – for example (148763) – six-figure map references to leave readers in no doubt about precise locations. These map references are to the National Grid, but with the ST and SU prefixes omitted. Explanation of the easily understood National Grid reference system is provided on all Ordnance Survey maps.

The photographs are generally my own, and to facilitate use of the book each chapter is divided under prominent sub-headings that with their page numbers are listed in the list of contents that precedes this introduction. Appended to this book is a brief bibliography and a comprehensive index of persons and places.

By attempting to be as informative as possible this book contains so much detailed information that I fear occasional errors may have been made. I shall therefore be pleased to be informed of any factual mistakes that readers, many of whom will have better knowledge of their own districts than myself, may discover.

It remains for me to acknowledge the very great help that I have received from the staffs of Wiltshire Reference and Local Studies Library and Wiltshire & Swindon Record Office at Trowbridge when researching this book and its two predecessors, and the encouragement of my publisher Dr John Chandler.

Ken Watts,
Trowbridge, Wiltshire,
November 2007

Notes relating to the Suggested Walks in Chapters 2, 3 and 4

1: As the maps of the walks are merely sketch maps they contain insufficient detail to be used as walking maps and are therefore no substitute for the relevant Ordnance Survey maps that with their definitive information on current public rights-of-way should be followed by all walkers.

2: Landranger Map 173 (Swindon and Devizes) covers all of the suggested walks, but some walkers may prefer to use the appropriate larger scale Explorer maps.

3: The walk directions include National Grid map references in round brackets e.g. (- - -) and also cross-references to relevant information in the text in square brackets, e.g. [- - -].

4: The letters N, S, E, and W in the walks directions obviously refer to the cardinal points of the compass. Walkers following the directions are therefore advised to carry a simple pocket compass.

5: The walk directions are believed to be correct at the time of writing but may become outdated by subsequent changes. Rights-of-way are sometimes altered, and those shown on the current Ordnance Survey map should always be followed when undertaking the walks.

1
Some General Aspects of The Wiltshire Cotswolds

IN ORDER TO AVOID the inevitable repetition that would take place if some subjects constantly recurred in the topographical and historical Chapters 2, 3, and 4, this chapter contains background information on a number of subjects that have influenced the topography, architecture and history of the Wiltshire Cotswolds. These subjects are covered in general terms but in some detail, the more important ones being architecture, dry-stone walls, sheep-farming, cloth-manufacturing and stone-mining, although several other less influential subjects are described, as listed in the schedule of contents on pages iii-v.

The Provenance of the Name
The Wiltshire Cotswolds

WHEN AS A WALK LEADER or in conversation I have mentioned the Wiltshire Cotswolds reactions are sometimes of surprise and at other times incredulity, but I believe that anyone who is truly familiar with the topography and architecture of north-west Wiltshire will understand my use of this term.

Having grown up and spent most of my life living near the southern end of the Wiltshire Cotswolds I have for long recognised their close relationship to the Gloucestershire Cotswolds, and have always regarded parts of north Wiltshire as being effectively part of the Cotswolds. One of my many justifications for titling this book *The*

Wiltshire Cotswolds is the fact that north-west Wiltshire has been included in the official Cotswold Area of Outstanding Natural Beauty that is the largest AONB in England or Wales. Although my title may be regarded by some as being controversial it in fact has a perfectly good official provenance in that the local authority has set up at Bathford beside the A363 five miles north-west of Bradford on Avon a stone with text informing passers-by that by following that road south they are entering the 'COTSWOLDS Area of Outstanding Natural Beauty'. Other facts that support my title are that The Cotswold Way Long Distance Path runs as far south as Bath

Cotswold sign at Bathford

and that the Cotswold Voluntary Warden Service starts guided walks from Colerne, Castle Combe, Sherston, Ford, Luckington and Box – all of which are within the area that I have defined as the Wiltshire Cotswolds – as well as from several other points around Bath.

Being an esssentially geological, topographical and architectural concept the extent of Cotswolds should not be defined by arbitrary man-made boundaries. That they are by common consent recognised to extend beyond the bounds of Gloucestershire into Oxfordshire is confirmed by the many publications that refer to the Oxfordshire Cotswolds. Wiltshire is recognised to lie at the very heart of the south country chalk but no reasonable person would argue that the chalk downlands do not extend beyond the boundaries of Wiltshire into neighbouring Dorset, Hampshire, and Berkshire (part of which has now become Oxfordshire), and many years ago the writers of the authoritative *Victoria County History of Wiltshire* recognised that the Cotswolds extend into Wiltshire by on one of their maps (on page 43 of Volume 4) showing narrow geographical bands running across north-west Wiltshire and designating one of these 'Cotswold Country'. Many topographical writers have however for convenience chosen to ignore the irrationality of using county boundaries to define the limits of particular styles of natural landscape and architecture and have regarded the Gloucesterhire-Wiltshire boundary as the southern edge of the Cotswolds. That many informed writers have on the other hand recognised that the Cotswolds extend south out of Gloucestershire into north Wiltshire I shall now show.

Edward Hutton in *Highways and Byways in Wiltshire* (1917) headed his final chapter containing his description of north-west Wiltshire 'The Foothills of the Cotswolds', and wrote: 'These hills are the lower heights of the Cotswold, and they stretch all the way from Bath and the Avon valley to Sherston and Tetbury on the extreme north-western boundary of Wilts, and so on into Gloucestershire'. At the beginning of his foreword to *The Buildings of England: Wiltshire* (1963) Sir Nikolaus Pevsner mentioned: 'the innumerable, always attractive houses of the Cotswold type in the north-west and north of the county', and in his 'Introduction to Geology' section of Pevsner's book Terence Miller remarked that: 'The Jurassic rocks of north-west Wiltshire are physiographically part of the dip-slope of the Cotswolds'. When discussing the Cotswold style of building in *The Gloucestershire Landscape* (1975) H. P. R. Finberg wrote: 'In reality the style is common to the whole belt of oolitic limestone from Dorset to Lincolnshire ; but in the Cotswolds it attains its highest degree of regularity and grace', and the *Everyman Encyclopaedia*, after indicating that the Cotswolds 'really commence at Bath' then states that they 'spread northwards into Gloucestershire'. *Everyman* also designated Malmesbury a Cotswold town, as did A. E. Trueman in *Geology and Scenery in England and Wales* (1949).

In Hale's *Portrait of Avon* (1981) John Haddon claimed that the Cotswolds even extended through north-west Wiltshire into the then County of Avon, mentioned in his chapter headed 'Cotswold Country' that the stone region of Avon 'was once known as the Southwolds', and asserted that this name was: 'particularly appropriate, for although the area belongs physically to the sweep of Jurassic limestone hills which make up the Cotswolds, it is rarely recognised as such'.

The area of the Cotswolds that extends across Wiltshire runs south-west from Tetbury to Bradford on Avon where the limestone plateau immediately north of the town is essentially Cotswold in character. This region of Wiltshire measures about twenty-four miles in length and an average of only about eight miles in width, and the local artist Robin Tanner summed up this region's character and emphasised the ways in which it resembled but also subtly differed from the Gloucestershire Cotswolds when he described in *Double Harness* (1987) how its:

> . . . stone houses with thatched or stone-tiled roofs and mullioned windows were a Wiltshire version of Cotswold: something less perfect perhaps: Cotswold with a rough, earthy difference . . . here, close to the Gloucestershire border, was a splendid building stone, but in deep rich dairy country.

Elsewhere Robin, in collaboration with his wife Heather Tanner, wrote in *Wiltshire Village* (1939):

> This [north-west Wiltshire] is, indeed, still Cotswold country. The soil is chiefly cornbrash, with occasional sandy loam or clay, and the limestone is apparent now in outcrops in those few lanes which remain white, now in disused quarries, and every where in the houses, that are as natural as animals' homes, fashioned out of the earth on which they stand. And surely

man has never found a kinder material to his hand than lies in this belt of oolitic limestone that stretches across the country from here to Yorkshire, throwing up its kindred houses, all the way.

My assertion that the Cotswolds extend across north-west Wiltshire has been recognised by other topographical writers. In his *Cotswold Country* (1937) H. J. Massingham defined the 'limestone country' as extending 'from the Dorset coast to Lincolnshire' and included in his book detailed description of the landscapes and buildings of north-west Wiltshire. He also in *The English Countryside* (1939) described the Cotswolds as a 'tawny band of wold that reaches diagonally from the Wiltshire Avon by Bath to the Warwickshire Avon by Evesham' and, when defining 'the wold proper' as extending 'roughly from Bath to Evesham', he echoed the words of C. B. Ford who in *The Beauty of Britain* (1935) described the Cotswolds as extending for 'about sixty miles, from the Wiltshire Avon by Bath in the south-west to the Warwickshire Avon by Evesham in the north-east'. Mr Ford also suggested that 'Cotswold thrusts down limestone feelers as far as Bath . . . where the stone building of Cotswold extends into the verdant pocket of Castle Combe', and nearer our time R. S. Barron used the uncompromising heading 'Wiltshire's Cotswolds' for one chapter of his *Geology of Wiltshire* (1967).

The title *The Wiltshire Cotswolds* that I have adopted for this book is therefore a perfectly valid name for this northern and north-western region of Wiltshire that is characterised by stone buildings and bridges built in a style that very closely resembles that of the Gloucestershire Cotswolds, and my title declares my agreement with the opinions of these writers that the Cotswolds extend into and across north and north-west Wiltshire where they are, in the words of Robin Tanner, 'a Wiltshire version of Cotswold'.

Some poets and topographers have in the past quoted a litany of place-names to give a flavour of the district that they are describing, and in this district I can offer the following attractive Wiltshire Cotswold place-names that spring immediately to mind – Stanton St Quintin, Easton Piercy, Littleton Drew, Ashton Keynes, Easton Grey, Leigh Delamere, Ditteridge, Yatton Keynell, Colerne, Broughton Gifford, Great Chalfield, and Monkton Farleigh. Readers of this book will discover many more.

Archaeology

WILTSHIRE IS RECOGNISED to be archaeologically the richest county in England but the majority of its visible prehistoric field monuments are located in the east and the south-east of the county around its great prehistoric centres of Avebury and Stonehenge.

In the Wiltshire Cotswolds Bronze Age and Iron Age field monuments are outnumbered by those of the Romano-Britons. In most regions Bronze Age round barrows exceed in number the larger and more imposing Neolithic long barrows but in this district round barrows are fewer as may be confirmed by referring to the distribution maps of archaeological field monuments in Part 2 of Volume 1 of the *Victoria County History of Wiltshire* which reveal that although the Wiltshire Cotswolds contain a number of long barrows, especially along the north-western edge of the county, round-barrows here are unusual apart from a few above the valley of the By Brook. It seems somehow appropriate that in this essentially stone region Neolithic (New Stone Age) long barrows with their monolithic stonework should predominate over Bronze Age earthen round barrows, although it should be recognised that in the stone districts of Exmoor and the Quantocks in Somerset not far distant from Wiltshire some round barrows were built of stone. It is therefore possible that on the shallow topsoils of the uplands of the Wiltshire Cotswolds some round barrows that may also have been built of stone may have disappeared as a result of being 'robbed' to construct dry-stone walls, as have been some of their long barrow predecessors.

Many of the chambered long barrows of the Cotswolds are of a distinctive type from the long barrows of the chalk downlands in that their burial chambers are placed around the perimeter of the barrow. These are known as the Severn-Cotswold type of long barrow and they will be described later (page 120).

The most obvious surviving field monuments of of the Iron Age are the hillforts which are numerous on the Wiltshire chalk downlands, although only two examples are recognised in the Wiltshire Cotswolds, these being Bury Camp promontory fortress and the Iron Age hillfort above Castle Combe that has been overlaid by a Norman castle.

The comparative scarcity in the Wiltshire Cotswolds of archaeological remains of the early prehistoric periods is compensated by the abundant remains of the Romans who were particularly active in this region. The old saying 'Scratch Gloucestershire and find Rome' is equally applicable in the Wiltshire Cotswolds which contain two major Roman roads, several Roman villas, and two Roman roadside settlements in Nettleton Shrub and at White Walls, both on the Fosse Way. This strong Romano-British presence within a comparatively small area is explained by the presence of the Fosse Way that

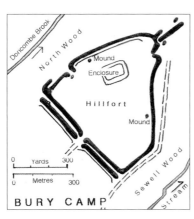

Plan of Bury Camp

crosses the north-western edge of this district between the Roman towns of Bath (*Aquae Sulis*) and Cirencester (*Corinium*) and was the Roman frontier zone at the time when the conquest was temporarily halted (as described on pages 41-2), and of the Roman western road from their capital at London (*Londinium*) to their recreational centre at Bath which crosses the southern end of the region.

Architecture

ALEC CLIFTON-TAYLOR in *The Pattern of English Building* (1972) expressed the essence of Cotswold architecture when he wrote: 'Nothing is more striking about Cotswold buildings than the visual accord which they achieve with the landscape in which they are placed', virtually echoing the sentiments of H. J. Massingham when forty years earlier he wrote of Cotswold architecture in *Wold Without End* (1932) that it: 'appears to grow straight out of the soil in grace and accord with it'.

In the the chalk downlands that cover more than half of Wiltshire architecture is incidental to the natural landscape but in the Wiltshire Cotswolds buildings are such prominent features in the landscape that they will figure prominently in this book. The universally admired character of the Cotswolds – in Oxfordshire and Wiltshire as well as in Gloucestershire – is largely due to the almost invariable use in its buildings of local oolitic limestone that, being the bedrock of the region, links the landscape to the buildings that have been built upon it by local master craftsmen who, using that stone, created buildings that by appearing to grow naturally out of the soil contribute so much to the Cotswold scene. This almost universal use of local stone for building was a matter of fortunate necessity rather than choice until the appearance of the canals and the railways in the 19th century provided cheap transportation into the region of alien and much inferior building materials. For a time the distinctive character of Cotswold architecture was in danger of being undermined by the introduction of these non-indigenous materials, but with the introduction in the 20th century of planning legislation a degree of control was introduced that is appropriately very stringently exercised in this region.

Just as it is sometimes difficult to decide when fine craftsmanship becomes art so is it difficult to decide when building becomes architecture. In his essay 'Under an Elm-Tree . . . ' (1889) the great Socialist craftsman-designer William Morris wrote of: 'the architecture proper of days bygone, when every craftsman was an artist and brought definite intelligence to bear upon his work', and when as a retired architect I reflect on the architecture – or is it the building? – of the Cotswolds I become very aware that few of the Cotswold buildings that we so much admire were designed by acknowledged designers. As is usual with vernacular styles they grew naturally as a result of the ability of many generations of highly-skilled local craftsmen who, fully comprehending the nature and capabilities of their native building stone worked within a long-established local tradition that allowed them scope for individuality, and instinctively built fine buildings while remaining to a great extent modestly unaware of the supreme quality of what they were achieving.

In early-Medieval times when stonemasons shared the secret allegorical associations known to the ecclesiastics who designed the great Gothic buildings that their masons built for them, those masons enjoyed considerable standing in society. The *Cotton Manuscripts* include depictions of Henry III, who surrounded himself with artists and masons, talking with his master masons. Out of the Guild of Masons emerged the Society of Freemasons that grew away from the stonemasons who then became mere working craftsmen receiving scant pecuniary reward for their work and generally not commemorated by monuments in churches or headstones in churchyards. Their monuments are the buildings – churches, manor-houses, farmhouses, barns, cottages and bridges – with which they adorned the Cotswolds that largely as a result of their efforts are now recognised as being an Area of Outstanding Natural Beauty. The Wiltshire-born architect Sir Christopher Wren often employed Cotswold masons on his great works, and when visiting the Cotswolds we may justifiably say of these humble craftsmen what was

Ball finial at Broughton Gifford Manor House

said of Wren on a Latin inscription in his St Paul's Cathedral that loosely translated reads: 'If you would seek his monument, look around you'.

These craftsmen also created the exquisitely carved and lettered 17th and 18th century table-tombs and headstones that are features of Cotswold graveyards, and their love of their work is reflected by the way in which they introduced subtle individual features into their work, for example the tiny mice that are carved scrambling over the ball-finials to the gatepiers at Broughton Gifford Manor House. The achievements of these craftsmen were recognised by H. P. R. Finberg when he wrote in *The Gloucestershire Landscape* (1975) a paragraph that, as he indicates, is equally applicable to the men who produced the similar work in the Wiltshire Cotswolds:

The fine school of stone-working craftsmen who rebuilt the manor houses also carried out a wholesale reconstruction of the villages and market towns. From 1570 onwards they built thousands of new farmhouses, cottages and barns. It was in this period that they evolved what is usually known as the Cotswold style. In reality the style was common to the whole belt of oolitic limestone from Dorset to Linconshire ; but in the Cotswolds it attains its highest degree of regularity and grace.

When we think of Cotswold architecture we tend to visualise groups of buildings with their walls, roofs, and window mullions constructed throughout of the indigenous local limestone. That these buildings were for an extended period built in an extremely traditional vernacular style was pointed out by the artist-writer Sydney R. Jones when he described in *England South* (1948) how the traditional Gothic-Tudor style for long persisted in this region where the masons only reluctantly accepted the classical Renaissance style:

> Gothic work advanced to great excellence in ecclesiastical and domestic building and persisted with remarkable tenacity in parts little affected by the changes of time. The wave of classicism that made Bath new and wonderful spread to the towns, manor-houses, and some of the villages. But whether Gothic or Renaissance canons were followed, the men who laid and carved the native stone by methods long known brought to their work something of imagination and poetry, a measure of their inheritance and themselves. Signs of graciousness in life, and reminders of the storied past, ancient custom and usage, abound in this geological division. Hills, vales, and lowlands and the gifts of the earth and artistry at every turn offer sermons in stone.

The intricate carved foliage and profuse and detailed statuary of the Gothic style demanded great skills from the stonemasons who were in that style allowed great scope for individuality, in for example the variation of the detail in successive column caps in many church nave arcades and the way in which Gothic masons often caricatured their

*Cottages in Church
Walk, Ashton Keynes*

colleagues when carving gargoyles and corbel-tables. The classical Renaissance style was generally plainer and less demanding, it was often repetitive, and being based on design manuals and pattern books it was more controlled. The master masons evidently resisted their loss of individuality involved in the introduction of this less demanding style for when possible they often continued to work in the old tried, trusted and familiar Gothic style.

The more imposing buildings of the Wiltshire Cotswolds are built of fine ashlar freestone, while the humbler barns and cottages tended to be built of the cheaper and more rustic limestone rubble. The beauty of Cotswold cottages is largely attributable to their small scale which was often achieved by restricting the height of their walls to about ten feet and springing their roofs from that low eaves level. This necessitated rooms in the roof zone being lighted through their gable ends or through dormer windows inserted into the roof slope – and sometimes both. A frequently-used alternative to dormers was to build a series of almost adjoining small gables at roof level along the main wall-face as a series of large gable-dormers which were then treated like gable ends, each gable being pierced by a single window. This arrangement was often used in almshouses, probably to visually minimise what in these sometimes large

The Lyte Almshouses at Kington St Michael

buildings might otherwise have been their institutional scale. Most cottages were built presumably for thermal reasons with tiny two-light upper windows, although at that time when artificial lighting was poor weavers' cottages in cloth-weaving areas were sometimes built with wide upper floor windows to provide the maximum natural light that was required for weaving.

That few cottages are as old as their owners sometimes believe was emphasised by Professor Hoskins when he wrote in *The Making of the English Landscape* (1955): 'There seem to be no true cottages left in England of an earlier date than the latter part of the seventeeth century', and also suggested that: 'most are probably eighteenth century in date'. This is relevant in the Wiltshire Cotswolds as elsewhere, as Hoskins emphasised when he wrote 'whole villages on and near the great Stone Belt, that crosses England from Dorset to the Yorkshire coasts, seem to have been built about the same time' – that is the late-17th century.

In most vernacular styles of architecture contrasting materials were used on roofs and walls – roofs of tile, slate or thatch above walls of stone, brick, or render – but Cotswolds buildings are, as described by

the local artist and writer Robin Tanner: 'as natural as animals' homes, fashioned out of the earth on which they stood'. The practically universal use of stone in its buildings prompted Massingham to describe the Cotswold style as being 'solidity, simplicity, and durability', and this solid unpretentious style also generally prevails in north-west Wiltshire where villages such as Castle Combe and Biddestone and the towns of Bradford on Avon, Malmesbury and Corsham bear such close affinities to their Gloucestershire Cotswold neighbours that Robin Tanner described this region as 'Cotswold with a rough, earthy difference'. One of these differences was that the Wiltshire Cornbrash rubble tends to be of a rather greyer colour than is the more golden rubble stone of Gloucestershire.

Cotswold Barn and stone walls south of Luckington

     The multi-gabled stone-built and stone-roofed street architecture of the towns and some of the larger villages of the Wiltshire Cotswolds where the cottages sometimes stand directly at the back edge of the pavements – at for example Malmesbury and Castle Combe, in the Flemish cottages at Corsham and the Lyte Almshouses at Kington St

Lower end of Castle Combe

Michael – also employs the vernacular Cotswold style. These street buildings are, as are so many of the rural cottages and fine manor houses of the Wiltshire Cotswolds, built in a style that would provoke no adverse comment were they to be relocated in Gloucestershire, nor would the stone bridges of north Wiltshire like the arched stone bridges at Easton Grey, Bradford on Avon and Castle Combe, the clapper bridge on the Broadmead Brook below Nettleton Shrub, or the low-parapeted stone packhorse bridge between Broughton Gifford and Whaddon, which are all essentially Cotswold in character. The bridges that I have listed are examples that spring immediately to mind, but there are many more, often with their parapets kept low in order to allow unrestricted crossing for packhorses carrying bulky bales of wool.

Flemish Cottages at Corsham

A popular misconception has arisen that age in buildings is synonymous with quality which is of course untrue. In the Cotswolds it probably arises largely because the natural weathering of limestone as it ages greatly enhances the appearance of all limestone buildings. This weathering can make ordinary buildings look good and good buildings appear exceptional, and this fact goes far towards explaining the immense contribution that its native limestone makes to the beauty of Cotswold buildings. Lichens love limestone and as soon as the stone is exposed to the atmosphere they colonise it with splodges of colour ranging from the brightest orange through blueish-greens to subtle light greys. The Georgian poet George Crabbe – who as the rector of Trowbridge often geologised in the stone quarries of Bradford on Avon – described the growth of lichen on limestone as:

> The living stains, which Nature's hand alone,
> Profuse of life, pours out upon the stones.

Walls of oolitic lime-stone also provide admirable backgrounds for the climbing plants for which the Cotswolds are noted, although if they are allowed to clamber over stone-slated roofs these plants can penetrate under the slates and damage the roof. A few words are necessary about these stone-slated roofs that contribute so much to the Cotswold style of building. Stone slates were obtained from quarries in which the

Lichen growth on a stone stile at Broughton Gifford church.

stone was naturally fissured and was therefore easily split into thin layers along its bedding planes, sometimes after being exposed to frost before its quarry sap had dried out. Robin Tanner described these fissured beds of stone as 'shaly layers that are all but ready-made ready-graded tiles packed in the soil'. Some north Wiltshire place-names commemorate the former specialist quarries from which stone slates were obtained, examples being Tile Pits at Hullavington and Tile Quarr at both Biddestone and at Sherston, 'quarr' being an ancient name for quarry. After they had dried out the riven slates were roughly trimmed by hand into the sometimes delightfully irregular shapes that were fixed upon the roofs, traditionally with oak pegs but in more modern times with nails. The great attraction of stone-slated roofs lies in their uneven texture and, as with limestone walling, the patina that they develope as they age which prompted the Edwardian architect Guy Dawber to describe Cotswold stone roofs as being: 'when old and covered with lichens . . . indescribably exquisite'. The great weight of stone slates sometimes distorted the lines of the roof by deflecting the roof structure, a circumstance that led the writer Clifford Bax to describe the stone-slated roof of the manor house

Castle Combe street, looking north

that he lived in at Broughton Gifford as having a 'many wrinkled surface'. The natural weathering of stone slates was accelerated by the facts that they vary in thickness, have uneven riven surfaces, and open pores. These factors encouraged the rapid growth of the lichens and mosses that with time adorns them with their beautiful patina, but unfortunately the moss growth that so much enhances the appearance of stone-slated roofs also carries the seeds of their destruction as moss retains moisture that can perish the limestone. This problem can be overcome by inserting growth retarding copper strips that remain effective for about 30 to 40 years, but these strips also inhibit the natural weathering.

The aesthetic attraction of Cotswold stone roofs is not entirely due to their texture and weathering. Their builders literally built into them

Graduated stone slates,
Limpley Stoke Church

subtleties that are sometimes not immediately apparent. Most common roofing materials such as slates and clay tiles are laid to equal overlaps creating an even texture over the entire roof. Cotswold roofers however traditionally laid their stone slates in diminishing sizes graded from large at the eaves to small at the ridge. They would have been instinctively aware that this traditional practice contributed immensely to the aesthetic quality of their roofs, although it is so subtle that even the normally meticulous Robin Tanner omitted to depict this gradation in some of his drawings and etchings, although his wife wrote of 'the graded tiles' on Cotswold roofs.. Cotswold roofers also became adept at 'sweeping' the stone slates into curves over the valleys at the intersections of their roofs and by so-doing enhanced the continuity of stone-slating over the entire roof and avoided the introduction of valley gutters in other materials such as lead. They also sometimes swept their stone-slated roofs into curved 'eyebrow' eaves above windows, at for example Monk's Chapel near Corsham, and they also very occasionally employed stone-slates as vertical slate-hanging such as I have noticed at Box and Turleigh.

Detail of Monk's
Chapel, Corsham

Cotswold stone roofs became so widely admired that they were sometimes used at some distance from the Cotswolds, an example that comes immediately to mind being the Norman St John's Church at Devizes in mid-Wiltshire that is now roofed with Cotswold slates that presumably replaced an earlier roof of sheet lead.

Dry-stone Walls

CLOSELY ASSOCIATED with Cotswold buildings are the dry-stone walls that appear in many of the stone districts of England but are a particular feature of Cotswold countryside, villages and towns. Their existence is explained by the enclosure of the countryside that took place when it was realised that large expanses of open upland, because they provided no shelter in winter made it impossible to control close-grazing to manure the land, were not entirely satisfactory for grazing amimals. It was then decided that smaller fields were in many respects better, and John Aubrey (1626-97) confirmed that enclosure of the

Cotswold dry-stone walls near Conkwell Grange, near Winsley

Wiltshire Cotswolds commenced in the late-16th century shortly before his time. After the monarchy was restored in 1660 the government first encouraged enclosure by private landlords wherever possible by agreement, but official enclosure of the common fields with the sanction of parliament followed and from about 1750 many Enclosure Acts ensured that enclosure proceeded with great rapidity. Much of north-west Wiltshire was enclosed by the late-18th century and the rest of the enclosures were largely completed soon after 1800. Although enclosure was intended to create smaller closes for grazing livestock, it also accommodated the newly-introduced systems of crop-rotation in which fodder crops such as turnips and clover alternated with wheat and barley. The practice of leaving fields fallow to recover their productivity was also eliminated by using livestock to graze and manure the enclosures to improve crop yields, and by the introduction of artificial fertilisers.

In most districts enclosure was effected by planting thousands of miles of hawthorn hedges to subdivide the countryside, but with so much rubble stone readily to hand it was achieved in the Cotswolds by building dry-stone walls rather than enclosure hedges. These stone walls are a feature of the Wiltshire Cotswolds from their extreme northern fringe north of Malmesbury, through the countryside around Biddestone and Corsham, and as far south as the limestone plateau around Winsley above Bradford on Avon. That the craft of dry-stone walling is very ancient is established by the presence of such walling in many Neolithic long barrows and the fact that such walls were mentioned by the giant Polyphemus in Homer's *Odyssey*, written in the late-8th century BC.

There tends to be a subtle difference between the dry-stone field walls of Gloucestershire and Wiltshire in that the former are, like their Neolithic predecessors in long barrows, generally built of slabs of stone almost as thin as stone slates, while Wiltshire walls tend to be built of larger stones like those used in rubble buildings. This is however by no means invariable, and it is noticeable that in some places thin stones are used in Wiltshire dry-stone walls, at for example Broughton Gifford.

Cotswold dry-stone wall near Oaksey Church

The term dry-stone reflects the fact that these walls are built entirely without mortar. Superficially they may appear to be merely piled-up rubble stone, but they are in fact skilfully-built structures that depend for their stability upon a combination of gravity and the friction obtained from the stones being carefully trimmed and fitted into the wall so that they effectively lock together. An old stone waller was once heard to say: 'There be more art, look, goes to the making of a dry wall than there does to a wet 'un'. Dry stone walls often consist of two outer faces of carefully fitted larger stones with occasional through stones to bond them together,

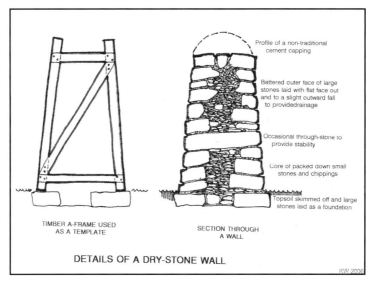

Profile of a non-traditional cement capping

Battered outer face of large stones laid with flat face out and to a slight outward fall to provide drainage

Occasional through-stone to provide stability

Core of packed down small stones and chippings

Topsoil skimmed off and large stones laid as a foundation

TIMBER A-FRAME USED AS A TEMPLATE

SECTION THROUGH A WALL

DETAILS OF A DRY-STONE WALL

KW 2006

the core of the wall – known as the 'hearting' – being filled with compacted small stones and chippings that were sufficiently coarse not to wash out of the open joints of the wall. The mortar-free nature of the walls allowed air to circulate freely and dry out the walls after rain, although as an additional precaution the stones were sometimes laid with an outward fall towards the face of the wall to encourage rainwater to drain away and not remain in pockets in the wall and cause damage by freezing and expanding in cold weather. Being dry-jointed dry-stone walls are flexible and can absorb settlement. This allowed their foundations to be minimal and the preparation for building involved little more than skimming off the turf and the topsoil, although large stones were often placed under the ends of walls, at gate openings, and at changes of direction.

Modern dry-stone walls are often capped with rounded in-situ cement copings. These keep out rain, prolongue the life of the wall, and also make theft of the capping stones more difficult, but cement cappings are disliked by traditional stone wallers for aesthetic reasons and because they add a rigidity to the wall that is disadvantageous in two respects. In the event of the dry-stone wall settling due to ground movement the stones of the wall drop away from the rigid coping leaving it bridging the gap in the wall, and if a farm or road vehicle accidentally collides with the wall the rigidity imparted by the cement coping drags down a longer length of wall than would have collapsed if there were no cement coping.

Dry-stone walling is a protracted and laborious occupation and I can recall when driving daily to work in Bath in the 1960s observing with great interest the slow progress of an elderly dry-waller building the extremely long wall up the north side of Winsley Hill opposite the south end of Conkwell Wood. A mason friend has recenly told me that this man was Richard ('Dick') Dagger, and that he is buried with a headstone in Bradford cemetery on the Holt Road, but for me his lasting monument is his wall up Winsley Hill.

'Dick' Dagger, Wiltshire Cotswold waller

It has been suggested that dry-stone walls are unfavourable to wildlife, although they encourage the growth of plants such as pennywort and ivy-leafed toadflax, and their open joints also allow small birds and mammals to explore them in search of food. Some wall-builders are said to have deliberately left small cavities in which small birds could nest, although they would never allow daylight to be visible through their walls. Dry-stone walls are today sometimes neglected due to lack of skilled labour or the high cost of rebuilding them, and they now sometimes become so overgrown with self-sown bushes that they appear to be hedges rather than walls. That such neglect is not a new development is indicated by the fact that when travelling across Wiltshire during the Second World War H. J. Massingham complained about seeing 'tumbled or gaping drystone walls'.

The tools used in dry-walling were few and generally consisted of a heavy walling hammer and a pick to shape the stones. Their builders also sometimes used leather palm protectors to protect their hands from being abraded by constant handling of the rough stones. To maintain a consistent section the stone-wallers often used an A-frame profile with almost vertical sloping legs which when used with string-lines ensured that the wall was built with a slight batter, the pointed top of the A-frame being cut off horizontally to provide the flat top to the wall. The stones were best laid as they were bedded in the quarry, otherwise when saturated and subjected to frost they were liable to laminate and disintegrate.

The limestone rubble used in these walls was generally obtained locally from surface quarries in neighbouring fields, and the words 'Quar' or 'Quarr' in place-names throughout this region indicate the former existence of such surface

Collapsed dry-stone wall south of Ashley

quarries, examples being Quar Close at Nettleton, at Malmesbury, and at Box, Quar Piece at West Kington, Quar Leaze at Grittenham, Leigh Delamere and at South Wraxall, and Quarr Hill and Quar Plantation both at Yatton Keynell.

Dry-stone walls sometimes incorporate Cotswold-style step-over stone-slabbed stiles consisting of a massive stone slab four to six inches thick set vertically as a barrier to stock, sometimes with stone steps resembling those of a mounting-block to help pedestrians to negotiate the stile. The explorer Speke was killed when his sporting gun discharged when he was scrambling over a dry-stone wall near Corsham (see page 209). These Cotswold stiles may be seen at many places in the Wiltshire Cotswolds, for example immediately west of the churchyard at Biddestone, in the wall of Broughton Gifford churchyard, on a footpath near the railway west of Monkton Farm south of Broughton Gifford, and

Stone stile south of Ashley

at the end of a short lane on the west side of the B3109 opposite the hospice at Chapel Plaister. Several examples also exist on the limestone plateau north of Bradford on Avon, including two opposite each other on the bend in the road a quarter of a mile south of Great Ashley (at 812616). There are many more, including an example with steps on the east side of the minor road through Westrop near Corsham that was incorporated by the local artist Robin Tanner in his etching entitled 'June' that he made to celebrate the end of the Second World War.

Courses in dry-stone walling for beginners are now run by the Drystone Walling Association whose contact numbers are available from Cotswold tourist information centres, and the Cotswolds Conservation Board annually organises dry-stone walling competitions and offers grants to help with the restoration and repair of dry-stone walls in some areas.

Farming and Industry

HISTORY IS ABOUT PEOPLE and, as is usual in rural districts, the people of the Wiltshire Cotswolds were employed in many activities. Among these were the solitary shepherds tending their sheep on the upland wolds, the quarrymen working in their stone quarries and mines, the builders and stonemasons who built cottages, farmhouses and barns and the occasional church and manor house, the stone-wallers who plied their lonely trade all over the district, the monks, nuns, and their lay-brothers in their monasteries and abbeys, the cattle, pig and arable farmers, the cheese and butter-makers in their dairies, the cloth workers in their cottages and woollen factories, and the lords of the manor and their families and servants in the manor houses that were generally financed by profits obtained from the cloth industry. Many of these people worked in or were associated with the farming and industries of the district.

Sheep Farming

ALTHOUGH SHEEP-FARMING was the predominant form of farming in the Wiltshire Cotswolds a good deal of mixed farming was also practised in this region and its cattle, pig and arable farming that provided essential diversity will be described later.

From the early-Middle Ages until comparatively modern times Cotswold sheep-farming produced an immense amount of wool that was initially exported to foreign markets although from the mid-14th century was woven into cloth locally. The monasteries were instrumental in the development of sheep-farming when, after being granted huge amounts of land, they improved their huge ecclesiastical estates by clearing their woodlands, draining the marshes, and developing their uplands into sheepwalks. In the early-Middle Ages the Abbots of Malmesbury prospered by expanding sheep farming on their immense north Wiltshire estates to provide wool for export to the Low Countries where much highly esteemed English wool was woven into cloth. The sheep that grazed the Cotswold Hills have been described as 'the sheet anchor of farming' and although they were raised mainly for their wool, prior to the introduction of paper their skins were made into the parchment that was used for written documents from the 3rd century AD until the end of the 15th century when paper-making was introduced into England and became a minor industry in this area (see later, pages 37-8). In the Middle Ages sheeps' milk was used to make cheese, but mutton was then as now not particularly popular and generally only the sheep that yielded inferior wool were butchered for meat. Mutton later became more important when in the 18th century it was produced to feed the expanding populations of the towns.

The Romans are said to have introduced Mediterranean breeds of large sheep into the Cotswolds to provide long wool, but from Medieval times the breed of sheep upon which the prosperity of the Cotswold sheep-farming and woollen industry was based was the celebrated Cotswold Lion breed that generated such immense wealth for the region that it was referred to as 'the golden hoof'. There is a tradition that this breed was developed by selective breeding from twelve Flemish rams brought to England in 1328 as part of the dowry of Philippa of Hainault when she married Edward III who a few years later instigated measures

Cotwold Lion sheep

that revived cloth-weaving in England. The Cotswold Lion was a very large sheep that carried a heavy shiny fleece weighing 15 to 20 lbs with strands of wool about 6 inches long. Around their necks they had ruffs which were thought to resemble manes and on their heads they grew top-knots, characteristics that were thought to make them resemble lions and explains the popular name of the breed. I have heard it said that when they were sheared a sample tuft of wool was left on their shoulders to provide an indication to buyers of the quality of the wool that they would produce the following year.

Michael Drayton (1563-1631) described the Cotswold breed of sheep in the following rather ponderous lines as:

> . . . the whitest kind ; whose brows so woolly be
> As men in her fair sheep no emptiness should see.
> The staple deep and thick, through, to the very graine
> Most strongly keepeth out the violentest raine –
> A body long and large, the buttocks equal broad
> As fit to undergoe the full and weightie load.

Cotswold AONB logo

and in the first English comedy *Ralph Roister Doister* (1553) a character says: 'Then will he look as fierce as a Cotswold lion'. Today The newspaper of the Cotswolds Conservation Board is called *The Cotswold Lion* and this breed of sheep is also depicted on the logo of the Cotswolds Area of Outstanding National Beauty. The breed is not quite extinct, but it was commemorated by the brewing of a pale bitter called Cotswold Lion to celebrate the anniversary of the founding of The Cotswold AONB.

The indigenous sheep of the Wiltshire downs was the Wiltshire Horn that was so-named because the ewes as well as the rams of this breed were horned. This long-legged very hardy goat-like sheep did not need to be sheared as it shed its wool naturally. In Medieval and Tudor times little attempt was made to improve the stock by selective breeding and until the end of the 18th century, when it was replaced by the improved Southdown and Leicester breeds, the rather nondescript Wiltshire Horn remained the principal Wiltshire sheep although I have been unable to establish the extent to which this breed gave way to the Cotswold Lion in the Wiltshire Cotswolds. It seems however inevitable that a breed that had been so successful on the Gloucestershire wolds would have been brought across the county boundary to feed on the wolds of north Wiltshire.

The flocks of the principal sheep owners often ran into tens of thousands, but sheep were not owned exclusively by the great lords and ecclesiastical magnates. Peasants and yeomen also kept sheep and dealt in their wool, and during the reign of Edward III the proportion of sheep owned by common people increased so rapidly that they ultimately owned more sheep in total than did the lords and abbots. Consequently during the Middle Ages the prosperity of all classes of society depended upon wool and Michael Drayton described in his *Polyolbion* (1622) a Cotswold ram and bell-wether being crowned with garlands for a rustic merry-making by peasants who recognised the importance of sheep to their prosperity.

During the latter part of the 14th century there was no appreciable increase in the national wool production and this situation was maintained until about 1460 when the Continental demand for wool for cloth-making suddenly increased and was satisfied by practically all the wool for Western European looms becoming supplied from England. At this time much arable land in the Wiltshire Cotswolds was converted into sheepwalks to satisfy the increased demand for wool and throughout the Medieval and Tudor periods sheep farming – and later the expanding woollen industry (see below, pages 20-7) – provided most of England's prosperity, a fact that is reflected by the woolsack that is incorporated in the seat of the Lord Chancellor in the House of Lords. After the Dissolution of the monasteries in the mid-16th century lay 'woolmen' took over the sheep farming and the prosperity that the now redundant abbeys and monasteries had for so long enjoyed.

Cloth-making

THE DISCOVERY of loom-weights at many archaeological excavations proves that weaving took place in England in prehistoric times, presumably on a subsistence only basis. Its continuation through the Romano-British period on a more commercial basis is revealed by the reputation that British cloth and woollen cloaks then enjoyed abroad, and by the fact that Diocletian's *Edict of Prices* in AD 303 included cloth among the maximum prices that traders were permitted to charge for various materials. In the late-4th century a list of Roman officials included in the *Notitia Dignitatum* mentioned an 'Administrator of the Imperial Weaving Works' as being responsible for supervising the provision of cloth for clothing the Roman army, indicating that a considerable amount of cloth-weaving took place in Romano-British times.

In 1312 at least one fifth of the population of Bristol – which had links with the nearby Wiltshire Cotswolds – was engaged in weaving, but cloth-making in England then declined for a time as English wool was generally exported to be woven into cloth in the Low Countries which practically monopolised the European weaving trade. This situation obtained until 1336 when, provoked by Louis of Flander's arrest of some English merchants, Edward III sharply reduced wool exports, offered inducements to attract immigrant weavers to England, and encouraged the export of English cloth. These measures led to the realisation that wool could be as easily be woven into cloth in England as in the Low Countries, and the subsequent revival in cloth-making was also helped by the introduction of the foreign weavers.

It has sometimes been argued that the tradition of Continental weavers coming to England is a myth but there is documentary evidence of Flemish weavers being invited and moving to England, their names are known, and according to Sir Arthur Bryant a Fleming called Thomas Blanket opened the first factory in Bristol in the reign of Edward III and there wove the item of bedding that still bears his name. These skilled immigrant weavers transformed the English cloth industry and they were welcomed by the ruling classes, but they were resented by the English workers and consequently tended to live in colonies which explains names such as Dutch Barton for part of Bradford on Avon and the Flemish cottages in Corsham High Street. The revival in cloth-making was also influenced by the introduction of fulling mills whose water-powered fulling stocks fulled (that is pounded) the cloth that had previously been laboriously trampled by men.

The decrease in the amount of wool exported from England is shown by the fact that in the mid-14th century England exported an average of 30,000 bales every year while by the end of the century only about 19,000 bales were sent abroad. The simultaneous increase in cloth-making in England was phenomenal. In 1348 a little under 4,500 cloths were exported, but by the end of the century this figure had increased by ten times to about 45,000, by the mid-15th century it was 54,000, and by 1550 the figure was 122,000 cloths, half of which emanated from the western shires. England had in two hundred years been transformed from being an esentially pastoral country that exported its wool into a flourishing cloth-producing nation that prospered by weaving and exported much of its cloth. The Cotswolds were at the head of this revolution, although many other parts of England including north-west Wiltshire now had flourishing weaving industries.

When Defoe journeyed through the Wiltshire Cotswolds for his *Tour through the Whole Island of Great Britain* (1724-26) he nominated Malmesbury, Castle Combe and Bradford as centres of the 'broad-cloth manufacture' that he described as 'this prodigy of a trade'.

In the early days of cloth-manufacturing weaving was usually done by men while the spinning was done by women, which explains the term 'spinster'. Both activities were undertaken by 'home-workers' in their cottages, spinning on hand operated spinning-wheels and weaving on manually-operated looms that were generally located on the upper floors of cottages. Weavers, like artists, preferred north-facing windows and their cottages were often built with wide windows to provide the necessary good light. The disadvantage to the cloth merchant of 'home-working' was that it necessitated constant transport of his materials around the various dispersed trades, as described by Defoe's when he wrote:

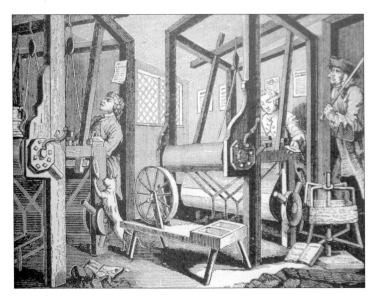

18th Century Hand Loom

Every clothier must keep a horse, perhaps two, to fetch and carry for the use of his manufacture to fetch home his wooll and provisions from the market, to carry his yarn to the spinners, his manufactures [i.e. his cloth] to the fulling mill, and when finished, to the market to be sold, and the like.

The merchants first delivered the raw wool to the cottages of the carders and spinsters and then collected the yarn and took it to the weavers. They then collected the cloth and successively carried it to the shearmen, the fullers and the dyers, and then by packhorse to the markets. The clothiers' horses were also later used to power the early gig-mills which raised the knap of the cloth, a process known as carding that had for long been done by hand with teazels held in carding frames.

This carrying of the product around at various stages to successive home-workers was obviously uneconomic and it prompted the cloth merchants to collect the workers into factories in order to obtain control of the entire cloth-making process in one place. These manufactures (or factories) were built along the streams and rivers that provided water for washing and finishing the cloth as well as the power to drive water wheels and fulling stocks. Riverside mill development now took place in the Wiltshire Cotswolds along the Bristol Avon, on its tributaries such as

The Evolution of
Weaving

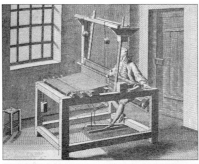

the By Brook, and even along tiny tributaries of tributaries such as Doncombe Brook north of Colerne.

By becoming wage-earners in loom-shops and factories the cloth workers lost their independence while the large clothiers prospered greatly and contributed immensely to the character of the region by financing religious establishments and building for themselves grand houses that were usually imposing and often beautiful. At Malmesbury William Stumpe, who was described by Leland in the mid-16th century as 'an exceding rich clothier', was for a time the greatest clothier in Wiltshire, especially when after the Dissolution of the monasteries he bought Malmesbury Abbey and its ancillary buildings from the Crown, and in the words of Leland filled 'every corner of the vaste houses of office that belonged to the abbaye [with] lumbes to weve cloth yn'. Aubrey wrote:

> Stumpe was a wealthy clothier at Malmesbury, in the time of Henry VIII. His father was parish clarke of North Nibley , in Gloucestershire, and was a weaver, and at last grew up to be a clothier. This clothier at Malmesbury, at the dissolution of the abbeys, bought a great deal of the abbey lands thereabout. When King Henry VIII hunted in Braden forest, he gave his majesty and the court a great entertainment at his house (the abbey). The King told him he was afraid he had undone himself ; he replied that his own servants should only want their supper for it. Leland says that when he was there the dortures and other great rooms were filled with weavers' looms.

The great clothiers now became so prosperous that alarm bells were sounded and in 1576 the landed gentry contrived to get an Act passed restricting to twenty acres the further amount of land that any cloth manufacturer was allowed to acquire in Wiltshire, Gloucestershire and Somerset. Nevertheless many yeoman families such as the Pooles of Oaksey and the Stumpes of Malmesbury succeeded in progressing up the social scale by becoming first large landowners and then landed gentlemen whose daughters the aristocracy were only too glad to marry for their large dowries and inheritances.

During the English Civil War the transportation of cloth from the woollen towns of Wiltshire to London was disrupted by the royalists whose headquarters was at Oxford. A meeting was convened in Marlborough at which the Wiltshire 'woolmen' negotiated an arrangement with the royalist governor of Donnington Castle near Newbury by which for a levy of £3 a waggon the trade would be allowed to continue unmolested.

After they had concentrated their workforces into factories the clothiers sometimes built massive multi-storey factories such as the late-Georgian Avon Mill at Malmesbury and the Victorian Abbey Mills at Bradford on Avon, the town at the southern end of the Wiltshire Cotswolds where the cloth industry flourished and survived for much longer than at Malmesbury. At Bradford the prosperous clothing families included the Halls, Hortons, Methuens, Cams and Yerburys, and in the 16th century Leland wrote: 'Al the toune of Bradeford stondith by cloth making'. The industry survived into modern times at Bradford, although the west country clothing trade went into decline because it persisted in manufacturing heavy broadcloths at a time when lighter cloths were demanded. In an attempt to satisfy this demand the west country clothiers in the early-17th century began weaving some of the finer mixed cloths called medleys incorporating some fine Spanish wool, but by the 18th century the industry was drifting away to the north where at the time when machinery and steam power were being introduced into the industry Yorkshire exploited the proximity of its coalfields to expand its cloth-making industry and concentrate on making the lighter cloths that were now becoming popular. Other factors that influenced the move of

Avon Mill and Weir, Malmesbury

Abbey Mill at Bradford

the industry to Yorkshire were the tardiness with which machinery was introduced into west country factories, and the fact that even after mechanisation had been introduced the west country workers insisted on maintaining their former piece-rates for their more mechanised production and by so-doing made their cloth uncompetitive. The decline in the west of England cloth industry accelerated in the depression that followed the Napoleonic Wars at a time when Yorkshire continued to expand its production. The long term impact of the woollen trade on the Wiltshire Cotswolds is however demonstrated by the fact that the former cloth-manufacturing towns of Malmesbury and Bradford remain the largest towns in the region, although its woollen industry finally died out in the mid-20th century.

Cloth-making involved a complicated series of operations that can be summarised as follows. When the sheep had been sheared the fleeces were bundled into bales and carried down from the upland sheep-walks on packhorses. The fleeces were then graded by the 'parter' who separated out the finer ones that were then 'scoured' (washed) and dried. The 'carder' (or 'scribbler') then separated out the coarser wool and impurities by combing them out using a handled board with wire teeth. Spinning – that is the conversion of the wool into spun thread known as 'yarn' – was then undertaken, originally by 'spinsters' using spinning wheels at home in their cottages but later in factories using machines known as 'spinning-jennies'. From the spinners the yarn went to the weavers who wove the yarn into the cloth that was fulled by 'fullers' by a process known as fulling, tucking or pounding that involved pounding the cloth in water. The Romano-Britons had added human urine to the water used for fulling cloth, but a substance associated with the oolitic limestone that was used in fulling was the Fuller's earth that from the Middle Ages was used to scour the cloth clean of grease and oil and also felt the coarse woven cloth into a fine smooth broadcloth. Prior to the invention fulling mills with their water-powered fulling stocks (massive timber mallets that pounded the cloth) fulling was done by men trampling on the cloth in swift-running streams which explains why fullers were sometimes known as 'walkers'. Any loose threads were then drawn out of the cloth by the 'rower' or 'carder' using wooden frames that held teazles which also raised the knap of the cloth enabling the 'shearman' to shear the cloth smoothe using massive hand shears. The 'drawer' then drew together the threads to fill holes and faults and the finished cloth was stretched taut on 'tenterframes' or 'racks' to dry, from which arose the expression of being 'on tenterhooks' for being in modern terminology 'up-tight'.

The invention in the north of England in the 18th century of machines, generally for the cotton industry, led to a number of labour-intensive manual operations in the woollen industry becoming mechanised. Some of these innovations initially benefitted the cottage weavers. The invention by Kay in 1733 of the flying-shuttle immediately enabled them to earn much more provided that they could obtain sufficient spun yarn, but for this they were compelled to compete and travel around collecting their yarn from widely dispersed cottage spinners. The demand for more yarn led to the invention in 1765 by Hargreaves of the 'spinning-jenny' in which one wheel drove multiple spindles, Arkwright's water-powered spinning machine followed in 1769, and in 1778 Crompton's 'mule' combined these two machines. During the years 1788 to about 1800 spinning machines were turning wool into yarn at such a rate that weavers were in great demand, but the weaver's trade was easily learnt and when their numbers increased a slump in wages set in, particularly as Cartwright invented the first power loom in 1785 and in 1801 the French silk-weaver Jacquard invented a loom capable of weaving complicated patterns.

Steam power was first introduced into woollen mills in the 1790s after having been initially developed to pump water out of coal mines, which explains why the first stationary steam engine, that was invented in 1689, being called 'The Miner's Friend'. This primitive engine was gradually improved throughout the 18th century and by the last quarter of that century the Boulton and Watt partnership was designing steam engines to order to power machinery in woollen mills. Steam power however came late to Wiltshire where coal was not readily available, but it became more popular after the introduction of the canal system in the early-19th century reduced the cost of transporting coal.

Because clothiers in the early days of the industry generally stored their wool at their houses, distributed it to the spinners and weavers in their dispersed cottages, and then collected the woven cloth, the only surviving buildings associated with the early woollen industry tend to be weavers' cottages with their wide windows that provided the necessary light for weaving, and the water powered fulling or tucking mills that appeared from the late-15th century along the Bristol Avon and the By Brook, often as adaptations of existing corn mills. Many of these water mills were small and have been destroyed, but their former existence is often revealed by surviving weirs, leets and channels that organised the water into sufficient volume to drive water wheels. After weavers had been gathered into factories wool stores and loom shops were often built in the gardens of the clothiers' town houses, as occurred at Bradford on Avon where the last woollen mill was built in 1875.

Cattle farming

WITH ALL OF THE EMPHASIS on wool as the basis of the prosperity of the Wiltshire Cotswolds it should not be assumed that sheep grazed the pastoral areas of the region to the exclusion of other animals. Sheep generally grazed the uplands while the river valleys and clay flat lands provided excellent lowland grazing for cattle. The existence of clay subsoils in the plain around Malmesbury is testified by the appearance on old large-scale maps of 'Old Clay Pit' (932887) one mile north and 'Old Brickilns' (913862) one mile south of the town.

Historically there is evidence that in the latter part of the Romano-British period stock-raising increased in Britain at the expense of agriculture and although much of this probably involved an increase in the number of sheep to produce wool it should be remembered that a tribute of hides was as easily collected from the native people as was a tribute of corn or wool, and that the Roman army needed a great deal of leather for jerkins, breeches, sandals, shield coverings, and tents. Cattle horns were also needed in early times to make a variety of objects including drinking-horns, and lard obtained from cattle or pigs was a staple constituent of the Roman army diet. Consequently many of the clay lowlands around the Bristol Avon were in Roman-British times probably devoted to cattle-farming that persisted through the ensuing Anglo-Saxon period when cattle-raiding became so rife that King Athelstan, who is strongly associated with this region, passed many laws against cattle-theft and obliged all men to report incidents of cattle-stealing.

Demand for leather continued throughout the Medieval, Tudor and Stuart periods when excellent grazing for cattle existed in areas such as Malmesbury Common (see pages 94-5) and the riverside pastures around Melksham (see pages 236-7). Some leather was probably tanned locally by tanners in pits, using as their tanning agent oak-bark obtained by men known as barkers from the Forest of Braden. Both tanner and barker became surnames, and somewhere in his ancestry the local artist Robin Tanner presumably had a tanner.

The *Gentleman's Magazine* in April 1752 reported an outbreak of cattle distemper around Malmesbury that necessitated some cattle being put down, and about a hundred years earlier Aubrey described the cattle of this region when he wrote: 'I have not seen so many pied cattle anywhere as in North Wiltshire. The country hereabouts is much inclined to pied cattle, but commonly [elsewhere] the colour is black or brown, or deep red'. These would have been the ancient longhorn breeds, and Aubrey also commented on the adverse effects of cattle-farming upon the local people in the following uncomplimentary passage about his fellow north-Wiltshiremen:

> . . . hereabout is but little tillage or hard labour, they only milk the cowes and make cheese ; they feed chiefly on milke meates, which cools their braines too much, and hurts their inventions. These circumstances make them melancholy, contemplative, and malicious ; by consequence whereof come more law suites out of North Wilts, at least double to the Southern parts. And by the same reason they are apt to be fanatiques . . .

In pointing out the litigious natures of his neighbours Aubrey was probably reflecting on the fact that although he never married he was financially ruined by law-suits arising as a result of his matrimonial problems!

None of the water-meadow systems that were created on so many of the rivers of south Wiltshire to provide an early flush of grass for animals appear to have been introduced on the rivers and streams of the north Wiltshire Cotswolds, although at their southern end the low-lying riverside pastures beside the Avon at Challimead south-west of Melksham and at Whaddon were famed for the quality of their grazing, and Melksham derived its name from the Old English *meoloc*, meaning milk.

Cheese-making

CATTLE WERE OBVIOUSLY FARMED for their milk as well as for leather, and since in early times it was difficult to keep it from going sour surplus milk was often made into butter and cheese. Of cheese-making on a commercial scale in this region Aubrey wrote:

> Now of late, about 1680, in North Wiltshire, they have altered their fashion from thin cheeses about an inch thick, made so for the sake of drying and quick sale, called at London Marlborough cheese, to thick ones, as the Cheshire cheese. At Marlborough and Tedbury [Tetbury] the London cheesemongers do keep their factors for their trade,

and he described Marlborough, that is only about twenty miles south-east of Malmesbury, as: 'one of the greatest markets for cheese in the west of England' where 'doe reside factors for the cheesemongers of London'. The expresssion: 'As different as chalk from cheese' arose to differentiate the sheep-grazed chalk upland areas of Wiltshire from the low-lying cheese-producing lands around Malmesbury.

Pig-farming

PASTORAL AND ARABLE farming were often inter-related and the waste products from dairying and brewing with the malt grown in the Wiltshire Cotswolds (see later, pages 30-1) was used to fatten local pigs. Some arable farmers and most cottagers kept one or two pigs to provide meat for their own tables, but some farmers farmed pigs on a commercial scale to be exported out of the area, particularly to London after the capital city had outgrown the capability of its immediate surroundings to feed it. Defoe confirms (again in his *Tour through the Whole Island of Great Britain* 1724-26) that:

> the farmers in Wiltshire, and the part of Gloucestershire adjoining, send a very great quantity of bacon up to London, which is esteemed the best bacon in England, Hampshire only excepted: this bacon is raised in such quantities here, by reason of the great dairies, as above, the hogs being fed with the great quantity of whey, and skim'd milk, which so many farmers have to spare, and which must, otherwise, be thrown away.

Apart from these locally farmed pigs there was much traffic in pigs that were driven in droves across the Wiltshire Cotswolds. For hundreds of years vast numbers of animals – especially cattle and sheep – were driven 'on the hoof' eastwards to feed the rapidly expanding population of London. Much of this droving by-passed the Wiltshire Cotswolds to their north or south, but many thousands of imported Irish pigs that were annually landed at Bristol were driven east towards London across the Wiltshire Cotswolds and then generally on through Calne where the pig droving trade is well-recorded. Because pigs were notoriously difficult to control a coffee house was opened at Calne in an attempt to lure the pig drovers away from the inns, a drunken drover in charge of a large drove of pigs being capable – or was it incapable – of creating immense havoc in the town. The trust books of the Calne Turnpike Trust on 23 July 1836 also minuted a decision to 'take immediate steps before the Magistrates against Pig Drivers who shall not keep their Pigs from the Foot Paths'.

The scale of this pig-droving trade is indicated by the fact that despite widespread evasion of tolls, in 1830 shortly before before the railways effectively put an end to droving 14,500 pigs from Ireland passed through Beckhampton turnpike gate east of Calne on their way to London.

Arable Farming and Malting

AS THE PROSPERITY of England for centuries depended upon wool production, in the competition for land pastoral grazing for sheep tended override the provision of land devoted arable crops, but although 'wold' means literally 'open uncultivated land' there was necessarily always a good deal of land devoted to arable crops in the Wiltshire Cotswolds. The Romans interfered very little with the agriculture practised in the Iron Age, although they introduced improved methods of drying corn in ovens, they stored it in improved storage vessels, and ground it in better rotary querns. Consequently arable production was increased, although much of it was literally swallowed up by the Roman army.

The difficulty of growing arable crops on the thin topsoils of the limestone hills prior to the appearance of artificial manures inspired the old saying that corn was 'as slow growing as Cotswold barley', and we have seen earlier that even after enclosure took place cattle and sheep continued to be used to manure with their dung the areas destined to grow arable crops. Ploughing for these crops in north Wiltshire was from very early times done by ox-teams and ox-ploughing survived in Gloucestershire and north Wiltshire well into the 20th century. This was because oxen were hardier than horses and pulled harder, they ate rougher food, and they consumed it more rapidly than did horses, and the north Wiltshire country writer Richard Jefferies wrote in 1883 of 'four oxen drawing the ancient wheeled plough' and also pointed out that they then 'made prime meat in due time', which was after working for about ten years.

Much of the barley grown in this region was as Defoe indicated used to make malt for brewing the beer that prior to the importation and popularisation of tea was the staple drink for working men and women, and for their children who were often given the small (that is weak) beer as a safe substitute for water that was then often polluted. The many local brewers and innkeepers of the district created a substantial demand for malted barley, and at Bradford on Avon for example thirteen alehouses are recorded as brewing in 1628 from 6 to 12 bushels of malt a week.

Barley was converted into malt by being first screened of extraneous matter. The grain was then steeped in water for two or three days and after it had swollen was placed on suspended malting floors consisting of thick clay tiles perforated with tiny holes in dark but well-ventilated malthouses. There it was allowed to germinate and grow for eight to ten days, being turned and spread and periodically sprinkled with water to ensure even germination under controlled conditions of temperature and humidity. Drying was achieved by lighting stoves below the floor to circulate hot air through its perforations, and by frequently turning the malt with wooden malting shovels. The finding of perforated floor tiles on a derelict site is often the only surviving sign of the former existence of a malthouse. After any stalks had been removed the dried malt was bagged-up into sacks and delivered to the brewery where it was crushed and mashed in hot water, boiled, and fermented to produce beer. Malting became a specialised activity because it demanded much more space than brewers were prepared to allocate to it, and this explains why specialist maltsters generally malted the barley and delivered it to the brewery. Place-name evidence suggests that many small local malthouses existed in the Wiltshire Cotswolds, but an examination of Victorian trade directories reveals only a few maltsters, possibly because they combined malting with other activities as did John Britton's father at Kington St Michael. There were in 1830 four maltsters at Malmesbury and three in 1848, and at Cricklade three in 1830 and two in 1848. Their apparent scarcity may be explained by the fact that the upland village of Marshfield – only a mile outside this region and just over county boundary in Gloucestershire – was a noted centre for malting and the remains there of many malthouses confirm the assertion of the artist Thomas Hennell who, when writing of malthouses in *Change in the Farm* (1934), stated: 'in the small town of Marshfield, for instance, there are said to have been eighty in living memory'. The malting industry at Marshfield died out in the second half of the 19th century when the large brewers took over the local small brewers and brought in their own malt in bulk. Barley-growing probably also declined in the Wiltshire Cotswolds at that time, although it should be remembered that barley was also used to make cheap brown bread for the poor who could not afford the refined white wheaten loaves that were eaten by the rich.

Stone and Stone-quarrying

I N *The Making of the English Landscape* (1955), the pioneer field archaeologist Professor W. G. Hoskins, after indicating that geology lies behind the English landscape, suggested that it was the duty of the historian to clothe the geological skeleton. This is particularly relevant in the Cotswolds where as I have already emphasised buildings were almost invariably constructed of the local stone.

A large part of north-west Wiltshire stands on the belt of sedimentary oolitic limestone rock that extends north-east from Dorset to Lincolnshire. The word oolite is derived from the Greek word for egg, and the Cotswold limestone of Wiltshire, Gloucestershire and Oxfordshire is sometimes known as roe-stone because when examined under a microscope it is seen to consist of granules that resemble closely-packed fish eggs. It is practically impossible to describe the beauty of this limestone when it has naturally weathered and become smothered with lichen growth. This weathering, that is best seen at close range on old gravestones in churchyards, on gatepiers outside manor-houses, and on milestones beside turnpike roads, was graphically described by the poet Edward Thomas when he recorded passing on one of his long walks in Wiltshire: 'Old milestones lichened as with battered gold and silver nails'. On new stone this weathering can easily be accelerated. When in the 1960s involved in reconstructing an 18th century turnpike cottage at the west end of Marshfield, only a very short distance west of the the Wiltshire Cotswolds, I specified that all of the aggressively new stonework was to be liberally painted with a solution of cow dung, soot and yogurt. Within six months this treatment rendered the new stone indistinguishable from the re-used two hundred years old weathered stone.

The rubble building stone and stone slates used in the Wiltshire Cotswolds were obtained from open surface quarries throughout the region between Malmesbury and Bradford, but the finer oolitic freestone used for the more important ashlar buildings was obtained from deeper layers at the southern end of the region where in modern times it has been commercially extracted from quarries and underground mines, for many centuries at Box and later at Corsham. Box stone was known in Roman and Saxon times, but the full potential of Corsham stone was not realised until the stone excavated in the construction of Box Tunnel in the 1840s (see page 192) was used to construct the railway village and works at New Swindon and was found to be excellent for building. It should be recognised that buildings in the Cotswold style and materials were sometimes built at some distance from the sources of this stone, and that the Cotswold style sometimes extends for some distance outside the limestone belt into areas such as the northern fringe of Wiltshire included in this book where builders sometimes used Cotswold stone and stone slates in their buildings.

The long history of stone building in this region may be briefly summarised as follows. Dry-stone walling was used in Neolithic long barrows such as Stony Littleton long barrow near Wellow that is surrounded by a dry-stone wall. Prehistoric man also used stone in a primitive way by setting up large unworked stone monoliths to form the chambers and portals of long-barrows such as Lanhill and Lugbury, and for forming loose-laid rubble foundations for his timber structures. The Romans, who quarried stone and marble in Italy and there used it expertly to build their extremely sophisticated clasical buildings, imported their methods into Britain where with their keen awareness of mineral wealth they were soon after their conquest using the limestone of this region for building and for sculpture, in for example in their baths at Bath, their fine town buildings at Cirencester, and in many of their their rural villas and temples.

Box Hill from the east end of Box

The pagan Saxons in their northern European homelands almost invariably built in timber and in Britain, despite marvelling at the surviving remains of stone-built Romano-British buildings, they continued this practice until they were converted to christianity. The royally connected St Aldhelm of Malmesbury must after visiting Rome have recognised the remains of buildings at places such as Bath and Cirencester as being Roman and it was Aldhelm who revealed to his people the stone quarries at Hazelbury near Box (see later, pages 34-5). After some of the christianised Anglo-Saxon aristocracy including King Ethelwulf and the future King Alfred had also made ilgrimages to Rome and also seen the stone-built architectural splendours of that city, the Anglo-Saxons although they continued to employ timber for their domestic buildings began to use the more noble and permanent stone for their carved crosses and for their more prestigeous buildings that they erected to the glory of God, a surviving example being their tiny church at Bradford on Avon.

The Normans had used stone extensively for building in Normandy and after the Conquest they rapidly built throughout England an astonishing number of stone-built castles, abbeys, monasteries, churches and manor houses, largely to overawe the native Anglo-Saxons and stamp their authority on the newly conquered land. The principal surviving example of their work in this region is the great abbey at Malmesbury.

The transportation of huge quantities of heavy freestone for ashlar work from the quarries to the building sites must in early times have posed immense transportation problems. The Romans and the Anglo-Saxons would almost certainly have transported stone for their stone buildings by water and this practice must have persisted throughout Norman and Medieval times when roads were so appalling that they were often impassible even to light traffic. Most of the freestone for ashlar buildings must then have been carried on barges along navigable rivers to points as near as possible to the locations where it was needed, and then transported short final distances by cart. We know however that in the late-16th century the stone for Longleat House was brought the twenty-five miles from Hazelbury Quarry near Box to Longleat on ox-drawn sledges.

The freestone from the southern end of the Wiltshire Cotswolds is generally known as Bath stone. This name is someting of a misnomer as although there were extensive stone quarries at Combe Down south of Bath, much of the finest Bath stone was obtained from Wiltshire mines and quarries at Hazelbury near Box and, particularly after about 1840 from the Corsham district where the light cream slightly coarse-grained stone known as Corngrit was mined. In the 18th century Bath stone was promoted as a business speculation by Ralph Allen after he bought the Combe Down quarries and it was exported and used in many places, although in London it was regarded with some suspicion and even derided as 'Cheddar cheese' because it was thought that in the then polluted London atmosphere it would be impermanent. There was some justification in this allegation as limestone is not chemically inert and it can react with the acidic fumes that are generated by smoke in a polluted environment. Another problem is that the blackening on stone caused by urban smoke is less acceptable on honey-coloured limestone than on the darker sandstones.

The building of the Kennet and Avon Canal and the coming of the railways provided an impetus to the marketing of the products of the Wiltshire stone quarries, initially because some stone was used in their construction, and later because they made the cheap transportation of stone great distances more practicable. In 1887 several stone companies amalgamated in order to promote the local stone under the name of The Bath Stone Firms which later became The Bath and Portland Stone Firms.

Stone-quarrying involved obtaining stone from near the surface, while in stone-mining the stone was obtained from deep underground workings. Bath stone is in fact the only major English stone that was mined rather than quarried. The best oolitic freestone was initially quarried from Box Hill until the construction of Box Tunnel in the 1840s revealed previously unknown beds of fine building stone which led to a huge network of tunnelled underground mine workings being excavated around Corsham.

The name St Aldhelm Box Ground commemorates the incident when St Aldhelm riding over Hazelbury Hill threw down his glove and ordered his companions to dig where it fell promising that they would find great treasure, they did so, and discovered the excellent freestone. These early quarries, that are now filled in, were located between Box and Hazelbury House north-east of Hazelbury Hill where Quarry Hill (830686) is marked on modern maps. They were at first granted to the monks of Stanley Abbey, Lacock Abbey, and Bradenstoke Abbey who quarried the stone that was used for early important ecclesiastical

buildings including the Saxon church at Bradford on Avon, Lacock
Abbey, and Monkton Farleigh Priory. The quarries were then for a time
owned by Sampson de la Boxe, the Lord of Box, but later some quarries
at Hazelbury were sold to rich individuals including Thomas Tropenell
in 1485 for building Great Chalfield Manor and Sir John Thynne in 1573
for his great Elizabethan prodigy house at Longleat near Warminster in
west Wiltshire. The story of St Aldhelm's discovery of the Hazelbury
quarries was recorded by John Aubrey in his Wiltshire Topographical
Collections which were collected by Canon Jackson and published in
1862:

Site of Hazelbury
Quarry from Box

Haslebury Quarre is not to be forgott, it is the eminentest freestone quarry
in the West of England, Malmesbury and all round the country of it. The old
men's story [is] that St Aldhelme, riding over there, threw down his glove,
and bade them digge, and they should find great treasure, meaning the
Quarry.

   Aubrey also described Hazelbury quarry as: 'the most eminent for
freestone in the western parts before the discovery of the Portland quarry,
which was about anno 1600', but by the 20th century most of the Bath
stone required to satisfy the now reduced demand was quarried in
Wiltshire from around Corsham.
   The oolitic freestone – the term means fine-grained and capable of
being sawn and worked in all directions – used for fine ashlar and carved
work came from the lower beds of stone. This deep-mined freestone
emerged soft from the mine and while in that condition was easily sawn

by hand, but before being used for building it had to be dried of its quarry sap and allowed to harden. To achieve durability it also needed to be bedded as it had lain in the quarry, otherwise it would laminate and disintegrate.

Just as in the Wiltshire downlands the chalk bedrock is sometimes over laid with 'clay-with-flints', the limestone bedrock of the Wiltshire Cotswolds is sometimes similarly associated with the coarse rubble limestone that is known as cornbrash and is usually found embedded in beds of clay. The name cornbrash arises from the fact that these clay beds containing the cornbrash – and brash means fragments of rock – were capable of growing good arable crops, as was noted by Aubrey when he described the country around Brokenborough near Malmesbury as being 'altogether upon a Stone-brash and very natural for Barley'. Because it often lays near the surface this cornbrash has been extensively used in rubble cottages and barns after being taken from the surface at many locations in Wiltshire, especially around Bradford on Avon and Winsley where the land still grows arable crops.

Stone mined from the underground mines at Box Hill (835694) was reached by means of inclined shafts or 'adits' driven into the hillsides. These sometimes ran for miles underground and the more than sixty miles of them in this district constitute one of the largest underground stone mines in the world. To prevent the roofs of the mines from collapsing much valuable stone had to be left in-situ in substantial supporting piers. Occasionally stone was extracted by vertical shafts, a method that led to the creation of an excavation called 'the Cathedral' that was for a time one of the sights of the neighbourhood being a hundred feet deep, shaped like a bottle, and with galleries driven out from it at three levels. From it excavated stone was lifted to the surface by a chain and a horse-gin, and after 'the Cathedral' was abandoned in about 1850 the quarrymen were in the habit of bringing their wives and girl friends to see it for an afternoon outing.

As was usual in industrial regions many of the Box quarrymen in the 17th and 18th centuries became ardent non-conformists and when in the mid-19th century they supported a Methodist preacher the uncompromising vicar of Box had him arrested. As Spring Quarry near the east end of Box Tunnel (at 854692) was used by the quarrymen for their non-conformist meetings it became known as Chapel Ground.

Prior to the Great War the disused underground workings around Bradford on Avon were found to be ideal for mushroom growing, using horse-dung from the Wiltshire racehorse stables as a manure. During the Second World War the vast underground galleries in the Corsham mines were used for storing ammunition, and in 1942 an aircraft factory was built there underground. In that war some redundant stone mines were also used to store the nation's art treasures.

After the Second World War artificial Cotswold stone walling

The Quarryman's Arms
on Box Hill

blocks, window mullions and surrounds, and 'stone' slates were invented as cheaper substitutes for the natural limestone. Although they are sometimes clever imitations of the real thing, because they are basically constructed of the denser and cheaper concrete they do not weather so beautifully. Their attractions are their cheapness, the fact that they are possibly more durable than the natural oolite, and that they require less maintenance. On the other hand they are aesthetically much inferior as being machine-made they are regularly shaped and do not readily acquire the attractive patina that age confers upon natural stone.

I can recall in the 1990s touring the Box underground stone mines in a conducted party. Shortly after this such tours were discontinued, but today anyone interested in the stone industry of this region should visit the Quarryman's Arms on Box Hill (835695). This former resort of local quarrymen standing among their cottages has displayed on its walls maps of the stone mines and a display of photographs and memorabilia surviving from the industry. This inn is rather difficult to find and prospective visitors should from a point near the bus-stop on the A4 on Box Hill (836696) a mile north-east of Box proceed south up Hedgesparrow Lane, enter Barnett's Hill, and at a junction turn right. The Quarryman's Arms is then found on the right a short distance along the lane. Although both Hedgesparrow Lane and Barnett's Hill are steep they are suitable for cars, and the inn has a car park. Another place well worth visiting is the Tourist Information Centre in Corsham High Street which has a room entirely devoted to the history of stone mining in this region.

Paper-making

PAPER-MAKING was introduced into Europe from the east in the 11th century although it did not reach England until the late-15th century at about the time when the first book to be printed in English came out in 1475. Printing then developed in England throughout the 16th century and it created a great need for paper to satisfy the demand for printed books. By 1588 Queen Elizabeth was issuing licences for paper-making and soon after this paper-making made its appearance in the

Wiltshire Cotswolds where for a time it flourished. An essential requirement for paper-making was an ample supply of very clean water and the By Brook admirably fulfilled this need. John Aubrey tells us in the 17th century that a paper mill which supplied brown paper to the Bristol market then existed at Yatton Keynell, but in fact at Long Dean, south of Castle Combe in the parish of Yatton Keynell. Aubrey's mention of the Bristol market reveals one of the reasons why paper-making was attracted to this district.

In its early days the paper-making process involved stretching a woven cloth tightly over a frame of the size of paper required. Another frame was then placed over this and the frames were then immersed in a vat containing a mixture of fibres and water known as 'stuff'. The frames were then shaken to spread the pulp evenly, the outer frame was removed, and the paper was pressed before being dried by being hung on long ropes in large drying sheds situated near the mills. The paper was then coated with size and machine-rolled to give it a glaze. Existing woollen mills were often adapted for paper-making as was the case at Long Dean,

Weavern Farm

and more paper mills were opened further down the By Brook. One of these at Slaughterford continued to produce paper until comparatively modern times, although the population of this small village was much reduced when one of the paper mills closed in the 1840s. The Rag Mill at Slaughterford converted rags into fibres for papermaking, and a mile and a half south of Slaughterford at the edge of Colerne parish the former *'Weverne'* woollen mill that is now Weavern Farm (841718) and was Wayworn Mill on Andrews and Dury in 1773, became the Weavern Paper Mill, and continued making paper until about 1860. Other paper-mills existed elsewhere in the parish of Colerne. One was on the tiny Doncombe Brook at the north edge of the parish, while another on the By Brook a mile east of Colerne at Widdenham was converted back into a woollen mill in about 1744 and is now Widdenham Farm (838710).

2
Malmesbury and the Northern Fringe,
including the
Fosse Way

THIS ACCOUNT of the topography and history of the Wiltshire Cotswolds begins at their northern end with two areas, that around Malmesbury and also the northern fringe of Wiltshire that extends from Malmesbury eastwards as far as Cricklade. The boundaries of the former are to its west and north the Wiltshire county boundary, to its south the M4 motorway, and on its east the A429 from Stanton St Quintin as far north as the county boundary. The northern fringe is the wedge-shaped area that runs east from the A429 to Cricklade and is bounded on its north by the county boundary and to its south by the B4040 road. Within these districts, that are defined on the map on page vi, are the historic towns of Malmesbury and Cricklade, the large villages of Sherston and Ashton Keynes, and a number of smaller villages including Brokenborough and Crudwell. The northern fringe between Malmesbury and Cricklade is included because although it lies away from the limestone belt and is topographically adjacent to the Upper Thames Valley, many of its buildings are Cotswold in style.

As it is one of the the remotest parts of Wiltshire the north-western area of the Wiltshire Cotswolds is not much visited. A glance at the definitive rights-of-way map reveals that it is rather lacking in public footpaths and that most of its ways are minor roads; motorists generally have little cause to enter this area west of the A429 other than to visit Malmesbury. This remoteness makes the countryside north and west of Malmesbury topographically an attractive part of Wiltshire that is also of historical interest. From the time during during the Roman Conquest when it was temporarily the frontier zone of Roman Britain (as described later, page 42) to the so-called Dark Ages it saw much military activity largely because it stood on the border between the often-warring kingdoms of christian Wessex and pagan Mercia, and later when, after they had become christian, the Anglo-Saxons were resisting the incursions of the pagan Vikings that began merely as sporadic plundering raids but developed into determined attempts to conquer Wessex.

The northern fringe of Wiltshire between Gloucestershire and the former Braden Forest to its south is better provided with footpaths than is the north-west of the county. It is also more populated as it contains a number of small settlements, the large village of Ashton Keynes, and the small town of Cricklade.

Geologically north-west Wiltshire stands on oolitic limestone rock or beds of cornbrash rubble embedded in a mixture of clay and sand, but in the northern fringe east of the A429 the geology is rather different. This region lies largely in the clay vale catchment area of the River Thames with its beds of river gravel, while in the southern part of this northern fringe a narrow belt of corallian limestone runs east from near Malmesbury past Charlton, and then widens out between Cricklade and Swindon. Elsewhere a band of cornbrash rubble runs north past Corsham, Chippenham, Charlton and Oaksey to Pool Keynes in Gloucestershire. These bands of corallian limestone and cornbrash have provided the stone that has been used to construct many of the buildings of this district.'

The Fosse Way

THE ROMAN ROAD that we know as the Fosse Way provides an appropriate subject with which to open this account of the historic Wiltshire Cotswolds because in addition to being essentially historic it passes through some of the finest rural topography of the region. This road derives its name from the Latin *fossa* meaning ditch from the ditches were excavated beside it to provide good drainage, and the Saxon weg meaning way. It ran north-east from Devon across England to Lincoln, and over the almost twenty miles that it crosses or borders north-west Wiltshire it survives as a public right-of-way, apart from its last mile across Kemble airfield just before it enters Gloucestershire. As is usual but not invariably the case with Roman roads, the Fosse Way for most of its length follows a gunbarrel straight line and in Wiltshire it generally survives as a hedge-lined byway linking Roman Bath (*Aquae Sulis*) to Cirencester (*Corinium*).

Roman roads were generally surfaced with gravel or flints but parts of the Fosse Way were paved with stone where it was available.

Fosse Way looking north from Ladyswood

When early in the 20th century A. D. Passmore sectioned the Fosse Way near Easton Grey he found that the road was originally surfaced with small limestone slabs set on a one foot bed of clay packed with limestone rubble, and much earlier William Stukeley recorded in his *Itinerarium Curiosum* (1776) seeing a stretch of the Fosse Way near Ilchester in Somerset that was in his words 'composed of the flat quarry stones of the country, of good breadth, laid edgewise', and looking 'like the side of a wall fallen down'. This phrase is interesting as if this construction applied throughout the Fosse Way its stones may have been removed and used to build some of the Saxon and Medieval stone buildings that stand near it.

The old road has survived because in the times of enclosure Roman roads were often left undisturbed. One 1765 enclosure award particularly stipulated that the Fosse Way should be left 'of the same width as it hath heretofore usually been'. In its early days the Fosse Way was not merely a road. After the Romans in about AD 60 made London (*Londinium*) the mercantile and financial centre of their Britannia Superior most of their main roads were constructed radiating from London. The Fosse Way is however an exception in that it crosses the major radial Roman roads, the explanation for this being that it originated as a military road which for a time serviced the temporary frontier of Roman Britain. As early as 1935 Geoffrey Boumphrey suggested in *Along the Roman Roads* that: 'Ostorius Scapulus . . . decided to consolidate his gains . . . and built a line of forts along the Fosse Way' while he disarmed the tribes in his rear before advancing into Wales. Tacitus confirms this, and I. D. Margary in *Roman Roads in Britain* (1955) indicated that the Fosse Way 'was formed originally along the line of an early occupation boundary, soon after the Claudian invasion'. That this was probably a wise precaution is suggested by the fact a few years later the Romans, while reducing the Druids of Anglesey in North Wales, had to contend with Boudicca's revolt in their rear.

Margary pointed out that: 'A Roman frontier, or *limes*, was accompanied by a road, to give rapid lateral communication in case of trouble . . . ', and the text to the *Ordnance Survey Map of Roman Britain* (3rd edn, 1956) states: 'AD 47. Ostorius Scapula, governor, draws a frontier from Trent to Severn'. In their *The Roman Conquest of Britain* (1973) Webster and Dudley pointed out that the 'Fosse Way has long been regarded as a military conception', but the road was not as has sometimes been suggested the actual frontier but the line of communication that serviced the frontier zone with troops and supplies. That the frontier zone extended beyond the Fosse Way is confirmed by the fact that as early as AD 49 the Romans were exploiting the Mendip lead mines to its west. The possibility that this temporary frontier was provided with a line of signal stations is discussed in Chapter 3 (pages 170-3).

After the 2nd Augusta Legion, commanded by the tough Roman commander Vespasian (AD 7-79) who had made his reputation on the Roman frontiers and was in AD 69 to become Emperor of Rome, had conquered the south country and secured the important lead mines of Mendip, Aulus Plautus in was in AD 47 succeeded as governor of Britain. His successor Ostorius Scapula decided that the Roman army had become over-extended and ordered a pause while the native tribes south of a line Severn to Trent were, as was recorded by Tacitus in *The Annals of Imperial Rome*, subdued before an advance was made into South Wales to reduce Caratacus, the defeated British leader who had fled into the west and was organising the opposition to the Romans by the Silures in Wales. The line of the Fosse Way then remained the approximate frontier zone while the conquest of Wales was completed during AD 47-51. In AD 52 Ostorius Scapula then died: 'worn out by the cares of office'.

Of the twenty miles over which the Fosse Way either forms the county boundary or crosses Wiltshire 9¼ of its miles are metalled and 10¾ miles are green ways. The absence of towns or villages along its route induces feelings of remoteness that are conducive to thinking, perhaps about the countless generations who for almost two thousand years have followed this ancient road, from the soldiers and roadmakers who during the *Pax Romana* would have been succeeded by civilians, civil servants, and Romanised Britons. to the Saxon armies that would have followed the road as they ranged around the countryside, as also would have the marauding Viking armies. The Fosse Way was also used in Medieval times, probably to reach Malmesbury out of the west and certainly by pilgrims making their way to Hailes Abbey in Gloucestershire (see page 137), until the time when the first new roads since Roman times began to be built. The Fosse Way then, apart from its now-metalled stretches, fell into disuse and became the remote byway that it remains in places today.

For those who may wish to walk the Fosse Way I shall now describe the old road progressively north-east from the Three Shire Stones to near Kemble.

From Bath the Fosse Way follows the line of the A4 until it leaves that road at Batheaston. At a quarry on Banner Down it (at 793687) joins a minor road and after changing direction to a little more east of north it

Three Shire Stones west of Colerne

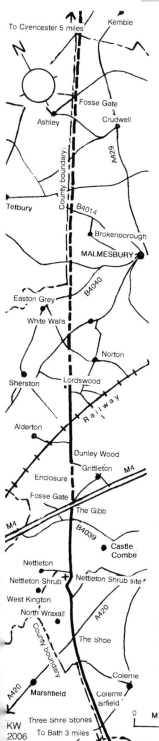

follows that road into Wiltshire past the Three Shires Stones (797703) that stand at the west side of the Fosse and appear to be the stones of a former Neolithic long barrow re-used in 1736 to mark the point where Somerset, Gloucestershire and Wiltshire then met. From these stones the Fosse Way continues along the minor road here coinciding with the county boundary along the west edge of Colerne airfield. At Doncombe Scrubs it departs from the county boundary and becomes for five miles a minor road past the Shoe Inn (formerly The Horseshoe: 808743) on the A420 and between Mountain Bower and North Wraxall.

When walking the Fosse Way in 1932 for his *Along the Roman Roads* (1935) Geoffrey Boumphrey commented how over its next stretch it became: 'less and less like a road and more and more like a lane' and noted how it: 'ducked down through a little valley by Nettleton Shrub, where traces of a Roman posting-station have been found (about 10 miles from Bath – the usual distance), and a mile further on it did the same in another little valley even more lovely – with a brook making the best of all noises over a little sluice'. The Nettleton Shrub settlement at the crossing of Broadmead Brook (at 822769 south of Nettleton Shrub) will be described later (pages 139-44). After after leaving Nettleton Shrub shortly before reaching Fosse Gate east of Lugbury long barrow (831786: see pages 144--5) the Fosse Way crosses the By Brook at Fosse Bridge under Gatcombe Hill (836789), as described above by Boumphrey. It then passes through a road intersection at The Gibb (838791) that was 'Gibraltar Turnpike' on the 1773 map by Andrews and Dury and 'Gibraltar' in Colt Hoare's 1819 *Ancient History of North Wiltshire*.

After passing through a tunnel under the M4 at Fosse Gate (840795) the Roman road enters the area that I have defined as the North-Wiltshire Cotswolds, and for seven miles continues to run roughly north-east, for a mile past Grittleton as a green way. Boumphrey mentioned how here the Fosse Way expanded to 'a full 60 feet' in width and became 'a noble road to walk along'. South of Oldlands Wood it passes through (at 844800) a virtually square earthwork enclosure measuring about 45 yards square with rounded corners that although it resembles a Roman marching camp was perhaps a more permanent camp or signal station created during the construction of the road. The Fosse Way often coincides with parish boundaries and is consequently mentioned in a number of Anglo-Saxon Charters, including the AD 956 Grittleton Charter in which

LINEAR PLAN OF THE FOSSE WAY IN WILTSHIRE

it is referred to as 'the public road which the ancients called *straet* [street] but which is now called *Fosse*.'

When they encountered small streams Roman engineers often built culverts to channel them under their roads. At the west end of Dunley Wood (853813) Boumphrey in 1932 commented on: 'In one place a little stream bridged by a great flat stone which looked as though it might have had an interesting history if only one could get at it'. From Dunley Wood the Fosse Way continues for three miles as a minor road and at the present Fosse Lodge (857820) the 1773 map marks 'The Elm and the Ash, Chapel Leaze in Ruins'. About half a mile beyond here the Fosse Way crosses the railway over a bridge and then continues as a minor road passing east of Lordswood Farm (at 870841). At a T-junction of roads north-east of Lordswood it again becomes (at 872843) a green lane for three miles past Sherston, apart from one short metalled stretch that provides a convenient place to park a car (at 880854) for a walk along the Fosse Way. Although designated public rights-of-way the unmetalled stretches of the Fosse Way in this area can be extremely muddy in winter and obstructed by brambles in summer. Margary in his definitive *Roman Roads in Britain* (1955) suggested that a [Roman] road branched north from the Fosse Way 1 mile south of Easton Grey [at 882858] passing close to Easton Grey House. From this point (882858) Geoffrey Boumphrey noted how 'a most un-Fosse-like track led straight ahead through a field', and soon stretched ahead 'widely set between walls'.

Fosse Way looking south from near Ladyswood

Half a mile east of Easton Grey an abandoned mill site (at 887872) marked on the first edition of the Ordnance Survey 'Foss Mill' may in view of its proximity to the nearby Roman station have been the site of a Roman mill. This Roman station, that was designated *Mutuantonis* (White Walls) by Colt Hoare and is described later (page 105), stood around the point where the Fosse crosses the Sherston branch of River Avon by a modern bridge (889871). Boumphrey wrote that 'when this bridge was put up, the footings of an old timber bridge were found which probably dated back to Roman times'. From White Walls the Roman road continues as a sometimes unmetalled byway described by Geoffrey Boumphrey as 'often 60 feet broad, sometimes raised above the fields on either side and dead straight uphill and down'. For much of its remaining length in Wiltshire the Fosse Way past Brokenborough and Crudwell coincides with the county boundary although opposite Brokenborough a bulge of Wiltshire formerly extended north-west of the Fosse Way (between points 911902 and 944950) to Tetbury. This bulge, that included Long Newnton and Ashley, was long ago transferred to Gloucestershire in a boundary adjustment and it is not included in this book.

Old mill race east of Easton Grey

Before reaching Cirencester the Fosse crosses (at 911903) the Tetbury branch of the River Avon (at 911902 north-west of Brokenborough) by 'a little bridge which is evidently very old and looks as though it was made for pack-horses' (Boumphrey). This bridge was 'Foss Way Bridge' on Andrew's and Dury's 1773 map. Two miles beyond this bridge the buildings on the Wiltshire side of the Fosse way opposite Long Newton (at 924921) occupy the site of an airfield (centred on 928920) that was created in 1940 as a decoy for Kemble airfield.

On the first edition of the Ordnance Survey the final stretch of the Fosse Way as it passes a mile and a half west of Crudwell is named 'Acman Street'. In its crossing of Kemble airfield the Fosse Way is no longer a right-of-way and it leaves Wiltshire and enters Gloucestershire shortly before reaching Jackaments Bottom about five miles from Cirencester.

Fosse Way river crossing at White Walls

The Area North of Malmesbury

HAVING BEEN HISTORICALLY generally devoted to sheep-grazing, barley-growing, and to a lesser extent stone quarrying, the long narrow wedge of Wiltshire that extends north of Malmesbury between the Fosse Way and the A429 is the least populated area of the Wiltshire Cotswolds. Its countryside remains largely open as a legacy of it having for centuries been used as sheepwalks by the abbey of Malmesbury, and walking in it is restricted by a deficiency of footpaths.

This district contains two villages in Brokenborough and Crudwell, the smallest and most remote being Brokenborough (917893) that stands well away from A-roads above the Tetbury branch of the Bristol Avon about half a mile east of the Fosse Way. Its older buildings around its church are stone-built, and Aubrey commented that the country around Brokenborough was: 'altogether upon a Stone-brash [i.e. Cornbrash] and very natural for Barley'. The principal historical interest in Brokenborough arises from the tradition that it was the site of the former palace of King Athelstan. This has generally been disbelieved, and the *Wiltshire Victoria County History* dismisses the story as 'implausible', but Aubrey believed it in the 17th century and a late-14th century chronicle written by a monk of Malmesbury claimed that a royal residence once existed at the manor of 'Kairdureburgh', and this according to *The Place-Names of Wiltshire* (1939) was the Celtic name for Brokenborough. The Malmesbury chronicle indicated that an early settlement at Malmesbury was destroyed when the hill upon which it stood was fortified as a castle called Inglebourne Castle, Ingleburne being the early name for the Tetbury branch of the Bristol Avon. The Saxon residents of Malmesbury were said to have then departed to

Brokenborough where the Kings of Wessex then lived, but to have returned after Maldulf founded his monastery at Malmesbury. Canon Jackson in the 19th century recorded a local tradition that Brokenborough was 'a 100 years older than Malmesbury', but the Malmesbury monk may have perpetuated a local legend or mistaken the remains of a Saxon settlement for the ruins of a Saxon palace. If such a palace existed it would presumably have been on the elevated land north of the church known as Goldhill. Thirteen years after King Athelstan's death Brokenborough was in AD 952 given to Malmesbury Abbey.

In describing Brokenborough Aubrey noted that 'the river embraces it like a horseshoe' and he also mentioned seeing at Brokenborough an 'old farme house moated' that was a grange of the great abbey. This has now gone, but a large early barn formerly stood on a moated site south of the church. When Aubrey was twenty-one an elderly man called John Bevin and his wife were in 1647 evicted from their cottage at Brokenborough and 'constrained to dwell in a hollow tree in the streete to the great harm of their lives they being ancient people'. A ten-bay double-porched late-Medieval monastic barn that also belonged to the abbey survives at Brokenborough whose church contains an early 13th century nave arcade on circular columns, a chancel arch with a squint, some good corbel heads supporting the roof, some remains of wall-paintings, and externally a timber bell turret, all of which survived restoration.

After the Reformation Brokenborough was as a manor belonging to Malmesbury Abbey in 1552 granted in an exchange deal to John Dudley, Duke of Northumberland. He sold it in the year that he was executed (1553) to Sir James Stumpe, the son of William Stumpe the Malmesbury clothier from whom it later passed by the marriage of a Stumpe heiress to the Knyvets of Charlton.

Crudwell Church

The only other village north of Malmesbury in this region is Crudwell (953927) that, as it stands on the A429, is much less remote than Brokenborough. It stands on a knoll, and Crudwell parish extended east over Eastcourt as far as Minety. Aubrey believed the bench ends in Crudwell Church to be 'the best and most substantiall I know of anywhere'. A mineral spring south-east of the church was reputed to transform milk into cream, and Aubrey rather improbably suggested that this spring explained the name of Crudwell when he wrote:

> At Crudwell neer to the mannoir house, is a fine spring in the street called Bery-well. Labourers say it quenches the thirst better than other wells . . . The towne, a mannoir of the Lord Lucas, hath its denomination from this well ; perhaps it is called Crudwell from its turning of milke into cruds.

Aubrey was inclined to be credulous and this seems to be a fanciful theory to explain the name of the village that was *Credvelle* in Domesday and is, according to *The Place-Names of Wiltshire* (1939), derived from 'Creoda's spring or stream'. At Crudwell the headwaters of the River Thames that flow through the village are spanned by a two-arched bridge.

Crudwell was in AD 850 given by King Ethelwulf to Malmesbury Abbey and at the Dissolution was acquired by the so-called 'Count' of Oxford, this being the 16th Earl John de Vere whose son Edward, who became the 17th Earl (1550-1604), was the impetuous court-poet who was believed by some to have been the writer of Shakespeare's plays. When Edward de Vere was nine in 1559 his father sold Crudwell to Sir Thomas Lucas and a hundred years later a Lord Lucas of Crudwell so distinguished himself in the royal cause in the Civil War that his daughter was created Baroness Lucas of Crudwell. After this family left in the 18th century the leading family at Crudwell became the Earles, a family of Bristol merchants who rose from being yeomen in the late-16th century to be minor gentry in the 18th after Sir Thomas Earle (d. 1696), a mayor of Bristol and an MP, inherited Eastcourt two miles east of Crudwell from his uncle.

A great gate to a manor house stood at Crudwell in Aubrey's time, and he also tells us that a large barn had recently been pulled down. In the 19th century John Britton saw and described this 'ancient gateway' which has now gone. The survival of a 15th century barn now convered to a dwelling a little south-east of the church suggests either that Aubrey was mistaken or that there were then two barns at Crudwell.

Charlton and its Parks

THREE MILES SOUTH of Crudwell and about a two miles north-east of Malmesbury is Charlton Park that is bounded to its west by the A429. The B4040 skirts the its south side and then passes through

Cottages at entrance to Charlton Park

Charlton village (962889) that until it was surrendered at the Dissolution of the monasteries was a manor belonging to Malmesbury Abbey. The park gates are at the west end of Church Street beside the much-restored village church. Pevsner mentions at Charlton a 'Handsome village street with divers attractive houses', although the only village building that he singles out for mention is the 17th century Village Farmhouse at its east end. The village is built largely of stone that presumably came from quarries shown immediately south of Charlton on old maps. Charlton's only building of real importance is its big house that stands out of sight within the extensive and strictly private former deer park.

At the Dissolution Malmesbury Abbey was bought by the clothier William Stumpe whose son and heir Sir James Stumpe, the MP for Malmesbury 1555-6, married a Bayntun lady from Bromham. They had no son and their heiress daughter Elizabeth married in 1566 Sir Henry

Charlton Church Tower

Knyvet (c.1537-1598) from a Cornish military family. His father Sir Henry senior (died 1546) had been Constable of Beaumaris Castle and his son Sir Henry of Charlton was disabled and lost 'both lim and blood' fighting against the French at the siege of Leith. Sir Henry junior became MP for Malmesbury, gained the approval of Queen Elizabeth, was knighted in 1574, and according to Aubrey in 1588 had a command in the forces that were assembled to oppose the Armada. He is commemorated with his wife Elizabeth, who died in 1585, by an imposing canopied tomb in the chancel of Charlton church.

The history of the park at Charlton is confused because the present home park around the mansion house had a virtually unknown predecessor called Stonehill Park about three miles east of Charlton that was presumably created by the Abbot of Malmesbury. The Stonehill Farm (983894) and Stonehill Wood (003893) of the current Ordnance Survey are on the site of Stonehill Park, and the

'Old Park' (984899) and 'Old Park Coppice' (997898) – now Park Copse – of the first Ordnance Survey also commemorate this park. The precise date of its emparkment is not known, but it was emparked and stocked with deer by the mid-15th century and a keeper was appointed to it in 1576. The Malmesbury to Minety road (B4040) probably bisects Stonehill Park that, after being for a time abandoned, was revived and re-enclosed with a park-pale fence by the Knyvets of Charlton in about 1610. It then covered about 400 acres and was designated 'Old Park', but when the huge new home park was created around the big new house the old park was disparked and turned over to grazing and agriculture.

Since the parks at Charlton are the first of several examples of Medieval deer parks to be mentioned in this book some details about the function and importance of such parks is appropriate as although they once occupied about two per cent of the land area of England deer parks are one of the most neglected elements of the Medieval, Tudor and Stuart landscapes.

A few parks may have existed in Saxon times but they were popularised by the Normans to provide them with recreational hunting, venison for the table, and buckskins for clothing. Since early parks were the prerogative of kings, noblemen, and prelates such as the Abbot of Malmesbury, who owned several parks in this region, they provided status symbols for their illustrious owners although later in the Medieval period many quite ordinary lords of the manor aspired to emulate their betters by owning deer parks which continued to be created until the time of James I. When the newly-rich men who had prospered from the Dissolution of the monasteries built ostentatious prodigy houses and surrounded them with landscaped parks that were stocked with deer that now became became simply ornamental working deer parks became unfashionable and their former existence was gradually forgotten and their importance and locations are now seldom recognised.

Charlton Park mansion

The fact that the word 'Park' was first appended to Charlton Park in 1580 in an account of a duel between Sir Henry Knyvet and Mr Moody of Garsdon in which Sir Henry was almost killed confirms that Charlton Park was a late creation as a deer park. Prior to the Dissolution the land that it occupies belonged to the Abbey of Malmesbury and it seems likely that the park around Charlton House was made to replace Stonehill Park when the first big house at Charlton was built soon after the Dissolution. It was emparked by the late 16th century and was listed in the 1583 *Note of Parks in the County of Wilts (State Papers Domestic)* as being two miles in circuit and owned by Sir Henry Knyvet.

In 1760 it covered only about 245 acres but by 1773 it had increased to about 675 acres. It was further enlarged in 1808 and today it covers about 600 acres. To its south and west it is partly walled with walls that are probably the surviving remains of the deer park walls that became usual in stone districts rather than the elaborate park-pale ditches and banks surmounted by fences that generally enclosed the earlier deer parks.

At the death of Sir Henry Knyvet Charlton was inherited by his second son Thomas Knyvet of Escrick (d.1622) who was instrumental in foiling the Gunpowder Plot. When it was rumoured that a catholic plot existed to blow up King James and his parliament Sir Thomas was, as a Gentleman of the King's Household, on 4 November 1605 ordered to search the basement of the House of Commons and there became suspicious about the vast quantity of logs stored for winter fuel. He had them pulled aside and discovered the barrels of gunpowder that had been placed by the plotters. Guy Fawkes was then found with fuses in his possession and it was to Thomas Knyvet that he is said to have confessed his intention of blowing up the Houses of Parliament together with King James and his entire family.

Katherine (1566-1633), the daughter of Sir Henry Knyvet and Elizabeth Stumpe, took Charlton to Lord Admiral Thomas Howard when she became his second wife in 1583. In 1603 he was created First Earl of Suffolk and it was Katherine who as Countess of Suffolk in about 1607 rebuilt the house with its four corner towers capped with ogee domes, many large flat-headed mullioned and transomed windows, and a classically influenced two-storeyed porch. Her husband fell from favour in 1618 but recovered some of his former standing before he died in 1626. Charlton Park was later remodelled and its internal court was roofed over as a saloon. As it stands today the exterior of the house remains essentially Jacobean while its interior is mostly Georgian. During the Civil War it was garrisoned by parliamentary cavalry, and in the First World War it became a Red Cross hospital, but after the Second World War it became a school and it is now divided into apartments.

Charlton Park is strictly private and no public footpaths cross it although a footpath follows the parish boundary from the A429 to the B4040 along its south-west edge. It is also surrounded by public roads that offer views across the parkland, but not of the house.

John Dryden at Charlton Park

AFTER THE CHARLTON ESTATE had passed to the Howard Earls of Suffolk the poet John Dryden (1630-1700) stayed at Charlton Park during the Great Plague and the Fire of London. Here he in 1666 wrote his *Annus Mirabilis* commemorating these momentous events and the disastrous Dutch Wars. Although he had inherited a small estate Dryden lived by writing and became one of the great literary figures of the Restoration period. His association with Charlton began after he addressed a poem to Sir Robert Howard, a son of the house. He then in 1633 married his sister and the following year collaborated with Sir Robert in writing the *The Indian Queen* which Henry Purcell memorably set to music. Dryden became poet laureate in 1668 and in 1670 historiographer royal.

Dryden's eldest son Charles (1666-1704) was born at Charlton and later when staying there the child suffered a serious accident. He was regarded as having been born in an evil hour and Dryden had pessimistically predicted that he would have a troubled life and this proved to be correct. While the child stood watching a hunt near the park gates at Charlton a cornered deer in attempting to leap over the stone park wall brought it down upon the boy. He was buried under the rubble and injured, but was dragged clear and survived. When he was twenty-three Charles Dryden was again seriously injured when he fell from a tower in the Vatican in Rome, but he also survived this accident, became a minor writer, and in the 1690s chamberlain to the pope. After returning to England he was drowned at the age of only thirty-three in 1697 while swimming in the Thames at Windsor. His father's pessimism had proved to be justified.

A Proposed Canal

THE WILTSHIRE WRITER and topographer John Aubrey (1626-1697) was for many years involved in a very early proposal for a canal linking the Thames to the Severn that anticipated by about a hundred and seventy years on a much smaller scale the Kennet and Avon Canal.

Among his papers Aubrey left details of this scheme for a canal linking London to Bristol that had been first proposed in 1626, the year of Aubrey's birth, by Mr Henry Briggs, the Savillean Professor of Geometry at Oxford. He when studying his maps had noticed the comparatively short distance between the Bristol Avon near Charlton and the Thames at Ashton Keynes and had originated the idea for cutting a canal between them. The fact that Aubrey indicated that the canal 'must run through Oaksey Park' is of interest as this is well north of a direct line and suggests that the proposal was for the canal to follow the Thames Valley west from Ashton Keynes approximately along the line of the Swill Brook, and near Oaksey swing south-west and pass south of Charlton to join the Bristol Avon somewhere near Malmesbury. The distance involved was according to Aubrey 'about three miles' but is in fact is nearer eight if it is assumed that the Swill Brook was not navigable.

The idea for this canal may have been prompted by the boat journeys and writings on inland navigation by the 'water poet' John Taylor (1580-1653) who was the subject of one of Aubrey's *Brief Lives*. After 'dropping-out' of Gloucester Grammar School this man was apprenticed to a London waterman and was pressed for the navy in which he served at the sacking of Cadiz in 1596. He then achieved fame for a number of eccentric journeys by water, including one in a paper boat that he described in *The Praise of Hempseed* (1620). Between 1630 and 1645 Taylor wrote some witty rollicking verse that gained him the patronage of Ben Jonson, and from 1645 until his death in 1653 he kept an alehouse at Long Acre in London where he is said to have 'diverted both court and city'. Aubrey met Taylor at Oxford in 1643 and may have visited him at his London tavern and discussed with him his escapades. Three years before Professor Briggs produced his canal proposal Taylor had in 1623 demonstrated the viability of making the Salisbury Avon navigable by rowing from London to Christchurch and then up the Avon to Salisbury. He described these exploits in *A New Discovery by Sea, with a wherry from London to Salisbury*.

After Professor Briggs had visited Wiltshire and viewed the terrain he remained 'very well pleased with his notion' but failed to obtain any encouragement. After his death in 1631 one of his friends, a Captain Francis Mathews from Dorset, revived the idea for the canal and succeeded in interesting Oliver Cromwell, but Cromwell too died in 1658. By this time Aubrey was interested in the proposal and as a member of the Royal Society he in 1660 introduced Captain Mathews to Lord William Brouncker, the President of the Royal Society who emanated from a Melksham family. The proposal was then shown to Charles II who during his exile would have become familiar with the extensive canal systems of the Low Countries having at Bruges lived in a house beside a canal. He later ordered the cutting of a long canal to supply water to his palace at Hampton Court.

The king recognised the virtues of the plan but in Aubrey's words 'money was wanting' and the proposal continued to lay fallow. When Mr Mathews died in about 1676 he left details of the canal scheme with his daughters and Aubrey in 1682, fifty-six years after the scheme had first been proposed, involved a Mr John Collins who discussed the idea with some barge-men who told him that they considered it a good scheme. Mr Collins also surveyed the topography and wrote up a proposal confirming that in his opinion that the original proposed route from Charlton to Ashton Keynes was the best, but in that same year (1682) he too died, according to Aubrey from a cold caught when surveying the route. The proposal was again placed before the Fellows of the Royal Society who liked the idea but were unable to finance the work. The next person to become involved was Mr Jonas Moore, the Surveyor to the Ordnance, but after he recommended an entirely different route past Wootton

Bassett the canal proposal that had been dogged by the deaths of so many of its supporters itself finally died – as in 1697 did its principal advocate John Aubrey.

Aubrey had however with great foresight written: 'I have been the more full in this account, because if ever it shall happen that any public-spirited men shall arise to carry on such a useful work they may know in whose hands the papers that were so well considered heretofore are now lodged'. In spite of these hopes another hundred years elapsed before the Kennet and Avon Canal was built to provide the long advocated and much needed through waterway across southern England.

Hankerton, Eastcourt House, and Cloatley

STANDING WITHIN A MILE of each other between Charlton Park and Oaksey are the village of Hankerton, the mansion known as Eastcourt House, and the hamlet of Cloatley. Hankerton (970908) had belonged to Malmesbury Abbey and it together with Cloatley to its east was at the Dissolution granted in an exchange deal to John Dudley, Duke of Northumberland. In the year (1553) in which he was executed for treasonably backing the spurious claim of Lady Jane Grey to the throne he sold them to Sir James Stumpe (d. 1563) of Charlton, and Hankerton and Cloatley then descended together with Charlton to the Howard Earls of Suffolk. Hankerton Church was remodelled in 1906 although its original west tower survived the reconstruction. Inside it there is a fine 1775 monument by Nollekens to Miles Earle from the family that had

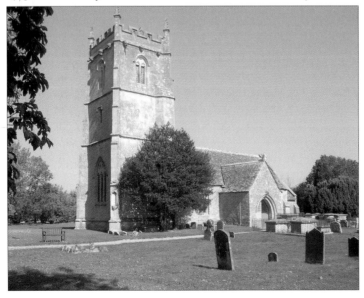

Hankerton Church

been at Crudwell two miles north-west of Hankerton but by this time had become associated with this district. Internal evidence suggests that Manor Farm at Hankerton had, before being re-modelled in the 16th century, been a manor house occupied by the Earles of Crudwell (see page 48) until the wealth that they amassed as Bristol merchants enabled them in the mid-17th century to build Eastcourt House nearby. Their presence at Manor Farm is confirmed by the dates '1707' and '1708' and the initials 'G E' for Giles Earle inscribed on barns in the farmyard.

An earlier Giles Earle of Crudwell had after being apprenticed to a notary in 1607 become a prosperous Bristol merchant and in 1648 MP for Malmesbury. At about this time he bought from Sir Nevill Poole of Oaksey the hamlet that was then called Eastcott equidistant between Crudwell and Hankerton, and there he built between 1648 and 1660 Eastcourt House (980919), a mansion house with mullioned and transomed cross-windows that is dated externally 1658 and internally 1662, but has a large later extension. When Sir Giles Earle died without issue in 1666 Eastcourt went to his nephew Sir Thomas Earle (d. 1696, see page 48) who also became a Bristol Merchant Venturer, was knighted in 1681, and was succceeded at Eastcourt by his son, another Sir Giles Earle (1678-1758). This man was MP for Chippenham (1715-22) and for Malmesbury (1722-47). As a Groom of the Bedchamber to George II when he was Prince of Wales Sir Giles became the most famous member of the family. He became a close friend of Sir Robert Walpole and obtained the lucrative post of Commissioner for Irish Revenue, but he also acquired an unenviable reputation for covetousness, coarse behaviour, and bad language. Lady Mary Wortley Montagu referred to him as 'a facetious gentleman' and after he fell from favour in 1741 he retired to Eastcourt where he died in 1758. His son, another Giles Earle (1678-1758), after acquiring the imposing Beningborough Hall in Yorkshire by marriage sold Eastcourt that is represented on Andrew's and Dury's 1773 map of Wiltshire as an extensively landscaped house designated 'Escot House'.

A minor branch of the Earles of Crudwell and Eastcourt was for a time at nearby Oaksey (991936) where in 1631 the rector Thomas Earle appealed to the Salisbury justices to release his son Thomas the younger, a clerk in holy orders, who was imprisoned for 'foule offences and misdemeanours' the nature of which is revealed by the elder Thomas Earle's offer to pay Richard Plumer ten pounds in compensation for his son's seduction of his wife!

Eastcourt was once occupied by Mr Walter Powell (1842-1881), a Welshman who was a director of the Penarth Railway Company. In the 1868 general election he defeated the Liberal son of the Earl of Suffolk of Charlton Park and became the Tory MP for Malmesbury where he became popular for regularly distributing coal among the Malmesbury poor and for building a reading-room in the town. He is however best remembered for his dramatic last act which was to take off in an air balloon and never be seen again.

According to local lore he took off from Eastcourt after being mortified by the failure of the Prince of Wales to fulfil an invitation to dine at Eastcourt but this was not the case. Newspaper reports indicate that he in fact took off on 10 December 1881 from Bath gasworks in a government air balloon called *Saladin*. Such passenger-carrying balloons had been invented in the late-18th century and were often used for scientific investigations. Mr Powell took off with two companions one of whom, a Captain Templer, was making observations for the War Office. When they apparently ran into difficulties off Bridport Mr Powell's two companions leapt from the balloon into the sea but he remained on board and the balloon, suddenly lightened of two of its three occupants, soared away and neither it nor Mr Powell were ever seen again. When relating the story in her *Gallipot Eyes* (1976) Elspeth Huxley amusingly suggested that this was a case of a captain who 'went up with his ship'.

At the Reformation the disreputable Tudor entrepreneur Sir William Sharington (c.1495-1553) of Lacock, who had clipped the coinage at the Bristol mint and was associated with Henry VIII's reckless brother-in-law Sir Thomas Seymour (c.1508-49) in preparing a rebellion against the boy king Edward VI, purchased lands around Malmesbury including Cloatley (982906) in 1542. By turning king's evidence he ensured the execution of Thomas Seymour but only narrowly escaped accompanying him to the block. John Warneford (d.1558) after being appointed steward to Sir Thomas Seymour purchased from Sharington first the lordship of the manor of Sevenhampton and then in 1543 the manor of Cloatley where he proceeded to live.

William Sharington, by Holbein

Cloatley Manor House (978909) stands north of the road from Hankerton to Upper Minety a short distance east of Hankerton church. This substantial partly-moated 14th century manor house became dilapidated and was reconstructed in 1986, but its outbuildings include a 17th century dovecot, a 1706 stable, and a barn built in 1707.

Oaksey

THIS HISTORIC LINEAR VILLAGE extends for about half a mile along the east-west road (at 990936) between the Cotswold Water Park and Crudwell almost three miles east of Crudwell. It once possessed a castle to its north and a small Medieval deer park to its south both belonging to the de Bohun Earls of Hereford who also owned

Monkton Farleigh manor that will be described later (see pages 211-14). The eminence of this family is indicated by the facts that a de Bohun married a daughter of Edward I and a female member became the queen of Henry IV and the mother of Henry V. Oaksey lies only half a mile from the boundary with Gloucestershire which reminds me to mention that a former part of Wiltshire north of Oaksey around Poole Keynes and Kemble is not included in this book as it was transferred by a boundary adjustment to Gloucestershire in 1897.

The former existence on Oaksey Common (at 995922) of a Roman kiln that yielded many tiles and bricks and probably provided materials for building Cirencester only five miles away establishes that the Romans were here. The village name, that means 'Wocc's well-watered land', appeared in Domesday as *Wochesie* and that name survived long enough for Aubrey in the 17th century to refer to it as *Okesey alias Woxy*. As a Saxon estate owned by Brihtric Oaksey was taken over soon after 1066 by the Norman Edward of Salisbury whose daughter Margaret of Salisbury early in the 12th century his took it by marriage to Humphrey de Bohun in whose family it remained for some time.

The de Bohuns were a powerful Marcher Lord family whose constant opposition to the autocratic excesses of successive monarchs from King John to Edward II helped to found democracy in England. Humphrey de Bohun and Margaret's son Henry de Bohun (died 1220) was after marrying a daughter of the Earl of Essex in 1200 made Earl of Hereford. In December 1253 Humphrey de Bohun (died 1275), the 2nd Earl of Hereford and the Constable and Marshal of England, was licenced to hunt hare, fox, cat and other wild beasts excepting deer in the Forests of Braden and Savernake. The de Bohun family was prospering and in 1302 Humphrey de Bohun, the 4th Earl (1276-1321), married Elizabeth, a daughter of Edward I. His successor John the 5th Earl (1306-1335) never married and was succeeded by Humphrey, the 6th Earl (1309-1361). The 7th Earl of Hereford, another Humphrey de Bohun (1342-1372), died without male issue and his daughters Eleanor and Mary divided his estates. Mary (died 1394) in 1380 married John of Gaunt's son Henry Bolingbroke and took Oaksey to him. When his father John of Gaunt died in 1399 Henry first became first Duke of Lancaster by inheritance and then King Henry IV when under great provocation he deposed the unpopular Richard II by force of arms. His son by Mary de Bohun then became Henry V who held Oaksey together with the other Duchy of Lancaster estates that continued to be administered separately under the Crown.

A small grass-grown mound at the edge of a small copse near the county boundary half a mile north of Oaksey is the motte of Norwood Castle (985944) of the de Bohuns. This little mound was described by Aubrey in the 17th century as 'a little cittadel, with a Keepe Hill, both moated round'. Beside this castle tump stands the mansard-roofed triple-

*Keep Mound of
Norwood Castle,
Oaksey*

dormered and stone-slated Dean Farm that has a Georgian south facade
applied to an earlier building.

From 1515 Leonard Poole (1477-1537) leased Oaksey from the
Crown at the time of Henry VIII, and this family held it until 1726.
Aubrey's knowledge of Oaksey probably dates from 1670 when as a guest
of Edward Poole he no doubt seized the opportunity to have a good look
at the antiquities of the estate. The Oaksey Pooles were a junior branch
of the Pooles of Sapperton who came originally from Cheshire, having
in the 15th and 16th centuries made a fortune out of wool, bought up
property, and married into the aristocracy. Sir Henry Poole (1563-1632),

Dean Farm, Oaksey

who was from 1614 an anti-royalist MP for Malmesbury and Cricklade, in 1615 obtained the lease of Oaksey where the manor house that stood in a field known as Church Woodfalls south of the church beside Minety Lane had been demolished by 1593. It was described by Aubrey as 'the ruins of an old seat of the Dukes of Lancaster, and a Chapell', and in the 19th century John Britton described its ruins as being 'a square area inclosed by a deep moat and embankment, and having a large mount at its north-east angle'.

Sir Henry's son Sir Neville Poole (1592-1651) was from 1640 the MP for Malmesbury and his son Sir Edward (1618-73) was MP for Wootton Bassett. At the start of the Civil War Sir Neville Poole, who had been knighted by James I in 1612 and was successively the MP for Malmesbury, Cricklade, and Cirencester, declared for parliament and in November 1642 successfully defended Marlborough against four hundred royalist cavalry commanded by Lord Digby, one of the most zealous supporters of the royal cause. The Marlborough garrison was then reinforced by parliament but in December Lord Digby returned with an army four thousand troops and stormed the town. Sir Neville escaped and returned to Oaksey where he died in 1651. Oaksey then descended through Sir Edward Poole who was MP for Chippenham in 1660 and for Malmesbury from 1668 until his death, Sir Neville (b. 1646), Sir Henry (b. 1672), and Sir Henry (d.1726) at whose death the male line of the Oaksey Pooles failed. Oaksey then went by the marriage of his daughter and heiress Finetta to Benjamin Bathurst, a younger brother of the First Earl Bathurst of Cirencester Park. She bore Benjamin no less than twenty-two children and then unsurprisingly expired, whereupon Benjamin married again and had fourteen more children by his second wife making his grand total thirty-six! He in 1732 he sold Oaksey to Sir Robert Westley who as he had become rich by supplying uniforms to the army was rather dismissively described by Britton as 'an army taylor'.

Some Maskelynes from the Purton family of the Astronomer Royal Nevill Maskelyne (1732-1811) lived at Oaksey for a time. A Nevill Maskelyne was the squire of Oaksey when he married the vicar's daughter Anne Bathe in 1692, and in the early-19th century the village registers reveal that a William Maskelyne was from at least 1817 until 1839 the tenant at Oaksey Park. At about this time a Maurice Maskelyne occupied Flintham House (981931) south-west of Oaksey. A Maskelyne's Copse (998914) exists at the east end of Flisteridge Wood.

In 1787 the majority of Oaksey manor was sold at auction in London to James Harris, the First Earl of Malmesbury (1746-1820) and a son of 'Hermes' Harris of Salisbury. James Harris was a diplomat who was given a peerage in 1788 and became Earl of Malmesbury in 1800. He appears never to have lived in the manor house, and in 1801 he sold Oaksey .

Oaksey Park is as a Medieval deer park of the de Bohuns much older than Charlton Park four miles to its south-west. In 1336 Oaksey was *le Park* in the *Calendar of Inquisitions post mortem* but it was never large and there are records that it was created as a 96-acre park within a wooden palisade between 1299 and 1347. In 1336 its area was 110 acres. Half a mile south of the church Park Farm (989925) has a long linear pond immediately to its south-east that may be the partial survival of a moat to a former parker's lodge. Having in 1399 become Crown property when Henry Bolingbroke usurped Richard II as Henry IV, Oaksey Park became a small royal hunting park. It was in 1419 stocked with a hundred beasts of the chase and again in 1591 with about a hundred deer. From about 1423 to 1595 the park was administered either by senior officials of the Duchy of Lancaster or by notable Wiltshire landowners. In 1427 a ruinous lodge existed in Oaksey Park, and from 1469 to 1481 a John Ferris was the parker at Oaksey, an appointment in which he was succeeded first by Sir Henry Long (d.1556), and then by Henry Herbert, Earl of Pembroke (d.1601) whose local deputy was Sir Thomas Knyvet of Charlton. Before 1591 the ruined lodge in the park was rebuilt by Sir Henry Knyvet.

In the 1583 *Note of Parks in the County of Wilts* Oaksey was in the keeping of Sir Giles Poole and was of limited extent, being only one mile in circuit implying an area of about 50 acres, a small size for a deer park and a halving of the 1347 area of 96 acres. Aubrey recorded Oaksey Park as being 'not above a mile about' and by mentioning 'the best oakes in the county' being at Oaksey confirmed a survey of 1591 that recorded Oaksey as being 'much beautified by the parke and the fair okes therein'. Between 1596 and 1598 the Crown sold Oaksey Park, although that enthusiastic hunting monarch James I is said to have still visited Oaksey for the hunting. A later Earl of Suffolk owner made a habit of of dropping acorns in the hedges of Oaksey Park in the hope that they would grow.

John Speed in 1610 showed a park pale on his map south-west of Oaksey and just outside the bounds of Braden Forest as defined in 1228. South of Park Farm the parish boundary coincides with the Swill Brook and probably also formed the south-west and south-east bounds of Oaksey Park and the northern boundary of Braden Forest. This is important as it places the park outside Braden Forest and is consistent with a 96-acre park a little under half a mile in diameter centred upon Park Farm. That a park symbol was shown by Speed in 1610 but not in 1695 by Morden suggests that Oaksey was disparked between these dates and although on Andrews and Dury in 1773 it was 'Oaksey House' the name 'Oaksey Park' re-appeared on both the first Ordnance Survey and the 1900 25-inch Ordnance Survey at Park Farm. The site is now undulating, enclosed and hedged, and it still has fine oak trees.

In 1938 Oaksey Park with Park Farm and its adjoining 'mansion' was sold to the Bruderhof, a primitive christian sect that had been expelled from Hitler's Germany. After the outbreak of the Second World War the German Bruderhof was viewed with great suspician which may explain why they soon left Oaksey. Oaksey Park was at this time littered with concrete blocks to deter enemy aircraft from landing. The Tudor Oaksey Park House was finally demolished in 1956 about 340 years after it was built, and Oaksey has also lost another old house with the demolition in 1966 of the Georgian Oaksey Moor House that stood a mile east of the village towards the now-flooded gravel pits. Old paintings of both are reproduced in Volume 14 of the *Wiltshire Victoria County History.*

The early buildings along the street in Oaksey village are built of stone with stone-slated roofs, and the village was designated a conservation area in 1975. It is unfortunate that modern motor traffic has necessitated the introduction into this straight-streeted mainly linear village of a traffic-calming system with all the road signs that this entails. As a result it is now rather difficult to imagine Oaksey in Medieval times when the great Marcher de Bohuns were its lords of the manor, or later times when the Plantagenet, the early-Tudor kings and James I are said to have come here to enjoy the hunting after Oaksey had become a royal manor. The historic past of Oaksey is perhaps best rekindled by after walking down its single main street venturing from its west end north along footpaths past Dean Farm to the old Norwood Castle site. Access to the park site south of the road through Oaksey is not so good as, although two public footpaths run south from Oaksey village towards Park Farm, there they end and there are no public rights of way cross the extreme southern end of the park towards the Swill Brook. The church, that stands at the centre of the village beside the earthworks of the former manor house, dates partly from the 13th century and on the outside of its north wall east of the porch displays one of only twenty-three *Sheila-na-gig* fertility figures that survive in England.

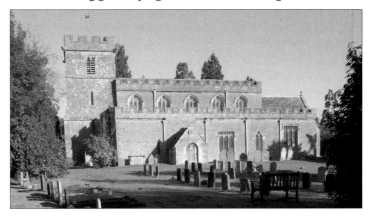

Oaksey Church

In modern times a famous resident of Oaksey was Geoffrey Lawrence, 3rd Baron Trevithin and 1st Baron Oaksey (1880-1971), the

English lawyer who as Lord Chief Justice of England presided at the trial of war criminals at Nuremberg in 1945. He was knighted in 1932, was created Baron Oaksey in 1947, and in 1959 succeeded his brother as Lord Trevithin. He bought Hill Farm at Oaksey before the Great War but was prevented by the demands of his busy legal career from living there until he retired in the 1950s. He is commemorated in Oaksey Church by a memorial carved with his arms (two Guernsey bulls) and lettered by Simon Verity from Minety. Another local resident was Elspeth Huxley who lived at Woodfolds (986933) on the east side of the lane that runs south from the road junction at the west end of Oaksey from 1941 until her death in 1997. She wrote many books of biography, local history, and autobiography, including the splendid *Gallipot Eyes: A Wiltshire Diary* (1976) based on her diary recording a year of her life at Oaksey that has provided me with much material on this district. The title of this book is taken from Aubrey's description of his fellow north Wiltshiremen as having 'gallipot eyes', a gallipot being a small earthenware glazed pot.

Woodfolds, Oaksey

The people of Oaksey seem to have enjoyed sporting and religious gatherings and long after its demise as a deer park steeplechase meetings were until 1914 held in Oaksey Park over a three and a half mile course that attracted the very best horses and riders. Grandstands were erected, the fences were stiff, and on one occasion a rider was killed. The Great War that marked the demise of so much of rural England then put an end to racing at Oaksey, the last race being run at Whitsun 1914. The present Lord Oaksey is the celebrated television horse-racing analyst.

Annual gatherings of Methodists who came from miles around were held at Oaksey where Methodism was at one time stronger than the church of England. They assembled in a field behind the chapel at Earl's Corner, the fork in the roads at the west end of the village (984935) near the intriguingly-named Bendybow. There the adults were entertained by a brass band that played hymns while the children were amused by treats and rides on farm carts. After the Second World War the Methodists declined in number and their chapel was converted into a dwelling house.

The Swindon to Stroud line of the former Cheltenham & Great Western Union Railway passes a half a mile east of Oaksey was built in 1841 originally with halts at Oaksey and Minety.

A short distance north of the Swill Brook and a mile east of Oaksey beside the Cotswold Water Park is Clattinger Farm (010933) where a farmhouse has existed for centuries. It was once occupied by a man who was derisively nicknamed 'Withypole' because he planted in his damp soil withies to fuel his breadmaking oven. He was in fact well in advance of his time as willows are now planted as coppice to provide renewable fuel. The fields of Clattinger consist of shallow topsoil over gravel and since they are liable to flood always been pasture land, have never been ploughed, and have never been treated with fertilizers. Consequently Clattinger Farm became in 1997 a National Nature Reserve administered by the Wiltshire Widlife Trust and internationally renowned for its wild flowers. The best times to visit are in April for its snakes-head fritillaries, that are locally known as 'Oaksey lilies', or towards the end of June for its meadow flowers. Good roadside parking exists near the Swill Brook Lakes (at 017937) and nearby is also the Swill Brook Lakes Nature Reserve containing lakes which offer good birdwatching, especially for water birds. More roadside parking is available at 017934.

Flisteridge Wood (995916) between Eastcourt and Upper Minety was as part of the manor of Crudwell granted to Malmesbury Abbey by King Ceadwealla in AD 681. Its unusual name was formerly *Flusridge* that may have been derived from 'fleece' at the time when Malmesbury Abbey was farming huge flocks of sheep. King John claimed Flisteridge Wood and by incorporating it into his extended Royal Forest of Braden deprived the abbey of its rights. This provoked a bitter dispute between the abbey and the throne but Flisteridge remained in the Forest and subjected to Forest Law with its severe penalties of mutilation or heavy fines for interfering with the royal deer. Flints excavated from Flisteridge Wood were in Victorian times sold to Crudwell parish council for roadmaking. No paths cross Flisteridge Wood other than one through its eastern edge, but the wood straddles the minor road from Eastcourt to Upper Minety.

A short distance south-west of Flisteridge Wood lies Cloatley Meadows Reserve (984906) that is reached by taking the Minety road for a mile east from Hankerton. This is another of the five Wiltshire Wildlife Nature Reserves that exist in this part of North Wiltshire. Being a grassland reserve celebrated for its wild flowers it is best visited before the hay is cut in July. Also near Upper Minety is the Emmett Meadows Reserve (011903) containing unimproved meadows which provide a fine display of wild flowers that are seen at their best in May to June.

Minety

THE VILLAGES of Upper Minety (009911) and Minety (027927) stand about a mile apart three miles south-east of Oaksey. Their church at Upper Minety contains a brass with kneeling figures in its aisle commemorating Nicholas Paulett (d.1609) who has sometimes been confused with his uncle Sir Amyas Paulett who was the jailer of Mary Queen of Scots.

At the time in the 13th century when Henry III was after marrying Eleanor of Provence granting preference to his wife's foreign relatives and supporters to the indignation of his English barons and clergy this church was the scene of an incident connected with this practice. A Braden forester called Little John with several companions took possession of Minety church on behalf of Queen Eleanor's uncle Peter of Savoy who was an unpopular foreign appointment as the Dean of Salisbury. Little John's intention was probably to seize the church dues for Peter of Savoy, but the Deans of Malmesbury and Cricklade promptly reacted by placing Minety under interdict and directing its parishioners to attend the church at Oaksey three miles away.

Some members of the family of the Buckinghamshire Penns settled at Minety and served Malmesbury Abbey as hereditary stewards. They were more famous as sailors and William Penn (d.1591) was the father of Giles who served in the navy with distinction. Giles's son was Admiral William Penn (1621-1670) who from 1644 served in the interregnum navy but after becoming a royalist in 1660 brought the Charles II home from his exile in Holland for his Restoration in his ship the *Naseby* that was appropriately renamed for the occasion the *Royal Charles*. Aubrey tells us that Admiral Penn was 'a man of excellent natural abilities, not equalled in his time for knowledge of naval affairs', and that he was born at Minety the son of keeper in Braden Forest, hence Penn's Lodge in the Forest about three miles south of Minety (at 026691). Braden was dissaforested by Charles I in 1630 to allow him to sell it to meet the debts that he had incurred while refusing to call the parliaments that would have voted him funds.

Admiral Penn's birth at Minety is questionable, although it is possible that he lived there. Britton quite specifically claimed that 'Sir William Penn, Vice-Admiral' was buried 'Near the south door of the chancel' of Minety church, but this may have been his namesake grandfather William Penn. After serving with distinction in action against the Dutch fleet in 1664 under the Duke of York, Admiral Penn was knighted and became Commissioner for the Navy and Governor of Kinsale. His son William Penn the Quaker (1644-1718) may also have lived at or at least visited Minety. After becoming a Quaker he was persecuted for his faith but still associated with the royal family. As the Quakers refused to defer to authority Penn is said to have once remained covered in the presence of Charles II who pointedly removed his own hat and when Penn enquired why he had done so the good humoured king replied: 'It is the custom of this place that only one man should remain uncovered at a time'. In return for a £20,000 debt owed to his long deceased father the Quaker William Penn in 1681 accepted from Charles II a large tract of land in America. He married an heiress and became one of the few large landowners to visit America where he founded Pennsylvania as a religiously tolerant state. In 1686 Penn in a vain attempt to persuade Aubrey to join him in America granted him six hundred acres of Pennsylvania, but ultimately Penn lost his fortune and died in England a disillusioned and penniless man.

Ashton Keynes

WATER INVARIABLY adds an extra dimension to landscape and the watery nature of Ashton Keynes (046940) has been emphasised by a number of writers. Here, at the extreme north boundary of Wiltshire three miles west of Cricklade, the Upper Thames having passed through the nearby Cotswold Water Park flows as a tiny stream, first through the north end of the village and then down its north-eastern edge that is known as Kent End from its associations in 1327 with a Ralf Kent. Another stream of the Thames flows south alongside High Road

Bridges on High Road looking south

through the middle of the village and joins the Swill Brook near Waterhay Bridge. These streams of the infant Thames almost surround the eastern part of Ashton Keynes with waterways, and the stream that runs down High Road is crossed by a number of little bridges that provide access to the houses and prompted the early-20th century writer Frederick Thacker to write: 'its host of little bridges is the peculiar, the perennial delight of Ashton Keynes' and also suggest that Ashton Keynes: 'possesses as many [bridges] in its tiny area as span the whole of the rest of the Thames'. Many of these former footbridges have now been enlarged into vehicular bridges. Edward Hutton also adopted the watery theme in *Highways and Byways in Wiltshire* (1917) in which he described Ashton Keynes as 'a little paradise with flowing waters everywhere', and also as 'a place of quietness immersed in a long peace'.

Since it is merely six miles from the Roman *Corinium* (Cirencester) it is not surprising that Roman finds have been discovered in and around Ashton Keynes, and aerial photographs have revealed a possible Roman temple east of the village at Cleveland Farm (068948). Too much emphasis should not however be placed upon the rather rectilinear street plan here that was noticed by Cobbett when he commented in 1826 on the: 'numerous lanes crossing and cutting the land into such little bits that that it must have been a large town', and later by Thacker who noted that: 'The village has several parallel streets, joined at the ends only'

In AD 899 King Alfred left the manor of Ashton to his daughter Aethelgeolfu who when she became its abbess took it to Shaftesbury Abbey. Ashton means 'farm by the ash tree', and the Keynes element of the name is a proprietorial suffix that arose when the village was owned by Guillaume de Cahaignes, Cahaignes being a village in Normandy. This man accompanied the Conqueror to England and fought at Hastings and was rewarded by being granted twenty-five English manors with among them Ashton Keynes that was inherited by his son Ralph who anglicised his name to de Keynes. By 1256 William de Keynes (born 1221) owned much of this district, but in 1330 the manor was transferred to Tewkesbury Abbey. After the Dissolution it was acquired by Anthony Hungerford and in 1682 it was sold to Sir John Hungerford. He conveyed the manor to another Sir Anthony Hungerford of Stocke near Great Bedwyn, allegedly as security for debts.

The church stands beside the B4696 at the western edge of Ashton Keynes (at 042944) and is approached from the village up a tree-lined walk called Church Walk. It was restored by Butterfield in the 1870s and contains a moving inscription to a child and

Ashton Keynes Church and Cross

Cross near Church Walk

his grandfather from the Hawkins family who died on the same day in 1658. It ends:

> The Grandsire & Grandsone hence both of them
> Past in one day to their Hierusalem

The child's probable father was John Hawkins who was born in 1621, was MP for Crudwell, and was also lord of the manor of Ashton Keynes in 1658, the year of this inscription.

Prominent features of Ashton Keynes are its four stone Medieval crosses. One in the churchyard has been reconstructed from several fragments as a war memorial while the other three – situated respectively at the end of Church Walk, in Park Place and in High Road – are ruinous. After the Anglo-Saxons became christianised they sometimes set up carved stone crosses for daily prayer, particularly in locations that lacked a church. Such stone crosses are a particular feature of this district and in addition to these at Ashton Keynes there are two at nearby Cricklade, one at Latton, fragments of a Saxon cross was found under Minety Church during reconstruction, and there were other crosses in nearby Gloucestershire villages, but the reason for four 14th century standing crosses being erected at Ashton Keynes has never been convincingly explained. During the 14th century monastic monks were becoming more worldly and were being supplanted in the estimation of the common people by the orders of wandering mendicant friars that appeared in the 14th century. Some of these crosses may be attributed to the emergence of these friars who practised an apostilic poverty that closely resembled the condition of the common people. They sometimes preached sermons that were political and egalatarian, as did John Ball during the 1381 Peasants' Revolt.

Some village crosses were probably set up as preaching crosses for these friars and were often set on steps that raised the preacher above his congregation. Their tall shafts were usually capped with ornamental heads that have now often been destroyed. After being originally places at which friars preached these locations often became market sites where the crosses became associated with trading rather than with religion. Aubrey tells us of markets that were held at the cross at his home village of Kington St Michael, and some of these crosses would have been elaborated by the addition of market shelters, as apparently happened at Castle Combe (page 133). Some incorporated crucifixes that would have rendered them idolatrous at the time of the Reformation and to the puritans of the 17th century, which explains why so many of these crosses are now ruinous, as are three of the four at Ashton Keynes.

To the left of Church Walk beside the churchyard is a deep dry ditch that appears to be the remains of a moat said to have enclosed a monastery. Such a monastery could have been founded here by the Abbey of Shaftesbury in the 10th century when it held Ashton Keynes. As they contained rich objects monasteries were at that time often raided by the Vikings and were sometimes moated to provide them with some security. Alternatively, this moat in its prominant position south of the church may once have surrounded a fortified Norman manor house built perhaps by the Keynes family, particularly as Church Farm Manor that now stands on the site is partly Medieval and may be an adaptation of an earlier manor house.

The ownership of Ashton Keynes by Shaftesbury Abbey also suggests the possibility that the village crosses may have been set up to replace 10th century Saxon crosses erected by the abbey to commemorate St Augustine's mission to this area four hundred years earlier (as described on pages 81-2). These may over the intervening four hundred years have become ruinous and been replaced by 14th century crosses set up when Ashton Keynes was transferred to Tewkesbury Abbey in 1330.

Cottage opposite end of Church Walk

Pevsner remarked on the situation of Ashton Keynes church: 'away from the village by the manor house'. From his description of the manor house as being 'SW of the church, across a field', as having: 'C17. Gateposts on the road', and being a: ' Good group with farm buildings', we know that he was referring to the now-abandoned stone-slated manor house that stands among its farm buildings west of the village (at 040942). This house, that now stands beside flooded gravel pits, was shown in 1773 by Andrews and Dury as being then occupied by 'Henry Whorwood' who after buying the house from Henry Chapman in 1762 some time later sold it to John Paul of Tetbury who decided that the house was too large for its estate and directed in his Will that part of it should be pulled down. Consequently when the Paul family finally sold the house in 1802 it was much reduced in size.

Mill House

Pevsner also noted the 'two-arch BRIDGE' and admired the 'delightful group of houses at the end of a lane [Church Walk] that continues as a footpath to the church'. Near the point where the way to the church becomes pedestrian is Mill House (043943) that was formerly a 17th century water mill. A mill on this site leased by Sir John Hungerford in 1576 was by 1913 converted into the dwelling that it is today. It has a millstone set high in its south gable and old photographs show to its rear a now demolished tall brick chimney, indicating that it was at some time converted to steam power.

At the extreme northern edge of Ashton Keynes, within Hall's Close that is sometimes known as The Battlefields, are the eroded earthworks of a motte and bailey castle that are marked 'Ring & Bailey' on the Ordnance Survey (048945). Excavation here by the Cricklade Historical Society in the 1960s exposed footings of a wall following the line of the bailey together with some 12th century pottery that suggested that the castle dates from the time of King Stephen's anarchy. It could be the castle at South Cerney captured by Stephen in 1139, South Cerney being less than a mile and a half to its north.

A stream of the Thames
in Church Walk

Churchyard cross and Richmond Tombs

In the 17th century an important Ashton Keynes family were the Richmonds who lived at Cove House that was also known as 'The Mansion'. Oliffe Richmond after coming to Ashton Keynes as a steward to Sir John Evelyn entered into advantageous marriages and eventually became lord of the manor by purchase from Sir John. A tragic story is told of two of his sons who served on opposing sides in the English Civil War. This did not diminish their brotherly affection and the night before the Battle of Newbury Henry Richmond decided to visit John after dark in the enemy camp. After evading the guards and finding his brother's tent he lifted the flap and his brother, startled by the sudden appearance of an apparent intruder, instantly shot him dead. In his grief John Richmond emigrated to America and his descendants are said to still occasionally visit Ashton Keynes. The Richmond table tombs are found between the churchyard cross and the church.

A windmill was documented at Ashton Keynes in 1758 and Andrews and Dury show a post mill south-east of Ashton Keynes (at about 052937). Windmills were introduced into England in the late-12th or early-13th centuries to augment the existing water mills. Being often built of timber they were vulnerable to fire and often short-lived, but we know that this mill still existed in 1790 as the parish registers for that year contain a reference to the death by a fall from his horse of a Thomas Arnold: 'at or near the turn of the road near the windmill in the Parish on the highway leading to Cricklade'.

The name of a tiny village two miles south-east of Ashton Keynes is spelt Leigh but is pronounced 'Lie'. Its original Medieval church stood (at 058928) half a mile north of the present village at the end of a lane near Waterhay but the villagers at some time moved away, possibly because the lane along which the old church was approached was

Leigh Church

frequently flooded in bad weather. Because of this the people of Leigh began in the 1890s to consider rebuilding their church nearer their village. Their architect Mr C. E. Ponting admired the old church and, as he recorded in the *Wiltshire Archaeological Magazine* (Volume 27), urged them to retain it and improve the access. The villagers however decided to dismantle their church and rebuild it in the village. Consequently the new church of All Saints (062921) at Leigh is a careful rebuilding by Mr Ponting in 1896 of the old church on the new site but with a new chancel, the 13th century chancel of the Old Church having been left as a mortuary chapel on its original site. In his *Highways and Byways in Wiltshire* (1917) Edward Hutton fulminated against 'the sad and disgraceful story' of the removal of Leigh church that he described as 'one of the most charming little churches in North Wiltshire'. He also recorded how 'the Society for the Protection of Ancient Buildings had urged the Wiltshire Archaeological Society to protest and save the little old church', and how 'the vandals had their way'.

The deserted chancel of the old church now stands forlornly beautiful in its ancient graveyard. From its west it looks surprisingly modern, and its simple, stark, whitewashed interior resembles the inside of a non-conformist chapel, but with a number of ornate 18th century painted biblical texts within elaborate painted surrounds. This remnant of the old church is in my opinion one of the most moving places in Wiltshire. It is often open and is easily reached by a short walk down the lane signposted 'The Chancel' that runs south-west out of the road (from 061929) a short distance south of Waterhay.

Chancel of Leigh Church

The Cotswold Water Park

MENTION OF THE WATERLOGGED nature of the site of old Leigh church leads into the subject of the Cotswold Water Park that adjoins Ashton Keynes. Although it is mainly in Gloucestershire, the water park occupies a northern promontory of Wiltshire that contains the Cotswold Community Centre (033956). In its entirety – that is including its Gloucestershire and Wiltshire sections – it is said to be the largest concentration of gravel pits in this country and as gravel extraction continues it continues to grow. At one time the site of the water park was lush Thames-side water meadows owned by the Abbey of Malmesbury, but long after the abbey was dispossessed at the Dissolution beds of oolitic gravel were discovered overlying the clay and that gravel has been extracted since the 1920s on a commercial scale creating the large expanses of now worked-out gravel pits that are now flooded and have been developed as a large multi-lake recreational and wildlife water park. A mile and a half east of Ashton Keynes (at 067932) is Upper Waterhay Wildlife Reserve.

Upper Thames near Cricklade

Cricklade

ALTHOUGH IT ADJOINS Gloucestershire Cricklade, situated at the extreme north-eastern corner of the region covered by this book (100935), is rather distant from the Cotswold limestone belt, but many of its buildings are built of stone in the Cotswold style and some are roofed with stone slates. After visiting Cricklade one is left with an impression of a small town of great antiquity that was once a place of importance, and this impression is in fact correct. Prior to the 18th century Cricklade was of importance, in Anglo-Saxon times because it stood on the borders of the kingdoms of Mercia and Wessex, and later because it stood at he point where the Roman Ermin Street crossed the River Thames, when both the Roman road and the river were important communication routes. Cricklade has now relinquished much of its former importance and become an attractive country town.

In Domesday it was *Crichelade*, the *lade* element – meaning 'passage' – being a reference to its situation at the Roman crossing of the Thames. When in early times roads were often impassible and rivers were used for travel and transportation, the Thames was a navigable waterway across southern England, and Cricklade at the head of the Thames navigation was one of the inland ports that then existed on navigable rivers throughout England. The town's position beside the Roman Ermin Street, which runs from Silchester (*Calleva Atrebatum*) to Cirencester (*Corinium*), also contributed to Cricklade's importance at the time in the Middle Ages when Roman roads were still the only surfaced long distance ways across England.

The present A419 by-passes Cricklade along the former Roman line of Ermin Street a short distance to its north-east. Excavations in Cricklade in 1953-4 revealed thousands of Roman sherds indicating a formerly unsuspected considerable Roman presence here, especially in the north-west part of the town. Dr T. R. Thomson, who collected much material for a history of Cricklade, suggested that during the Roman conquest Cricklade may have been the site of a Roman camp at the crossing of the Thames, and it is an interesting fact that the Saxon fortifications take the same rectangular form as a Roman camp. Other known Roman sites in the area include that at Kingshill Farm (117926) beside Ermin Way a mile south-east of Cricklade.

The Saxon fortifications were built in the 9th century AD when Cricklade became one of the towns fortified for the defence of Wessex against the Vikings. After experiencing great difficulty dealing with Viking armies after they retired into camps which they had fortified with earthworks, King Alfred (849-899) decided to take a leaf out of the enemy's book and fortify about thirty sites as strong points in his defences. These were generally re-fortified prehistoric hillforts, Roman towns with repaired walls, or new fortifications around existing settlements, Cricklade being an example of the latter. They were known as *burhs* and a feature of the *burh* system was that no point in Wessex was intended to be more than about twenty miles from such a refuge, although the historian Asser complained that the 'ealdormen' responsible for building some of the *burhs* often failed to finish or sometimes even commence some of them. The only *burhs* created in the Wiltshire Cotswolds were at Malmesbury and Cricklade, this being because this northern frontier of Alfred's Wessex adjoined Mercia which was a generally friendly and still largely Saxon kingdom whose King Ethelred

(d. 911) recognised Alfred as his overlord and was married to Alfred's daughter Ethelfled. Both Malmesbury and Cricklade are both closely associated with Roman roads which then facilitated the rapid movement of armies around the countryside, and they both also controlled rivers up which the shallow-draughted Viking longships could penetrate deep into the Wessex countryside.

Although the *burhs* were instigated by Alfred much that we know about them comes from the *Burghal Hidage* that was compiled after his death in about 911-19 as a record of the number of hides attached to each of the Wessex *burhs*, a hide being the amount of land needed to support a peasant household and a unit of tax assessment that in Wessex generally amounted to about 40 acres. Each *burh* was manned by one man from each hide. Domesday later adopted the word *burh* for all towns whether fortified or not, and the term later became 'borough' meaning a town represented in parliament. In Cricklade we have a fine example of a Saxon burh contained within a square enclosure with sides measuring a little less than 500 yards and the present High Street running across it, as shown on the plan below.

The fortifications consisted of an earthen bank 20-30 feet wide revetted with ashlar stone from Blundon Hill. This stone was later used

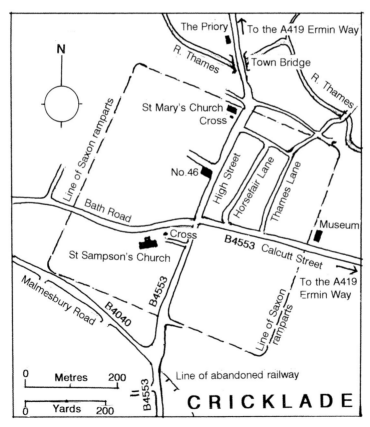

by the townspeople to reconstruct their houses and the fortifications where still visible are now merely low eroded banks that because they contained much Roman material were long thought to be Roman, although as they also include Saxon pottery. They survive at several places and are best seen on the south-east side of the town where a section cut in 1949 by the local historical society revealed an earthen embankment but no wall. Another excavation on the north-west side of Cricklade was made in 1952 with similar results except that some evidence of a wall was discovered. Despite these defences the Dane Canute seems in 1016 to have succeeded in plundering Cricklade as recorded in the *Anglo-Saxon Chronicle* entry that reads: '1016. In this year came Canute with one hundred and sixty ships, and with him ealdorman Eadric, and crossed the Thames into Mercia at Cricklade, and then turned into Warwickshire'. The 'ealdorman Eadric' who accompanied Canute was Eadric Streona, his Saxon ally who we shall meet later at Sherston (pages 98-102), and the mention of 'one hundred and sixty ships' suggests that the Vikings rowed up the Thames to Cricklade in their longships which were the symbol of the Vikings. These ships were shallow in draught and even when fully laden could negotiate both open seas and row up creeks and rivers.

King Athelstan in about AD 928 stipulated that mints must be sited in fortified places and we know that there was a mint at Cricklade because examples of coins minted there range from the reigns of Ethelred, when there were five moneyers at Cricklade, to that of William Rufus. The Cricklade mint then appears to have been closed down in 1242 when mints were reduced in number to two.

Some evidence suggests that about a hundred years after the Norman Conquest a castle was built at or near the already fortified town of Cricklade. In the *Acts of King Stephen* that records events during the anarchic mid-12th century Civil War between Stephen and Matilda we read:

> At that time, 1142, William of Dover, a skilful soldier, and an active partisan of the Earl of Gloucester [who supported Matilda] took possession of Cricklade, a village delightfully situated in a rich and fertile neighbourhood. He built a castle for himself with great diligence, on a spot which, being surrounded on all sides with wastes and marshes, was very inaccessible.

The mention in this account of Cricklade by name and the fact that the description fits its location suggests that this castle may have been at Cricklade, rather than at nearby Castle Eaton where Leland in the mid-16th century saw the remains of the castle that explains the name of the hamlet.

Despite its declining fortune in the Middle Ages Cricklade has two good churches. The largest stands a little west of the High Street (at

St Sampson's tower from the Thames

099936) and is dedicated to the Cornish-Breton St Sampson who is traditionally said to have taught at Cricklade. It is a large cruciform church with a huge late-Gothic crossing tower that is a landmark for miles around from the flat surrounding countryside. Hilaire Belloc may have had Cricklade in mind when he wrote in *The Historic Thames* (1907):

> There are dozens of reaches upon the upper Thames where little is in sight save the willows, the meadows, and a village church tower, which present exactly the same aspect today as they did when that church was first built.

St Sampson's Church and cross

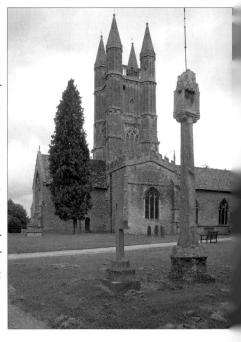

The tower of St Sampson's was built soon after the Reformation in 1551-3 at the joint expense of two benefactors one of whom was the John Dudley, the Duke of Northumberland (c.1503-1553) who despite being married to a daughter of Protector Somerset managed secure the downfall and execution of Somerset and his brother Lord Thomas Seymour who were executed because they stood in the way of his political ambitions. He was then himself executed for treason in 1553. The other tower benefactor was a local Hungerford lord of the manor from the family who already had a chapel in St Sampson's built by Sir Edmund Hungerford (d.1484). Internally the tower has a fine vaulted ceiling and above its crossing arches much carved detail including a good deal of heraldry, mostly of John Dudley as first Earl of Warwick and Duke of Northumberland. St Sampson's churchyard contains the remains of a late-14th century market cross that was moved here from

*St Sampson's Church
tower interior*

the High Street when the old town hall was demolished to make room
for a new one in the mid-19th century.

The other Cricklade church also stands west of of the High Street
near at the Saxon ramparts at the north entrance to the town (at 101938).
St Mary's, that is now the catholic place of worship, is a delightful small
church of Norman foundation. When it was restored in 1862 Roman
bricks were found. In its churchyard stands a fine cross that is a rather
less elaborate example than is the cross at St Sampson's.

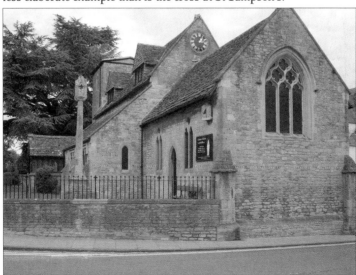

*Cross and St Mary's
Church*

Across the river a little north of the St Mary's Church is the site of
a Priory (101939) that was founded before 1231 and was described by
Aubrey long after it had been dissolved in 1535 as resembling St Ebbe's
at Oxford. Its buildings were later Georgianised and are now the houses

Georgianised Priory

numbered 1-3 High Street. Associated with this Priory was St John's Hospital that was founded by Henry III's chaplain Warin as a guest house for wayfarers and is said to have lodged wounded Crusaders who were brought by barge up the Thames to Cricklade, a suggestion that seems to be supported by John Britton's indication that a house at Cricklade belonged to the Knights Hospitallers who succeeded the Knights Templar. This establishment was granted wayleave for horses and carts collecting fuel for the brethren and the poor through the Forest of Braden.

Pevsner pointed out that the best houses at Cricklade are at the south end of the High Street, although many of the town's ancient houses have been re-fronted, an example being No. 46 High Street at the junction of High Street and Gas Lane whose unpretentious exterior conceals a timber-framed Medieval building.

In the times when the economy of Wales was dependent upon exporting cattle into England large droves of small black Welsh cattle were driven 'on the hoof' along the so-called Welsh Ways into England, mainly to feed the rapidly increasing populace of London. Some of these droves came down Ermin Street past Cricklade to join the Ridgeway at Fox Hill and continue eastwards to be slaughtered at Smithfield Market, although some were driven to rich English pastures to be fattened, as were those seen by Cobbett who wrote in his *Rural Rides* of seeing:

> . . . between Cricklade and Cirencester in separate droves about 2000 Welsh cattle on their way from Pembrokeshire to the fairs in Sussex. The greater part of them were heifers in calf. They were purchased in Wales at from £3 to £4.10s (£4.50p) each. They would fetch from £6 to £8.

The poet Edward Thomas recalled meeting in about 1911 'an old man who remembered helping the Welsh drovers with their black cattle there sixty years ago', 'there' being Ermin Street north of Cricklade. Large droves of Welsh and Cotswold sheep also came down Ermin Street past Cricklade on their way to the great sheep fairs at East Ilsley beside the Ridgeway in the Berkshire Downs. Ralph Vaughan Williams, who composed the ballad opera *Hugh the Drover* (1920), was born near Ermin Street on the Wiltshire border at Down Ampney a short distance north of Cricklade, but the hero of his opera was a horse-drover who provided mounts for the army.

Another vital commodity that was transported through Cricklade was salt that was in early times needed for preserving meat, for flavouring food, and for disinfecting, and also symbolised purity in primitive societies. Salt was obtained from coastal saltings or from natural inland brine springs, and was distributed on trains of packhorses along a system of saltways. James Turle suggested in *England all the Way* (1935) – and place-name evidence appears to support his assertion – that a saltway ran south from the salt-producing area of Droitwich and crossed Wiltshire on its way to Christchurch on the south coast. It went according to Turle through Worcester, Cheltenham, Cirencester, Cricklade, Marlborough, and Pewsey, and then down the Salisbury Avon to Christchurch, and through Cirencester and Cricklade it was recorded in 1591 as *Saltharpesweye*.

The residents of Cricklade would have been surprised when one September day in 1643 at the end of the 'royalist summer' during which the king's cause had been generally triumphant the Earl of Essex, having achieved one of the finest military exploits of the English Civil War, unexpectedly descended on the town with his parliamentary army consisting of four thousand cavalry and ten thousand foot. Essex had partly redressed the situation by marching the last surviving parliamentary field army in southern England out of London and across the royalist front at Oxford and relieving the siege of the strategically important city of Gloucester. He then needed to get his army safely back to the parliamentary headquarters in London and after feinting north towards Worcester he marched his army down Ermin Street and was at Cricklade from 16-17 September. A contemporary account reads:

> We advanced from Ciceter [Cirencester] five miles to a village called Letton, where our London Brigade was quartered for the night: the Lord General, with his army quartered a mile further at a market town called cricklet; at the village aforesaid were ten cavaliers, who were sick and lame, and brought here to be quartered, who when they heard we were marching to this place, found their leggs and run away.

This parliamentary army consisted of about four thousand cavalry and their horses, ten thousand infantry, their artillery and wagon trains, and no doubt many camp followers. Its impact on Cricklade must have been immense and the residents must have watched its departure with some relief. Although harassed by Prince Rupert's cavalry Essex successfully led his army east through Aldbourne Chase and after being brought to action at Newbury succeeded in returning it to London undefeated.

Because of its earlier importance Cricklade for long retained its status as a parliamentary borough. Its 18th century electors took their elections extremely seriously and it was said that after canvassing for months they at the election devoted several days feasting and drinking. Candidates according to Ralph Whitlock were in the habit of offering the townspeople ridiculously high sums for mundane objects in return for their votes, and matters became so corrupt that the problem was referred to parliament. Even in those days of rampant political corruption parliament felt obliged to act and in 1782 passed an 'Act for preventing Bribery and Corruption in the Election of Members to serve in Parliament for the Borough of Cricklade in the County of Wilts'. In later times Cricklade was for twenty years silently represented by the great GWR locomotive engineer Sir Daniel Gooch (1816-89) who after surrendering the seat wrote: 'I have taken no part in any of the debates, and have been a silent member. It would be a great advantage to business if there were a greater number who followed my example'.

During the 19th century Cricklade was served by two canals and a railway line, all of which are now redundant. A branch of the Wilts and Berks Canal known as the North Wilts Canal ran north-west out of Swindon and after going east of Purton passed through the west edge of Cricklade before at Latton Basin (087954) joining the Thames and Severn Canal. The railway line through Cricklade was a branch of the Midland and South Western Junction Railway that ran through the town on its way to Cirencester. It was built in 1882-3 in the face of strenuous opposition from the Great Western Railway Company and suffered several financial crises before being rescued by the exertions of Samuel Fay who left the company after seven years in 1899 in very good order. The line has been long been closed.

Immediately north-west of Cricklade beside the A419 is North Meadow (097946) that since 1973 has been a Thames-side National Nature Reserve and a Site of Special Scientific Interest. This reserve is now mostly owned by the Nature Conservancy and is designated 'Lammas land' because from Lammas Day (1 August) until Lady Day (25 March) it was grazed by cattle and horses owned by the inhabitants of Cricklade and was then during the summer months left to grow hay. Visited at some seasons North Meadow appears to be a perfectly ordinary meadow of no particular interest, but from April to May its flowering masses of the once common but now rare snakes-head fritillaries attract large numbers of visitors to see a sight that was once common in this district.

Fritillary flowers

North Meadow from
near Cricklade Bridge

North Meadow is of historic as well as botanical importance because under an 1824 Enclosure Act plots were allocated and marked with stones, some of which survive and are protected. A footpath runs round its perimeter from its entrance (at 100944), and North Meadow may be reached by a short walk along the Thames Long Distance Path north-west from near the Town Bridge at the north edge of Cricklade. Visitors are requested to keep to the paths to avoid trampling the fritillaries.

Four miles south of Cricklade at the east end of Braden Forest towards Swindon is the large village of Purton that contains a number of buildings in the Cotswold style, but is beyond the bounds of the Wiltshire Cotswolds as defined for this book.

St Augustine and the Celtic Bishops

IN THE LATE-6TH CENTURY AD the popes at Rome claimed to be the christian heirs to the failing Roman Empire and although Rome was then being reduced to ruin by pagan invaders Pope Gregory the Great (c.540-604), after according to legend seeing some British children in the slave market at Rome, conceived the idea of evangelising western Europe including Britain. In AD 596 he despatched to England his friend Augustine (d. 604) with forty other monks on a mission to bring the Celtic church into conformity with Roman practices and attempt to convert the then still largely heathen Anglo-Saxons. After spending some time at Canterbury Augustine in 597 went to Arles and after being there consecrated Bishop of the English he returned to Canterbury and set about expanding Roman christianity westwards. The Romano-British christianity that had survived in Cornwall, Devon, and Somerset and Wales was ascetic, monastic, non-diocesan, and evangelistic, while the Roman popes with the splendours of Rome ever before them built opulent churches and conducted an elaborate form of chrisianity. Augustine's instructions were to offer the Celtic christians the unity and organisation that was lacking in the English church which the Roman church could provide.

The principal Celtic church was at Bangor in Wales and in 603 Augustine met the British bishops at some unknown location. The Hwiccas, a midland christian kingdom whose southern border was the Upper Thames, were then at war with their neighbours the then pagan West Saxons, and the meeting was arranged somewhere on the border between the two kingdoms near the Upper Thames. As Roman roads were then still the principal communication routes Augustine could easily have reached the Cricklade area from his base at Canterbury by following Watling Street to London, continuing west along the Roman road through Staines to Silchester, and from there following Ermin Street to Cricklade, a total journey of about 120 miles. Bede in his *History of the English Church and People* (Chapter 2 of Book 4) says that the meeting took place at a site that became known as 'Augustine's Oak', and it is possible that 'The Oak' shown on the first edition Ordnance Survey a mile and a half north of Cricklade towards Down Ampney was the site of the meeting, particularly as a former curative well east of Down Ampney (at 114965) was known as St Augustine's Well. St Augustine and his monks may in accordance with their instructions have evangelised the entire boundary area around Cricklade, which could explain the proliferation of Christian crosses in the area – four at Ashton Keynes, two at Cricklade, and one at Latton. The fact that Hailstone Hill (see below) is believed to derive its name from the Old English *halig-stan* meaning 'holy stone' and was crowned by a chapel dedicated to St Helena, who claimed to have discovered the Cross of the Lord at Jerusalem in 326 AD less than 300 years before St Augustine's mission, seems to support this theory. Although they are of much later date, crosses may have originally been set up to commemorate this mission and been replaced by later crosses as they became derelict.

Augustine's mission failed because the Celtic bishops refused to co-operate with him, according to Bede because he failed to treat them with respect. The Celtic church then retained its independence of Rome until AD 664 when Oswiu the King of Northumbria ruled in favour of Rome at the Synod of Whitby.

Hailstone and Fulk FitzWarin – outlaw

IMMEDIATELY NORTH-WEST of Cricklade is Hailstone Hill (083943) that was once crowned by the standing stone and a chapel that are mentioned above and are now gone. We also know that Hailstone was also the site of a deer park from the *Close Rolls* that in 1236 recorded a gift by Henry III to Fulk FitzWarin III (d.1256) of two fallow bucks and ten fallow does for his park at *Halweston*. *The Place-Names of Wiltshire* (1939) confirms that *Halweston* was an early name for Hailstone, although it was *Halegstone* in the perambulations of Braden Forest. Hailstone Hill may be reached along a minor cul-de-sac road that runs north-west out of Cricklade, or by several public footpaths.

In 1201 Fulk FitzWarin, probably the father of Fulk FitzWarin III who was the recipient of the royal gift of deer mentioned above, rebelled against King John over a ruling which deprived him of his estates. The king's ruling seems to have been unjust as it arose as the result of bad feeling which had arisen between FitzWarin and Prince John when they were boys many years earlier. The incident is recorded in the Anglo-French *The Story of Fulk FitzWarin* written in the early 13th century:

> It happened one day that John and Fulk [FitzWarin] were alone in a chamber playing chess. John took the chess board and struck Fulk a great blow with it. Fulk, feeling hurt, kicked John hard in the stomach, so that he banged his head against the wall, became dizzy and fainted. Fulk was frightened, and was glad that there was no one in the room but themselves. He rubbed John's ears and brought him round. John went wailing to his father the king [Henry II]. 'Hold your tongue', said his father, 'you are always squabbling. If Fulk has done what you say, you probably deserved it'. He called his tutor and ordered him to be well beaten for complaining.

John was a man who could harbour a grudge and soon after becoming king in 1199 he seized the FitzWarin estates. These included Whittington Castle near Cheltenham that was later the home of Dick Whittington (c.1350-1423) who married a FitzWarin lady, which may explain his ownership of Whittington Castle, and went with his legendary cat to London where he made good by becoming three times Lord Mayor. After his estates were seized Fulk, together with his three brothers William, Philip and John and some adherents said to number in all fifty-two, took to the woods in the Forest of Braden which then straddled a vast expanse of of north Wiltshire, and there led an outlaw existence.

At this time a man declared outlaw forfeited all his land and goods, and it was legitimate for anyone to kill him. This applied until the time (1327-77) of Edward III when it was decided that only a sheriff could legitimately kill an oulaw, although surprisingly the law of outlawry was not repealed until 1938. Unlike his legendary contemporary Robin Hood, who was said to be similarly at odds with King John's Sheriff of Nottingham, FitzWarin now found himself at war with the monarch himself. He and his adherents must have been very desperate or extremely bold because near at hand were two powerful and militant great officers of state in Sir Alan Basset (d. 1232), Justiciar of England at Wootton Bassett, and William the Marshal (d. 1219), the Marshal of England at Marlborough Castle.

Forests were in those days great tracts of land that had been reserved by the Norman kings as hunting reserves and the FitzWarin gang lived a Robin Hood like existence in Braden Forest, robbing waggon trains including at least one of King John's, and cultivating the support of the local people. Their exploits were recounted in Mr T. Wright's *History of Ludlow*:

> Fulke and his company went to the Forest of Bradene where they remained some time unobserved. One day there came ten merchants who brought from foreign lands rich cloths and other valuable merchandise, which they bought for the King and Queen of England, with money furnished from the royal treasury. As the convoy passed under the wood, followed by twenty-four serjeants-at-arms to guard the King's goods, John Fitzwarine was sent out to enquire who they were. John met with a rude reception ; but Fulke and his companions came forwards, and, in spite of their obstinate defence, captured the whole party, and carried them into the forest. When Fulke heard that they were the King's merchants, and that the loss would not fall upon their own heads, he ordered the rich cloths and furs to be brought forth, and, measuring them out with his lance, gave to all his men their shares, each according to his degree and deserts, but each was served with large measure enough. He then sent the merchants to the King, bearers of Fulke Fitzwarine's grateful thanks for the fine robes with which his majesty had clad all Fulke's good men.

A manuscript in the Bodleian Library at Oxford describes how Fulk and his band were in the second year of King John's reign subjected to a siege in Stanley Abbey near Calne:

> Fulco Fitzwarine took refuge, July 2nd [1201], in the Abbey of Stanley and was there besieged, together with his followers, for fourteen days, by almost the whole county and by many others who had flocked to the place. But he came safe in the peace of the church, and was reconciled in the following year.

From this account it seems that Fulk was reconciled to both the church and to King John who in 1203 revoked his outlawry and granted his claim on Whittington Castle. In 1207 he married a lady called Matilda, and in 1210 and 1214 he loyally accompanied John to war in Ireland and France. He is then said to have again lost the king's favour as a result of making war upon his neighbours and in 1215 he joined the disaffected barons who were waging the Magna Carta War upon the king.

For a time after King John's death in 1216 Fulk was out of favour with John's nine-year-old son Henry III who bestowed many FitzWarin lands on his own favourites. He was again outlawed in 1217 but the gift of bucks in 1236 by Henry III (mentioned above, page 83) implies that the FitzWarins had then reached some accommodation with the throne and again been forgiven. It appears that even by the turbulent standards of his times Fulk FitzWarin was a very troublesome subject.

Latton and Eysey

L ATTON AND EYSEY are two rural parishes situated immediately north-east of Cricklade and separated from one another by Ampney Brook. Latton (093955) stands within a promontory of Wiltshire that projects north from Cricklade past Hailstone Hill into Gloucestershire and, since it stands beside the Ermin Way, it is not surprising that Roman finds are found here. These include fragments of two Roman columns that may be seen at the south-west corner of the churchyard and more Roman remains, including a Roman pavement that was unearthed near the village in the 17th century. When a watercourse was being straightened towards Cricklade in 1866 a Roman coffin and a hoard of fifty-five Roman coins were found, as was another pavement two miles north of Latton.

Latton was held in late-Saxon times by a thane of Edward the Confessor and in Domesday it was held by a Norman priest called Reinbald (or Regenbald). On the Cirencester road about 300 yards beyond the canal bridge a decapitated ten foot high octagonal-shafted cross stands on the wide approach to the church. This church is part Norman and part Perpendicular and was remodelled by Butterfield in 1861. Latton is also situated on the former Wilts and Berks Canal that was abandoned in 1914, and at Latton Basin (087954) the North Wilts Branch of the Wilts and Berks joined the Thames and Severn Canal where a toll house, a lock chamber, and a stone-lined basin survive.

On the redundant Wilts and Berks Canal a mile and a half south-east of Latton (at 113553) is Eysey – sometimes Eisey – that may be reached by a pleasant one mile stroll from Cricklade long the banks of William Morris's 'Upperest Thames'. St Mary's Church (117941) at Eysey existed as early as 1195 but was demolished in 1844. It stood on a footpath that runs west to east across Eysey Hill and its existence presumably indicates the former presence here of a village, particularly as the original church was replaced by a later one that survived until 1953 when it too was demolished. An 1810 Buckler painting of the original church was reproduced in *WAM* 57. Earthworks at Gastons (114911) between a bend in the Thames and the deserted graveyard of the former church on the hill at Eysey were on some modern maps designated the

'Hamlet with medieval origins', although the historian of Cricklade Dr Thomson believed that they were military works thrown up by parliamentary troops during the Civil War in anticipation of a battle that never took place.

At the Dissolution Latton and Eysey were bought by Sir Anthony Hungerford of Down Ampney and with these two tiny places my account of the fringe of Wiltshire north of the B4040 ends.

We will now move west to North-West Wiltshire where I will first describe

Malmesbury, the 'Queen of hilltop towns'

A PHOTOGRAPH captioned 'Queen of hilltop towns, Malmesbury as seen from the far side of the Avon' in Michael Wood's *In Search of the Dark Ages* (1981) first made me aware of the dramatic approach to Malmesbury that may be enjoyed by parking near Westport Bridge (928872) on the Foxley road to the west of the town and entering it on foot from this direction. To do this you follow the green field path along the Sherston branch of the Avon, turn left and cross the river at a former mill site, climb the paths up the hill, and enter the town through the site of the former Postern Gate that stood a few yards west of the Market Cross. It always seems to me a shame that most people who come to Malmesbury approach it from the A429 to its east and never experience the drama of entering the old town from this direction and seeing it in all its glory on its high hill. The Wiltshire artist Robin Tanner knew and loved this approach and wrote of his longing: 'to celebrate [in an etching] the ancient town of Malmesbury, especially the Abbey on the skyline seen from the bridge over the stream at the foot of the hill on which it stands'. In 1984 late in his life he realised this ambition when he made an etching of Malmesbury from this direction, incorporating in it some elements from elsewhere and, because of the town's associations

Malmesbury seen from west, with abbey (left)

Modern Housing by the river, Malmesbury

with St Aldhelm, entitling it *Aldhelmsburgh*. Some other interesting opinions of Malmesbury are H. J. Massingham's who suggested in his *Cotswold Country* (1937) that 'Malmesbury would make a good end or beginning to any country' and that 'as a pause in this pilgrimage of stone it is without compare', and that of the artist-writer S. R. Jones who in *England South* (1948) praised the view of Malmesbury as seen from its south across the river at Daniel's Well (931872) and described the old town as: 'a place of seclusion and great charm'.

Although Malmesbury features little in the *Anglo Saxon Chronicle* it remains an essentially Saxon town with at its heart the abbey that was founded in Saxon times and, despite its obvious Norman grandeur, is now semi-ruinous and a mere shadow of its former self. Malmesbury was one of Alfred's fortified *burhs* and a town whose history is of most interest in the Anglo-Saxon and early-Norman periods, as was recognised by Michael Wood when he in his *In Search of the Dark Ages* drew attention to the importance of its situation 'on what was then the border between Wessex and Mercia'. Malmesbury grew up on a hilltop described by Leland as being 'wonderfully defended by nature' between the Tetbury and Sherston branches of the Bristol Avon, and because of its strategic position it has long been thought that this hilltop was must have been occupied in prehistoric times. Excavations in 1998-2000 (see *WAM* 99: 105-164) have now confirmed its 'extended occupation during the Iron Age'.

Malmesbury is particularly associated with the activities of four ecclesiastics – the missionary monk Maldulf, its first bishop St. Aldhelm, the historian-monk William of Malmesbury, and the powerful Bishop Roger – but the monarch to whom Malmesbury is most indebted is Alfred's grandson Athelstan (c.895-939) who succeeded in uniting all of England under his rule and rebuilt Malmesbury Abbey after it had been destroyed during Alfred's resistance to the Danes.

To the West Saxons Malmesbury was Ingleburne and here in about AD 630-650 a Celtic christian mission was established by an Irish monk called Maldulf (d. 675) who gave the town its modern name that is derived from 'Maldulf's hill'. Dedications of some churches in nearby Somerset suggest that some early missionary work had been undertaken across the Bristol Channel by Welsh christians and it seems likely that the Celtic Maldulf built his mission upon elements of Romano-British christianity surviving from a little over a hundred years earlier. His monastery still existed in the time of the historian William of Malmesbury in 1140, and some 'long-and-short' work surviving in a cottage gable at Westport in west Malmesbury suggests that this cottage may once have been a Saxon church, although a masonry building such as this would probably date from late in the Saxon period. Maldulf's monastery soon established a reputation for learning and piety, and to it came St Aldhelm (c. 640-709), who is believed to have been related to the West Saxon Kings. When Maldulf died in AD 675 he was succeeded by Aldhelm who after becoming the first Abbot of Malmesbury converted Maldulf's Celtic mission to Roman christianity and introduced the Benedictine order at Malmesbury.

Aldhelm was the first Anglo-Saxon scholar to write in Latin and the first Englishman to obtain a European reputation. He became so popular that when in 705 he became Bishop of Sherborne his monks persuaded him to continue to be their superior at Malmesbury. At Sherborne he he built a new church but as he grew older his many responsibilities caused him to complain about 'the burdens of pastoral care' and after he died doing the rounds of his diocese at Doulting in Somerset his body was brought to Malmesbury for burial, its overnight resting-places along the way being marked by stone crosses.

Several centuries later the Malmesbury educated Anglo-Norman monk William of Malmesbury (c.1095-1143) became the abbey librarian and the first important English historian after Bede. It was William who recorded the amusing story of his fellow monk Elmer (sometimes Oliver), who flourished a few years before the Norman Conquest and:

> by some contrivance fastened wings on to his hands and feet, in order that, looking upon the fable as true, he might fly like Daedalus, and collecting air on the summit of the tower had flown for more than the distance of a furlong ; but, agitated by the violence of the wind and the current of air, as well as by the consciousness of his rash attempt, he fell and broke his legs, and was lame ever after. He used to relate as the cause of his failure, his forgetting to provide himself a tail.

Twynnoy Tombstone

When wandering around Malmesbury Abbey churchyard one cannot help having a guilty smile at the misfortunes of this daring early aeronaut, and also at the sad fate of a Malmesbury girl called Hannah Twynnoy who, as related on her tombstone in the abbey churchyard, in the yard of the White Lion Inn at Malmesbury, in 1703 attempted to befriend a tiger from a travelling menagerie and was killed by the tiger. Her tombstone relates: 'For Tyger fierce, Took life away, And now she lies, In bed of clay, Until the Resurrection day'. The fate of the tiger is not recorded!

The sole mention of Malmesbury in the *Anglo-Saxon Chronicle* was in 1015 when during the Viking wars Ealdorman Eadric Streona — who we shall meet later at Sherston (pages 98-102) — lured two northern lords Siferth and Morcar into a room at Oxford and murdered them, whereupon:

The king [Ethelred] then confiscated all their property, and ordered Siferth's widow to be seized and brought to Malmesbury. Then, after a short time, prince Edmund [Ironside] came and abducted the woman against the king's will, and made her his wife.

The circumstances of this incident were that Eadric Streona brutally betrayed and murdered Siferth and Morcar for allegedly opposing King Ethelred. Siferth's widow Ealdgyth was then incarcerated in the monastery at Malmesbury from where Ethelred's militant son Edmund Ironside abducted and married her.

The Normans as had their predecessors recognised the strategic importance of Malmesbury. They rebuilt the abbey in stone and replaced the Saxon abbot with the Norman Thorold of Fécamp. Malmesbury then suffered from the predatory ambitions of two bishops. When the abbey was being rebuilt as a fine stone building after being destroyed by fire Bishop Herman of Ramsbury coveted it and attempted to make it the centre of his bishopric but his hopes were dashed by the objections of the monks. Old Sarum then became the centre of Herman's diocese but some time later according to William of Malmesbury Bishop Roger of Salisbury (c.1065-1139) – a mighty prelate who presided over the nation's administration, finances, and justice, and was regent in 1123-6 – annexed Malmesbury 'as far as he was able to his See'. To the indignation of the monks and burgesses he built a castle adjoining the abbey and also added defensive walls with gateways around the top of the hill upon which Malmesbury stands. The smaller Postern Gate (933873) a short distance west of the Market Cross provided access to the town from the River Avon to its west. A 12th century 'substantial stone wall' revealed by the 1998-2000 excavation was probably the remains of the wall built by Bishop Roger who died in 1139 after being deprived earlier in that year of his offices by King Stephen. The positions of these defences, including the gates, are shown on the sketch plan overleaf.

The tradition that there was then friction between the abbey and the garrison seems to be confirmed by a letter from the pope that authorised the abbot to excommunicate members of the garrison for depradations upon the abbey. It may have been recollection of Malmesbury's former resistance to his father Henry II that persuaded King John, when embroiled in the revolt of his barons in 1216, to grant permission to the monks of Malmesbury to 'pull down the Castle and build there at will'. In 1542 Leland described the Malmesbury defences as: '4 gates by the names of est, west, north and south, ruinus al. The walles in many places stand up: but now very feble', but a 'bird's eye' drawing made of Malmesbury during the Civil War shows the town with substantial walls and triangular bastions that were probably slighted when the parliamentary garrison quitted the town in 1646.

Abbey crossing arches

The precise location of Bishop Roger's castle is uncertain although it may have been to the west of the abbey on the site of the present Old Bell Hotel that was formerly known as the Castle Inn. Bird in his *History of Malmesbury* (1876) stated that: 'The castle stood on a neck of land between the abbey and Westport'.

We know from William of Malmesbury that in 1142 Malmesbury Abbey 'in size and beauty exceeded any other religious edifice in England'. Bishop Roger, who died in 1139, may have planned Malmesbury Abbey church that is now a magnificent mainly Norman part-ruin with a blind-arcaded western tower, an exceedingly richly carved Norman porch with a series of receding semi-circular arches, and a later south front with nine pointed clerestorey windows. The immense height of the isolated surviving crossing arches at the east end of the ruins provides an indication of the former massive scale of the building, and as I write (in 2006) the parishioners are proposing to obtain more room by extending the abbey westwards towards the neighbouring inn.

Abbey south front and porch

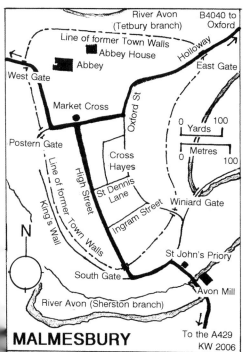

Malmesbury was in 1327 one of several abbeys which refused the body of the unpopular Edward II for burial after he had allegedly been foully murdered in Berkeley Castle. This refusal may have been due to his notorious reputation, or perhaps because there was an element of doubt about his death as some contemporary Continental evidence suggests that he escaped abroad and that the body which was eventually buried at Gloucester was not that of Edward II.

When in 1471 Henry VI's fiery Queen Margaret landed at Weymouth during the Wars of the Roses, and marched her Lancastrian army north intending to cross the Severn and join Jasper Tudor's Lancastrians in Wales, Edward IV advanced with his large Yorkist army out of London to intercept her. After evicting many alleged Lancastrians from Cirencester he allowed his army to be decoyed south to Malmesbury which he occupied on 1 May. After realising that he had been duped and that that the Lancastrians had got ahead of him King Edward set off in pursuit and on 4 May caught and decisively defeated the Lancastrians in the bloody Battle of Tewkesbury. Almost two hundred years later Malmesbury saw more military activity in the English Civil War when William Waller took the town for parliament on 21 March 1643 and wrote triumphantly to his commander-in-chief the Earl of Essex informing him of the exploits of his colleagues, including Sergeant Major Burghell who had entered the royal camp at Sherston as a spy. Waller was then forced out of Malmesbury, although parliament later regained and garrisoned it against the king.

At the Dissolution of the monasteries Malmesbury Abbey was valued at £1507 and sold to a local clothier named William Stumpe (d.1552) who has been censured for installing his looms in the monastery buildings but seldom given credit for giving the parishioners the great nave of the Norman abbey as their parish church.

After Stumpe's death in 1552 the woollen industry at Malmesbury began to decline and by the late-18th century was virtually extinct in the town. At the end of that century, however, a tentative attempt was made to revive it by a Bradford clothier called Hill who after experiencing trouble introducing machinery at Bradford moved to Malmesbury and in 1790 built Avon Mill (936839) down beside St John's Bridge at the southern entrance to the town. His enterprise failed and his massive Georgian mill with its multiple windows was soon adapted to manufacturing silk. Other minor industries practised at Malmesbury in the 19th century were gloving and the lace-making that became a cottage industry practised by the women in most of the cottages.

Avon Mill

As a young reporter the Wiltshire country writer Richard Jefferies (1848-87) sometimes walked fifteen miles each way across Braden Forest from Swindon to Malmesbury in connection with his duties as a local newspaper reporter. Under the pseudonym 'Geoffrey' he wrote *A History of Malmesbury* that was printed in twenty-one chapters and an appendix in the *North Wilts Herald* in 1867.

The picturesque winding streets of Malmesbury are lined by many fine houses, and Malmesbury has one of the finest market crosses in the country described by Leland as:

Market Cross

a right faire and costly piece of work in the market-place, made all of stone, and curiously vaulted, for the poor market folks to stand dry when rain cometh, There be eight great pillars and eight open arches, and the work is eight square ; one great pillar in the middle beareth up the vault.

The usually irascible William Cobbett approved of this cross and suggested that it was 'worth a journey of hundreds of miles' to see. A predecessor of the present cross was built by Abbot William de Colerne (d. 1296), a man who according to Canon Jackson was: 'famous for improving the creature comforts of the monks', and was said to have at Malmesbury 'planted vineyards and laid out gardens'. From near the market cross the grounds of the abbey are entered through a castellated arch flanked by two apparent lodges that are in fact two of the 'blind' house prisons that were built in many Wiltshire towns and villages to accommodate minor local offenders and more serious offenders on their way to other destinations. These Malmesbury examples with their substantial nail-studded doors are easily missed. On the site of the former abbot's lodging east of the abbey stands the fine Elizabethan Abbey House that was originally built by the Stumpe family.

At the bottom of the town near the river and a short distance from St John's Bridge and the Avon Mills are some almshouses that occupy the site of the former 13th century Hospital of St John of Jerusalem founded in 1263 by the Knights of St John. Leland noticed in the 1540s this 'poore hospitale' for which the Malmesbury people assumed responsibility in 1633. It was then maintained as an almshouse until 1948 when it housed some poor widows. Today all that remains of the old hospital is in a gable end a single blocked pointed archway that was probably its entrance.

St John's Hospital

King's Heath

Droveway over King's Heath looking west

I F MALMESBURY IS LEFT by crossing St John's Bridge and proceeding south along the former Kingsway (now the A429), the King's Heath (905851) – now generally known as Malmesbury Common – lies west of the road south-west of Malmesbury. Heath means literally 'flat waste tract of land often covered with shrubs' and its ancient name recognises King's Heath to be a form of landscape that is unusual in Wiltshire, namely a wide flat heath used mainly as pasture land and devoid of water apart from the drainage ditches that flank some of the straight causeways that carry several public rights-of-way across the common. King's Heath is historically as well as geographically interesting. The king of its name was Athelstan (c. 895-939), a grandson of King Alfred who in recognition of 'their assistance in my Conflict against the Danes' in about AD 930 granted to the burgesses of Malmesbury five hides of his large estate 'near to my town of Norton'. This land became known as King's Heath.

The precise nature of the services rendered by the burgesses to Athelstan are not known. The grant amounted to about 570 acres of which each of the commoners was allotted one acre to cultivate or graze animals. It now survives in an amended form and my understanding is that today about 250 commoners retain rights and that the land is now rented out as farms, each commoner being paid his share from the rental proceeds. The commoners must be residents of Malmesbury and a ceremony for initiating the them is still held at St John's Almhouses in Malmesbury High Street. The rights are jealously guarded and the story used to be told of a frail old Malmesbury commoner who steadfastly refused to go into the workhouse for fear of losing his rights at King's Heath insisting: 'King Athelstan hath kept I all my life and King Athelstan shall keep I till I die'. Today 'Athelstan's Day' is still observed locally on the second Tuesday after Trinity.

When early in the 17th century common lands were being appropriated by private enclosure a Malmesbury glover complained that rich people had: 'divided and severed . . . the Heath with ditches and hedges . . . to their own profit'. The commoners reacted violently by levelling the enclosure fences, and after their ringleaders were arrested they were freed by a sympathetic keeper from Cole Park. A Robert Berry then emerged as the leader of the commoners and disturbances continued for some time.

Thomas Hobbes of Malmesbury

A CELEBRATED SON of Malmesbury who was extremely proud of his place of birth was the philosopher Thomas Hobbes (1588-1679) who is described in *The Oxford Companion to British History* (1997) as 'the greatest political philosopher to have written in the English language', although his views attracted little following in his lifetime and he achieved little general recognition until the 19th century.

Hobbes was the son of the minister of St Mary's church in Westport on the neck of land outside the now-demolished west gate of Malmesbury. John Aubrey found and recorded his birthplace as being: 'at his father's house in Westport, being that extreme howse that pointes into, or faces, the Horsefayre ; the farthest howse on the left hand as you goe to Tedbury, leaving the church on your right'. Hobbes was born prematurely when his mother became distressed by news of the Spanish Armada, and was brought up by an uncle after his father fled after striking an ecclesiastical colleague. After graduating from Magdalen Hall at Oxford he devoted himself to study and private tutoring, and was fortunate in 1603 when the Cavendish family of Hardwick in Derbyshire approached his college for a tutor for their son who had had stipulated that he wanted no 'greybeard'. As the 15-year-old Hobbes satisfied this requirement he obtained the appointment and remained with the Cavendish family for most of his life, apart from a period after 1640 when he fled to France for fear of being accused by the Long Parliament of advocating royal absolutism. From 1647 he was mathematical tutor to the exiled Prince Charles.

Thomas Hobbes

For his masterpiece of political philosophy on 'the matter, Forme and Power of a Commonwealth Ecclesiastical and Civil' Hobbes chose the title *Leviathan* (1651), this being a Hebrew word for anything large or formidable. The monster of his book was the sovereign power, and Hobbes propounded the theory that: 'The condition of man . . . is a condition of war of everyone against everyone' that could only be countered by the exercise of supreme power. By advocating the case for an absolute monarch demanding complete obedience from his people

Hobbes alienated both the royalists and their opponents. For a time he was out of favour with Prince Charles who believed that his book was intended to encourage Cromwell to take the crown, and also with the puritan church which suspected him of atheism. In 1652 Hobbes returned to England where he submitted to the Council of State and was allowed to live in London but was forbidden to publish anything on controversial subjects. At the Restoration Hobbes although embroiled in controversy from all sides recovered royal favour. Aubrey recorded Charles II's opinion that he 'thought Mr Hobbes never meant him hurt', and he was even granted a pension of £100 a year which it is said was never paid! Parliament retained doubts about him and seriously debated whether the Great Plague and the Great Fire of 1665-6 were God's punishment on the country for harbouring such an atheist as Hobbes, but he contrived to escape censure, possibly as a result of intervention on his behalf by the king.

Leviathan *title page*

John Aubrey greatly valued his friendship with Hobbes and much of what we know about him comes from Aubrey's life that was published in his *Brief Lives*. We know for example that Hobbes was extremely proud of being a Wiltshireman and retained 'a little touch of our pronounciation . . . to his dyeing day', and the title page of *Leviathan* proudly declares its author as 'Thomas Hobbes of Malmesbury'. Some of Aubrey's recollections of Hobbes are unforgettable, for example that: 'In his old age he was very bald . . .: yet within door, he used to study, and sit, bareheaded, and said he never took cold in his head, but that the greatest trouble was to keep the flies from pitching on the baldness', and that as he did much of his thinking when out walking Hobbes had an ink-horn fitted into his staff to enable him to record his thoughts as they came to him.

When he was eighty-six Hobbes, claiming that he had nothing better to do, translated *The Iliad* and *The Odyssey* which were published in 1682, and with his last words he originated the expression: 'I am about to take my last voyage, a great leap in the dark'.

Avon feeder west of Sherston

The Headwaters of the Bristol Avon

ITS RIVERS CONTRIBUTE much to the topography and the history of the Wiltshire Cotswolds and for centuries they literally drove the cloth-making and the later paper-making that were the early industries of the region. The principal river is the Bristol Avon that is so-named to distinguish it from the Salisbury Avon, and has been said to 'sweep from the Cotswolds to the

Mendips'. Its total length from the source of its longest feeder to the point where it enters the Bristol Channel amounts to about 62 miles over which it drains most of north-west Wiltshire. Around the Upper Bristol Avon beds of oolitic limestone are interlayered with beds of clay that provide the region with its riverside pastures.

The two streams that form the headwaters of the Bristol Avon are its northern branch, generally known as the Tetbury or Long Newnton branch, and the Sherston branch. The former rises a little west of the Fosse Way near Tetbury in Gloucestershire and follows a meandering course south-east past Brokenborough to Malmesbury, while the larger Sherston Branch rises near Badminton in Gloucestershire and flows a little north of east through Sherston and Easton Grey. The crossing of the Sherston branch by the Fosse Way near Easton Grey was described

Tetbury Avon north of Malmesbury

earlier (page 44), as has the contribution that the two Avon streams make to the strategic strength of Malmesbury. The Tetbury branch passes north of the town as a beautiful wide river lined with trees and some light industrial establishments, while the Sherston branch is more rural and open as it flows south of Malmesbury. After flowing around the town and almost surrounding it with water the Avon streams unite a short distance east of Malmesbury, leave the area that I have designated the Wiltshire Cotswolds, and as the middle stretch of the Bristol Avon the now combined streams flow south through the claylands around the Somerfords, the Seagrys, Chippenham, and at Melksham re-enter the region covered by this book as the Lower Bristol Avon that after flowing through Bradford on Avon leaves Wiltshire along the beautiful Limpley Stoke Valley, as described later (page 239).

Sherston Church from Square

Sherston and John Rattlebones

ABOUT FIVE MILES WEST of Malmesbury near the head of the
Sherston branch of the Bristol Avon is Sherston (852858), a large
village that was once known as Great Sherston to distinguish it from the
smaller Sherston Pinkney to its north-east. Sherston's rectangular village
centre, that is now inevitably devoted to car parking, is suggestive of a
market square and John Aubrey confirms that before his time Sherston
had a market. The village is also said to have been built within a
fortification of which some signs remain in a partly destroyed defensive
bank and ditch of uncertain date (at 851860) that the local topographer
John Britton (1771-1857) recorded seeing 'to the west of the church'.

    The church which stands aside from and north of the square has
an imposing lofty tower whose upper stages are Georgian in date but
Gothic in style. They were built in 1730 by a Colerne master mason
Thomas Sumsion (c.1672-1744) whose persistence in designing in the
Gothic style in the first half of the Georgian 18th century illustrates the
practice in this region of continuing to design in the Gothic style long
after it had become extinct elsewhere. Sumsion was paid £1.15s. (£1.75p)
for his 'draught' for this tower, and the churchwardens' accounts also
record a payment: 'to Moses Rice for his sons goeing to Cullourn
[Colerne] to give notice to Thom^s Sumption to come the second time'.

    A battle between the Dane Canute (sometimes Cnut: c.994-1035)
and the Saxon Edmund Ironside (c.981-1016) is generally thought to have
been fought near Sherston in 1016 when these men were disputing the
throne of Wessex. Doubts have been expressed about Sherston being the
site of this battle, although Henry of Huntingdon nominated its location
as *Sceorstan* and the early translators of the *Anglo Saxon Chronicle*
stated that the two men: 'fought another battle after midsummer at

Sherston'. Albany Major in his *Early Wars of Wessex* (1913) also believed that the battle took place here, and most modern historians including Professor Stenton in the Oxford *Anglo-Saxon England* (1943) and P. Marren in *Battles of the Dark Ages* (2006) have also accepted Sherston as the venue. Its precise site is not known and it may have been fought astride the Fosse Way along which both armies probably came to Sherston. From this battle arose the story of a probably legendary local character called John Rattlebones whose name is commemorated in the name of a public house near Sherston church. The legend is a strange one, and it is necessary to set it in its historical context.

Rattlebones is alleged to have flourished fifty years before the Norman Conquest at the time when the Saxon Ethelred II (968-1016), known as 'the Unready', had ruled so ineffectively that he had in 1014 been forced to fly into exile in Normandy and been supplanted as king by the Danish king Sweyn Forkbeard. Ethelred's reign was blighted by the fact that when he was a boy his retainers at Corfe in 978 AD treacherously murdered his predecessor and half-brother King Edward the Martyr. Consequently many Saxons were opposed to him, especially when after marrying as his second wife (a Norman lady called Emma) he proposed to supplant his Saxon sons by his first wife and replace them with Edward, his semi-Norman younger son by Emma. These facts made

Sherston Church

Ethelred extremely unpopular and had allowed Sweyn to seize the throne of Wessex. He had also alienated his supporters by his excessive reliance on the low-born Eadric Streona, known as 'the Greedy', who with his brothers dominated his court and acted as Ethelred's hit men in eliminating all opposition.

Eadric Streona was described by the Saxon scholar Professor Freeman as 'a man of low birth, shrewd intellect' and 'of an eloquent tongue'. He initially attained eminence by his sheer effrontery and skill at speech-making, in 1007 he had become Ealdorman of Mercia, and between 1009 and 1012 he advanced rapidly in Ethelred's hierarchy. In 1012 he further consolidated his position by marrying one of Ethelred's daughters.

When Sweyn Forkbeard died in February 1014 the Saxons invited Ethelred back on condition that he ruled more justly than he had done in the past. He accepted and came home, but he was now terminally ill and it was left to his third and eldest surviving son, the militant Edmund Ironside, to lead the Saxon opposition to Sweyn's son Canute who was the new Danish claimant to the throne. Edmund while nominally representing his father's interests in fact pursued his own aspirations to the throne while Eadric, as the king's son-in-law and principal lieutenant, remained loyal to Ethelred. Despite this Eadric has generally been characterised as having betrayed the Saxons because by supporting King Ethelred he was obliged to oppose the Saxon claimant Edmund Ironside, and having earned Edmund's enmity when Ethelred became terminally ill he had no option but to ally himself with the Danes.

Rattlebones Statue

Both Edmund and Eadric now raised Saxon armies but in 1015, with Ethelred dying and the Saxons divided, Eadric fearful for his future if Edmund succeeded joined the Dane Canute taking with him many of the West Saxons. Ethelred meanwhile lingered on while Edmund fought Canute and Eadric in a campaign that had now developed into a straight fight for the throne. Battles were at this time generally rather casual encounters usually resulting from accidental meetings, but Edmund and Canute deliberately sought each other out and fought a series of pitched battles throughout southern England. When they met at Sherston contemporary evidence indicates that Canute and Edmund personally commanded the opposing armies. Canute's skald Otto the Black – a skald being a Scandinavian poet – confirms that Canute personally commanded the Danish army, and Eadric Streona was said to have at the battle attempted to create panic among the Saxons by crying out that Edmund was slain, proving that Edmund was personally in command of the Saxons. The *Anglo-Saxon Chronicle* confirms that Eadric was at Sherston 'assisting the host against King Edmund', and also implies that the armies fought each other to a standstill in a battle which was bloody but inconclusive, and that despite the presence of their respective kings themselves broke off the engagement. It reads:

> Some time previous to this king Edmund had made his way out of the borough [of London], and had taken possession of Wessex, and all the inhabitants submitted to him. Soon after this he fought against the host at Penselwood, near Gillingham, and fought another battle after midsummer at Sherston, and there was great slaughter on both sides, and it was the armies themselves [implying not the leaders] who broke off the fight.

At the Battle of Sherston Rattlebones was said to have fought nobly and done great execution among the Danes. John Britton, after informing the readers of his *Beauties of Wiltshire* (Volume 3) that the room over the porch of Sherston church was: 'the place in which, according to tradition, King Edmund slept the night before the battle of Sherston', conceded the very obvious fact that the porch was 'of much later construction'. A rudely-wrought three-foot high and much-weathered statue on a corbel on the east face of the porch of Sherston church has been claimed to represent Rattlebones who according to the legend when wounded in the stomach clapped a tile (presumably a Cotswold stone tile!) over his wound and fought on. Some authentic character may have provided the basis for this legend that was still extant in the 17th century when John Aubrey wrote:

> In the wall of the church porch [at Sherston] on the outside in a niche [actually on a corbel] without inscription or scutcheon is a little figure about 2 foote and a halfe high, ill done which they call Rattle Bone, who the tradition is did much service against the Danes when they infested this part of the countrey ; the figure resembles more a priest than a soldier ; something looks like a maniple and his Robe is a kind of cope. The old woemen and children have these verses by tradition, viz.:

> Fight well Rattlebone
> Thou shalt have Sherstone.
> What will I with Sherstone doe
> Without I have all belongs thereto?
> Thou shalt have Wych and Wellesley,
> Easton toune and Pinkeney.

The name 'Wych' is now apparently lost although *Sherstoneswyk* appeared in the 1356 *Assize Rolls*, 'Wellesley' is evidently the modern Willesley, 'Easton Town' is the north-eastern part of Sherston, and Pinkney lies to its north-east. The statue on the porch of Sherston church appears as Aubrey suggested to be wearing a pallium, that is a cloak or stole marked with crosses at the front and back issued by the pope to his archbishops as a mark of authority, and it is probably a representation of St Aldhelm who was buried nearby at Malmesbury in AD 709.

King Ethelred 'after much trouble and wretchedness' died in April 1016 leaving Canute and Edmund contending for his throne. The latter after being decisively defeated in Essex in October 1016 withdrew wounded into Gloucestershire and on an island in the Severn at Deershurst he and Canute later in 1016 agreed to divide England between them, Edmund taking Wessex and Canute Mercia and Northumbria, with a proviso that the survivor should take all. When Edmund died a few weeks later Canute in accordance with the agreement assumed full sovereignty as the first Danish ruler of all of England which he continued to rule for almost twenty years until his death in 1035. Although universally distrusted Eadric Streona was for a time allowed to retain his control of Mercia but at the first opportunity Canute had Eadric and a number of other potentially troublesome Saxon nobles executed in 1017.

But how are we to explain the strange Rattlebones legend? Just as the Romano-Britons when assailed by the Saxons in the 6th century rallied around half-legendry figure of Arthur, it is possible that the Anglo-Saxons, when their expectations for a Saxon Wessex were extinguished by the unexpected early death of Edmund Ironside and the succession to his throne of the Dane Canute, may have consoled themselves by creating the legend of Rattlebones as a local Saxon hero.

Towards Badminton in the countryside west of Sherston is Sopworth (827863), a tiny village that is so isolated that it has generally been missed by topographical writers. After spending many years studying Wiltshire history and topography and exploring its countryside,

Cotswold-style farm at south end of Sopworth

Sopworth remained the one Wiltshire village that I had failed to visit. When belatedly I arrived at Sopworth I found a nice Cotswold-style village containing a number of good buildings, including at its southern end a fine Georgian manor house and a nice 17th century farmhouse with stone cross-windows associated with a cluster of farm buildings built in the vernacular Cotswold style. The small 13th century church of St Mary to the east of the village is less interesting as it was heavily restored in 1871, although as so often with Victorian reconstructions its original tower has survived. The church contains a window depicting the three Marys that was designed by Burne-Jones and probably made by Morris and Company.

Easton Town, the Goodenoughs, and Pinkney

Richard Goodenough

To ITS NORTH-EAST and virtually adjoining Sherston is Easton Town (860864) that was the home of two men who were involved in a conspiracy to assassinate Charles II and his brother James, Duke of York. *Court Rolls* record the presence of Goodenoughs at Easton Town in 1585 when the family appears to have resided at Lower Farm (860862) adjoining Pinkney Park. By the 17th century the Goodenoughs had become a powerful local family many of whom became attorneys-at-law its most notable members being Richard Goodenough (died 1692) and his brother Francis. The former is described in the *Dictionary of National Biography* as a 'conspirator and attorney of bad repute' who after becoming a rather disreputable Under Sheriff of London for several years seems to have shared that office with his brother Francis. Being protestants the two brothers in 1683 became involved in the Rye House Plot that was hatched in London to secure a protestant succession by murdering the nominally protestant Charles II ('the Blackbird' of the plot) and his catholic brother James Duke of York ('the Goldfinch'), and declare the protestant Duke of Monmouth king. The plotting took place in several London taverns and Richard Goodenough was as Under Sheriff of London called upon to make out lists of potential protestant sympathisers. Although undoubtedly implicated the Goodenoughs were not principals in the plot, although Richard is on record as having been willing to contribute substantially towards financing it. The plan was to intercept the royal party as they returned from Newmarket races near Rye House in Hertfordshire but because of a fire at Newmarket the royal party left early. This threw the plot into confusion, the authorities became aware of it, and the Goodenough brothers fled to the Low Countries and were outlawed with a price of a hundred pounds on Richard's head. Two of the ringleaders – William Lord Russell and Algernon Sidney – were executed, and another, the Earl of Essex, committed suicide in the Tower.

In the Low Countries Richard Goodenough ingratiated himself with the Duke of Monmouth and became his Secretary of State. After the catholic James II succeeded at the death of Charles II Richard in 1685 took part in Monmouth's invasion of England during which he became paymaster to the rebel forces, at Taunton complained that 'none of note came in', and that Monmouth's force never had as many as six thousand men. After Sedgemoor Goodenough was captured attempting to take ship in Devon and sent to London. The normally unforgiving James II granted him his life on condition that he turned king's evidence against his fellow rebels and his written 'information against the Earl of Stamford' dated 1 November 1685 has

Prater's at Easton Town

survived. When summoned to give evidence in court he failed to appear and Dean Swift alleged that he fled to Ireland where he had family connections and there continued to practice law and died. There appears to be some doubt about this as he was officially pardoned in 1687 and although in a letter sent to his brother at Sherston in July 1689 he seems to have particular knowledge about the siege of Londonderry his letter also indicates that he was equally well-informed about the daily happenings in parliament.

Richard Goodenough made his Will in 1690 as a gentleman of 'the Middle Temple, London', and among the Goodenough tombs under a yew tree in Sherston churchyard is that of Richard Goodenough who died 16 April 1692 aged 77. He was after his death recorded as having lived in a large house at Easton Town that in a deed of 1718 was described as 'a messuage and lands in Easton Town in the possession of Thomas and Francis Goodenough, gents'. Richard's children were named Thomas, Richard, John, Francis and Rachel, and an account book kept from 1710 to 1725 by a Francis Goodenough (died 1728) reveals him executing much 'work don in and ab't Prater's' where he lived from 1700 and where his father Richard is known to have lived. This house was presumably Prater's Farm at Easton Town on the west side of the minor road that runs south-east to Ladyswood. This Francis Goodenough, who is commemorated on another tomb as dying also aged 77 on 26 August 1728, is obviously not Richard's brother and fellow conspirator but Richard's son. Another of his sons, also named Richard Goodenough, practised law in Dublin and may have been confused by Dean Swift with his namesake father. This son too seems to have died in 1752 at Sherston where he had inherited much of the Goodenough family property.

Easton Grey village and bridge

Easton Grey, Foxley and Bremilham

ROUGHLY MIDWAY between Sherston and Malmesbury is Easton Grey (881873), a small stone-built village with at its centre a group of houses described by Pevsner as a 'nice group'. The five-arched bridge over the Sherston branch of the Bristol Avon probably dates from the 16th century, and overlooking the river from its north is the late-18th century Easton Grey House. The village name means 'East farm' while the 'Grey' element commemorates John de Grey who held the manor in 1243.

Easton Grey stands a mile west of the Fosse Way and at the point a short distance east of the village where the Fosse Way crosses the Avon is the Romano-British site known as White Walls (890871). This linear settlement extended for about half a mile along the Fosse Way on either side of the present bridge, and for about fifty yards on either side of the Fosse. It probably originated as a *mansio* (see later, page 140) and associated with it is a detached Roman site in Whitewalls Wood (890876) beside the B4040. Among the many Roman objects found at White Walls are a relief of four figures inscribed 'CIVILIS FECIT' and the head of a statue of a goddess that was found in 1810 (for further information see the excavation report in *WAM* 99, 165-189).

On the opposite side of the Fosse Way from Easton Grey about one mile south-east of White Walls are Foxley and Bremilham, two former adjoining

Easton Grey House from the south

*White Walls Roman
Station*

parishes of which only Foxley (897859) survives as a tiny village with a five-bay 18th century manor house and a 17th century square dovecote with a gable on each of its faces. On their 1773 map Andrews and Dury show Foxley House (892860) as belonging to 'Lord Holland', although in a painting of about 1800 reproduced in the *Wiltshire Victoria County History* (Volume 14 facing page 220) the house is shown as being then ruinous. The gateposts of this former mansion of the Lords Holland survive at the bend in the road at the west end of Foxley (at 893860).

The Lords Holland were descended from Sir Stephen Fox (1627-1716), a poor boy from Farley in south-east Wiltshire who after assisting Prince Charles in his flight across his home district after the Battle of Worcester became a great financier, served Charles II in exile in Holland, and was after the Restoration made the Paymaster to the Forces. He originated the idea for Chelsea Hospital and in a long career also served James II, William of Orange, and Queen Anne.

*Gatepiers to the former
Foxley House*

When many years later their manor house in south-east Wiltshire was burnt down in 1744 the Fox family moved to London where they demonstrated some of the financial acumen of their famous ancestor by buying up land in Mayfair and the West End of London and building Holland House. Sir Stephen Fox produced a late family that included his second son Henry (1705-74) who was born when his father was seventy-eight. He obtained Foxley in the following circumstances in 1758 after he had become a successful politician. John Ayliffe of Grittenham had bought the manor in 1600 and the manor house was built by George Ayliffe (d. 1722) after he moved to Foxley in 1688. A Judith Ayliffe (d.1737) left it to her cousin Susanna Strangways (d. 1758) who was married to Thomas Horner, and she left it to her daughter's brother in law Henry Fox. In 1763, five years after he obtained Foxley, Henry Fox became Lord Holland, his elder brother having in 1756 become Earl of Ilchester. The most eminent member of the family was Henry's third son the Liberal statesman Charles James Fox (1749-1806) who would have known Foxley as his father acquired it when Charles James was nine. Foxley remained in the ownership of the Fox family until the late-19th century when it had become merely a farmhouse. The fact that Foxley was *Foxelege* in Domesday and Foxlegh in 1227 establishes that

Foxley Church and Farm

its name originated long before the Fox family became its owners. In 1675 a walled deer park that enclosed about 150 acres existed north of the manor where Foxley Grove (892869) is shown on the modern map, but by 1760 immediately after Henry Fox acquired the manor the park had been disparked. Part of the park wall survived until 1986. Foxley Church (897859) on the triangular Foxley Green is a rebuilding of a largely Perpendicular church.

Bremilham is a redundant place-name that has disappeared from the current Ordnance Survey maps. It was a small settlement a short distance east of Foxley at a bend of the Avon near the 18th century triple-arched stone river bridge (903863), situated in lush pastures north of Cowage Farm (903861) where Bremilham Mill survived until comparatively recent times. Cowage Farm is an L-shaped 18th century house with in its farmyard a small modern mortuary chapel that was built in 1874 on the site of the chancel of a proprietary or field church built by

a landowner that was pulled down in the late-19th century after the *Cowage Farm,* demise of the Bremilham settlement and the proximity of Foxley church *Bremilham* had made it redundant. Stories are however told of a dispute between the farmer at Cowage and the church authorities. The site of Bremilham is crossed by a footpath that runs north from the road past Cowage Farm, and also by a footpath that runs north-east from Foxley church to Hyam Wood.

Norton Manor House

A mile and a half south of Foxley is Norton (886843), a small village with a very fine manor house that was extended in about 1900. Two of its facades have semi-classical gabled two-storeyed porches with attractive primitive Ionic columns that were added in 1623 to older elevations with mullioned casement windows. Its older west front has modern additions. In his youth the antiquary John Britton (see pages 149-51) used to stay at nearby Maidford (892845).

Henry Fox and the Tockenham Forger

A T ABOUT THE TIME in 1758 when Henry Fox acquired Foxley he became involved in the celebrated case of John Ayliffe (c.1718-59), the Tockenham forger. The manner in which Fox had inherited Foxley from its former owners the Ayliffes is described above (page 107), and a wall monument in Foxley Church to George Ayliffe who died in 1722 confirms the Ayliffe presence at Foxley in the early-18th century, although according to the *Gentleman's Magazine* for 19 November 1759 John Ayliffe was 'born near Blandford, in Dorsetshire, of a very good family'. The fact that he was not among the eminent persons of Blandford listed by Hutchin's in his *History of Dorset* (1861-64) may be due to his alleged illegitimacy or to his crimes. John Britton in Volume 3 of *The Beauties of Wilts* gave John Ayliffe's birthplace as Tockenham, three miles south-west of Wootton Bassett and a mile and a half south of Grittenham where his father was said to have been a servant and his mother the housekeeper to a man named Gerard Smith. John seems to have been illegitimately related to the Ayliffes but to have adopted their name, presumably with the family's agreement. Despite their comparatively humble stations his nominal parents, perhaps helped by their employer or by the Ayliffes, sent John to Harrow School and he became a schoolmaster at Lyneham free school three miles south of Grittenham.

John Ayliffe

After marrying the daughter of a rich clergyman John Ayliffe lived beyond his means and ran into debt. Being illegitimate he was excluded from any Ayliffe inheritance, although when the legitimate Ayliffe heiress married Henry Fox's elder brother Stephen Fox, the Earl of Ilchester, Henry arranged for John Ayliffe to become steward to Mrs Strangway-Horner of Mells in Somerset who may have been Henry Fox's mistress. She then seems to have taken up with John Ayliffe who became steward of her estates in Wiltshire and Dorset, but in 1753 he was dismissed. Apparently resentful at being excluded from any Ayliffe inheritance, and despite being in comfortable circumstances, John still had ambitions. The Fox family were related to the Fox-Strangways of Dorset and possibly as a result of this connection John Ayliffe built for himself at Blandford Forum in Dorset a richly furnished house that he could ill afford, and after running deeply into debt he forged Henry Fox's signature on a presentation to the rectory at Brinkworth between Malmesbury and Wootton Bassett. When the forgery was exposed Henry Fox generously forgave him, found him another post, and probably because forgery was then a capital offence did not prosecute.

Ayliffe appears to have had expectations from Mrs Strangway-Horner's estate but she left everything to her former friend Henry Fox, although stipulating that some provision should be made for Ayliffe. Mr Fox complied by leasing Russley Farm in north-east Wiltshire to Ayliffe at a rent of thirty-five pounds for three lives — his own, his wife's, and his son's. Disappointed at missing out on another inheritance and while accepting Mr Fox's lease of Russley, Ayliffe having escaped retribution for his earlier misdemeanours attempted to raise funds by more frauds. He forged Mrs Strangways-Horner's signature on a document leaving him £3,000 and an annuity of £420 and then, in April 1759, threw caution to the winds by forging a copy of Mr Fox's lease of Russley to raise a mortgage on the estate. As the lease provided insufficient security for the loan that he needed he inserted five pounds instead of the actual thirty-five pounds as the rental, forged the signatures of Mr Fox and the witnesses, and persuaded a clergyman to become security for the substantial sum that he borrowed. When he defaulted on the interest payments on the loan the ruined clergyman committed suicide.

To conceal his crime Ayliffe had persuaded the lenders into an oath of secrecy, but when the interest was not forthcoming they approached Mr Fox to take on the mortgage. The disparity between the original lease and the forged copy was then revealed and Ayliffe was arrested and imprisoned in Newgate. Prison regimes were then very harsh but Mr Fox again demonstrated his generosity by paying for Ayliffe to be well fed and comfortably accommodated in prison. Ayliffe repaid this generosity by writing to Mr Pitt, who was then secretary of state but effectively prime minister, indicating that he had information about Mr Fox that would prejudice his position as a minister of state. Hearing of this Mr Fox finally abandoned Ayliffe to his fate and he was tried, found guilty, and sentenced to be hanged.

Ayliffe's appeals to Mr Fox for help now fell on deaf ears but he still expected to be reprieved. On the morning of 19 November 1759 set for his execution he seems to have at last realised the gravity of his position and delayed matters by dragging out his time with the chaplain who later wrote an account of his distracted behaviour. On his way by cart to Tyburn he continued to prevaricate and asked to speak to a friend of the deceased clergyman whom he had ruined, all to no avail. He was hanged and his last words were printed in a pamphlet entitled *A Genuine History of the Life, Character and Confession and dying Words of John Ayliffe, Esq., who was executed at Tyburn, 1759 for Forgery*. His life was later told in John Britton's *Beauties of Wilts* (Volume 3, pages 43-90).

The *Dictionary of National Biography* relates a rumour that Henry Fox had framed Ayliffe out of sexual jealousy, and that Fox's political career was ruined when his political opponents heard of this. Perhaps because of this rumour there was much sympathy for John Ayliffe and his punishment was regarded as excessive. He left a widow and son aged about eleven, and in 1761 a pamphlet appeared entitled *The Case of the Orphans and Creditors of John Ayliffe, Esq., for the opinion of the Public, etc.* Charles Churchill (1731-64), a dissipated political friend of the radical John Wilkes, wrote a long poem called 'Ayliffe's Ghost', and his books and effects were sold in a six-day sale at his house at Blandford in Dorset where he was living at the time of his crime.

Corston and its West Park

CORSTON IS A SMALL VILLAGE on the A429 about three miles south of Malmesbury. It was in AD 701 granted by King Ine to Malmesbury Abbey and in a Saxon charter of AD 956 it was *Corsa-tun*

Corston Church

meaning the 'tun of Corsa'. The A429 that runs from Chippenham to Malmesbury through Corston was as already mentioned known as early as AD 931 as the *Kingweye*, and beside it about a mile south of Corston (at 914826) stands Kingway Barn. Corston Church (926839) was rebuilt in 1881 and 1911 but it retains some Perpendicular features, although a painting of the church made in 1809 reveals that its charming little spired bell-cote perched on its west gable did not then exist. Immediately west of the A429 at Corston were extensive stone-quarries.

In the early-Middle Ages – when ecclesiastics as well as monarchs and noblemen owned deer parks which provided them with status as well as with sport and venison – West Park Wood was, as Corston West Park, one of several deer parks owned by the Abbot of Malmesbury. It appeared as *Westpark* in *Eton College Documents* of 1453 and as 'West Park' on Andrews and Dury where it is depicted as a small oval park of about 75 acres with a copse at its centre. The names of West Park Wood (917842), West Park Farm (913844), and Lower West Park Farm (914847) still appear on modern maps north of the Gauze Brook west of Corston village. A public right-of-way runs west from Corston towards West Park Farm and passes a little north of West Park Wood.

William Collingbourne and Bradfield Manor House

B ESIDE THE GAUZE BROOK about half a mile north of Hullavington stands the manor house (896830) of the ancient manor of Bradfield that was from Norman times held by the Mortimers. Edward IV's grandmother Anne was the Mortimer heiress and when he usurped the throne in 1461 Bradfield was merged with the Crown. From 1445 until 1466 it was held by John Russell (died c.1472), and from him it passed by marriage to John Collingbourne who in 1476 settled Bradfield on his son William Collingbourne (d.1484) who, despite holding a royal manor and several royal appointments, in 1483 incurred the wrath of the Yorkist usurper Richard III by intriguing with the Lancastrian exile Henry Tudor and writing and circulating some defamatory verses deriding the usurper's government and the power wielded by his henchmen. At this time Richard III was insecure on the throne that earlier in 1483 he had usurped from his boy nephew Edward V.

Collingbourne (sometimes Colyngbourne) held extensive lands in Wiltshire and his name suggests that he came from Collingbourne near Ludgershall in east Wiltshire. This suggestion is supported by several official appointments that he held in that district. He was for example in 1441 granted for life Everleigh Park near the Collingbourne villages, and in 1462 and 1482 he was also appointed keeper of the nearby royal deer park at Ludgershall. In 1478 he acquired Manton in the Kennet Valley west of Marlborough and about ten miles north of Collingbourne, and at the time of his execution he also held a lease on the former Templar estate of Temple Rockley in the downs north-west of Marlborough. He also owned lands at Shaw and Lydiard, west of Swindon and adjoining the Elcombe estate that was owned by Richard III's particular friend and favourite Francis Lord Lovel who featured as 'Lovel our dog' in Collingbourne's verses. We also know from the sole surviving personal letter of Richard III that Collingbourne had been the Wiltshire steward to King Richard's mother Cecily Neville as in that letter Richard suggested to his mother that a certain person should 'be your officer in Wiltshire such as Collingbourne had'.

Bradfield Manor House, that was with Quidhampton in Wroughton near Swindon inherited by the Collingbournes from the Russells in 1472, seems to have been William Collingbourne's principal residence. It was a simple stone-slated late-Gothic six-bay manor house, of which two bays formed a late-Medieval hall with 15th century pointed windows. A sketch by Aubrey of Bradfield drawn 'by remembrance' is reproduced here.

"Bradfield howse drawne by remembrance." J.A.

John Aubrey's sketch of Bradfield Manor

Some of the wings and the gatehouse drawn by Aubrey have now been removed and Bradfield now consists of a straight six-bay range with attached at its north-east end an early-17th century four-storeyed block that is also stone-slated. Pevsner described Bradfield as:

East wing of Bradfield Manor

The rare survival of a C15 hall, 'in the old Gothic fashion', says Aubrey, i.e with transomed two-light Perp windows, two to one side, one blocked to the other. The roof is also still visible, though only in the attic. It has collar-beams on arched braces.

William Collingbourne and many of the Lancastrian Wiltshire land magnates had reluctantly come to terms with the Yorkist Edward IV's usurpation of the half-mad Lancastrian Henry VI, but at Edward's sudden death in 1483 they found Richard III's usurpation of his boy nephew unacceptable, particularly as it was generally believed that he had arranged the murder of the two sons of his brother Edward IV in the Tower. In these circumstances Collingbourne, rashly in view of the ruthlessness with which Richard had disposed of his opponents, wrote his verses which included the couplet:

The older west wing of Bradfield Manor

> The Cat, the Rat, and Lovel our Dog
> Rule all England under the Hog.

He affixed copies in prominent locations including the door of St Paul's Cathedral in London, and also amplified his rhyme in more verses which ran:

> Catesby was one whom I called Cat,
> A craftee lawyer catching all he could ;
> The second, Ratcliffe whom I named a rat,
> A cruel beast to knaw on whom he could,
> Lord Lovel barked and bit whom Richard would,
> Whom I did rightly term our dog ;
> Wherewith the rhyme I call'd the King a Hog.

the 'Hog' reference being to Richard III's badge that was a blue boar.

These verses enraged Richard III who was already anticipating a military challenge from Henry Tudor who after Richard's usurpation and execution of the Duke of Buckingham for treason at Salisbury had become through his mother Margaret Beaufort the principal Lancastrian claimant to the throne. Richard resolved that an example must be made of Collingbourne, although the story that he was tried for writing his verses is incorrect and appears to have been originated by the historian Edward Hall who in his *Union of the Two Illustre Families of Lancaster and York* (1548) wrote:

> Yet the wild worm of vengeance wavering in his [Richard III's] head he could not be contented with the death of divers gentlemen suspected of treason, but also he must extend his bloody fury against a poor gentleman called Collingbourne for making a small rhyme . . .

Although Collingbourne's verses probably provoked the action against him he was in fact tried for conspiring with Henry Tudor who had appeared off the south coast during the 1483 rebellion, although the revolt was so poorly co-ordinated that it had been suppressed before he could land. After that rebellion Henry Tudor returned to Brittany where many Lancastrians joined him in exile. Collingbourne however remained in England and was arrested and tried in London. He was found guilty and sentenced to be hanged, drawn and quartered on Tower Hill. In carrying out this barbarous sentence executioners sometimes allowed their victim to hang long enough to become unconscious, but in Collingbourne's case the executioner, perhaps under orders, cut down and disembowelled victim while he was still fully conscious. It was rather improbably reported that as he was ripped open he was heard to mutter: 'Jesus, more trouble'. The following year his sufferings were revenged when Henry Tudor landed in Wales and after marching at the head of an army into England defeated and killed Richard III at the Battle of Bosworth and assumed the throne.

Collingbourne's estates were technically forfeited but in fact remained in his family. It has been suggested that Richard III would not allow their father's treason to penalise his heiresses Margaret and Joan, but such merciful generosity seems to be alien to Richard III's character and it may have been Henry Tudor as Henry VII who settled the Bradfield estate upon George Chatterton who had married Margaret Collingbourne and Quidhampton on James Lowther, the husband of Joan.

Past Bradfield runs the railway line from Wootton Bassett to Bristol that enters this area at a point on the A429 a mile east of Bradfield at Kingway Barn (913826) and then runs west for about six miles past Bradfield, crosses the Fosse Way a little east of Alderton, and leaves the area near Acton Turville in Gloucestershire. This line was a late construction by the Great Western Company in 1903. Elsewhere in the Wiltshire Cotswolds a now dismantled branch railway line once ran beside the Avon from Great Somerford to Malmesbury.

Stanton St Quintin

S TANTON ST QUINTIN (906799) lies immediately north of the M4 motorway in the extreme south-eastern corner of the region that I have designated the north-Wiltshire Cotswolds. In Domesday it was *Stantone* meaning 'stone town', the St Quintin being a later suffix arising from a Herbert de Sancto Quintino who held the manor in 1211.

In 1874 a Roman villa was discovered in Stanton Park (at 896796) during the digging of an earth to encourage foxes to be hunted. Although tentatively examined in 1910 this villa has never been properly excavated. The 1910 investigation uncovered a room with a hypocaust and established that either an early villa had been overbuilt by a later one or that parts of another villa had been incorporated into it. A public right-of-way that runs west from Stanton Church through Stanton Park passes the villa site. Since this is the first of several Roman villas that will be mentioned in this book the origins, function and decline of the Roman villa merits a little explanation. As soon as Britain had become Romanised the houses that we now know as Roman villas began to appear in the countryside, not necessarily as luxurious dwellings with hypocausts, mosaic floors and wall-paintings. In Britain they ranged in fact from the functionally squalid through merely comfortable to luxurious, the earliest being generally the simplest and the latest the more elaborate examples built when peace had been established. Many of the villas built in the Wiltshire Cotswolds, often related to the Fosse Way and the Roman towns at Bath and Cirencester, would have been occupied by wealthy Romano-Britons who had within a generation of the Roman conquest adopted Roman standards. Villas served as both dwelling houses and farms from which the surrounding countryside was farmed and were often built on the sites of former native dwellings, sometimes around courtyards and associated with barns, stables, corn-drying ovens, workshops, and accommodation for the farm workers some of whom would have been slaves. The workers' quarters were however not generally so primitive that they needed to be hidden away from the villa. Later villas included heated bath houses that were often at an extremity of the villa or completely isolated to minimise fire risk. When Romano-British society disintegrated early in the 5th century AD these villas tended to be abandoned. Few seem to have been deliberately destroyed by their owners who would have fled into the towns expecting to return. When this did not happen their villas would generally have become ruinous by the time that the Saxon colonists arrived and in some places evidence has been found of native squatters or Saxon invaders lighting fires on the mosaic floors of Roman villas using their roof timbers for fuel and sometimes accidentally or intentionally burning down the entire buildings.

The church at Stanton St Quintin has several good Norman features including a doorway that Pevsner, after deciding that it was 'highly puzzling', suggested might be 'made up of parts of two dates'.

Stanton Church

The church was reconstructed by the Victorians and the upper part of the tower is pseudo-Norman. The manor house has been demolished but an 1808 painting of it is reproduced in the *Wiltshire Victoria County History*, Volume 14, facing page 220.

Documentary references indicate that a windmill whose location is unknown existed at Stanton St Quintin in 1361, but regarding the position of the early-Medieval Stanton Park (895798) we are better informed although we do not know when or by whom it was founded. Land owned by the Abbot of Cirencester west of Stanton St Quintin had been emparked by 1236, which suggests that the abbot may have created the deer park and, although it was mentioned as *The Parke of Stanton St Quintin* in the 1602 *Longford Papers*, it was probably disparked at the Dissolution. Of this park Aubrey wrote in the 17th century:

'The parke very large, comes to the house. Yet is remaining part of the wall of it, built with mortar, and overgrown with ivy ; the highest that I know to any parke. Likely of old here were kept stagges'. The unusual height of the park wall evidently persuaded Aubrey to probably correctly assume that the larger red deer 'stagges' had ben kept in Stanton Park rather than fallow deer which were usually the park deer species. Today some of the park walls survive, now rather derelict and reduced to only about three feet high after having probably been quarried for building stone. As depicted on the first edition Ordnance Survey map 'Stanton St Quintin Park' covered about 275 acres which is is a fair size for a deer park and consistent with Aubrey's description of it as being 'very large'. Deer parks consisted of mixed woodlands to shelter the deer and open glades in which they were hunted but today Stanton Park survives as a wood of much the same configuration as was shown by Andrews and Dury in 1773, although Aubrey's statement that the park 'comes to the house' indicates that the park formerly extended much closer to the village than does the wood that is still called Stanton Park.

Murder in Stanton Park

T HE *Gentleman's Magazines* for June and September 1764 carried accounts of the murder in Stanton Wood of a black sailor called George Hartford by a fellow sailor called William Jacques. According to those accounts the murderer was arrested at Devizes, convicted at Salisbury, and hanged in a field at Stanton St Quintin, but the local Wiltshire writer John Britton, who came from nearby Kington St Michael, wrote a slightly different version in his *Autobiography*. In Britton's account the two men had been observed together in Malmesbury and at Stanton, and later the same day the murderer was seen walking rapidly through Kington where he enquired the way to Chippenham. According to Britton he killed and robbed his negro companion and within an hour the body was found by a woodman. The alarm was raised and Jacques was arrested at Chippenham, was tried, found guilty, and sentenced at Salisbury, and was brought back to near the scene of his crime and hanged on Stanton Common in a violent thunderstorm watched by most of the inhabitants of the surrounding villages. Britton recalled seeing the gibbet at Stanton from which he had been hanged.

More information about the murder is provided by June Badeni who in her *Wiltshire Forefathers* pointed out that William Jacques was the son of the vicar of Leigh Delamere. This would have been the Henry Jacques (1708-86) who was buried at St Mary's Church at Devizes twenty-four years after his son committed the murder, and was also probably related to 'Old Jacques' of Kington St Michael whose pre-

Reformation recollections of the nuns at Kington St Michael Priory were recorded by John Aubrey in the 17th century (see page 153).

William Jacques had gone to sea and after being paid off with £28 for a voyage on *HMS Stagg* had at the Green Dragon Inn at Malmesbury met by chance an old shipmate, a coloured man called George Hartford who had also been paid-off and so also had money in his pockets. The two men then accompanied each other south towards Jacque's family home at Leigh Delamere and near a pond called the Black Pool in Stanton Park Jacques bludgeoned his companion to death, took his money, and then continued walking through Kington St Michael. He was apprehended at Chippenham wearing the victim's neckerchief and at his trial at Salisbury confessed to both this murder and three others, and was sentenced to death and hanged on Stanton Common north of Stanton St Quintin between Upper and Lower Stanton at a place called Stockwood. Andrews and Dury in 1773 show the gallows in 'Upper Stanton Field' at a point (about 900808 west of Lower Stanton St Quintin) that is now covered by modern buildings associated with Hullavington airfield. A bush near the site of the hanging was for long known as Jacque's Bush, and the victim George Hartford was buried on 26 May 1764 at the west end of Stanton churchyard.

Grittleton and Alderton

FROM STANTON ST QUINTIN we now move a few miles west along the M4 corridor past Leigh Delamere to a remote area around the Fosse Way near the county boundary with Gloucestershire that contains a number of villages in Grittleton, Alderton, Luckington, and Littleton Drew.

In 1828 a siversmith called Rundell died and bequeathed the immense sum for that time of nine hundred thousand pounds to his great-nephew Mr Joseph Neeld (1789-1856), the MP for Chippenham. Mr Neeld then embarked upon a huge spending spree buying up properties in north Wiltshire, and in 1831 he also married Lady Caroline Ashley Cooper, a daughter of Lord Shaftesbury. A society scandal then ensued when immediately upon their return from the honeymoon Lady Caroline left her new husband and took out a suit against him, the problem apparently being that she had discovered that a little girl running around the house was a daughter of Mr Neeld by a French lady. When the couple met to discuss the matter furious allegations and recriminations were made and recognising that reconciliation was impossible they separated. The subsequent court case was acrimonius and the press seem to have for some reason demonstrated much animosity towards Mr Neeld. The *Morning Herald* and the *Wiltshire Gazette* reported the scandal with great relish, and the latter by describing the case as 'the face of Low Life Above Stairs' implied that Mr Neeld had married above his station.

Among the local estates that Mr Neeld purchased were Grittleton (860800) three miles west of Stanton St Quintin, and Alderton (840830) a little over two miles north-west of Grittleton. Neither of these villages are of much historical or architectural interest and, by dismissing Grittleton Church as being 'terribly over restored' and that at Alderton as being 'a Neeld church', Pevsner implied that both villages had suffered from the no doubt well-intentioned attentions of Mr Neeld, whose son Sir John Neeld undertook further restoration of Grittleton Church in 1865.

The lordship of Grittleton and the substantial Grittleton estate had been acquired by the Houlton family when Joseph Houlton (d.1731) married as his second wife Priscilla White, the sister and heiress of Walter White of Grittleton. The Houltons had made their fortunes as clothiers at Trowbridge and Bradford on Avon, and Andrews and Dury show Grittleton House in 1773 as owned by 'Robert Houlton Esq.' In 1828 Lt-Colonel John Houlton of Farleigh Hungerford, who was Sheriff of Wiltshire in 1808 and 1809, sold the house and the lordship of Grittleton to Mr Neeld who embarked upon a rebuilding programme that included building a new Grittleton House on the site of the former 17th century manor house south of the church. For this project he initially employed as his architect Henry Clutton who many years later in 1853 rebuilt the chancel of Steeple Ashton Church near Trowbridge. After work had commenced architect and client quarrelled and Mr Neeld replaced Clutton with James Thompson, an architect friend of the local Wiltshire topographer John Britton. The two architects between them produced an architecturally monstrous house consisting of a hideous agglomeration of unrelated elements that was still unfinished when Mr Neeld died in 1856. It is now a school.

The early-18th century Meeting House adjoining the grounds of the big house at the south end of the village street escaped the attentions of Mr Neeld who became a generous benefactor in the Grittleton area. The fact that he continued to employ James Thompson to at his expense design Alderton Church in 1845, Leigh Delamere Church in 1846, the school at Sevington in 1847, and Chippenham Town Hall in 1848, suggests that he was pleased with his performance. Sevington School is now run by a trust as a typical Victorian village school containing many educational artefacts from the period.

With Grittleton Mr Neeld also acquired Alderton village (840830) that he regarded as being 'in a state of decay'. Here the lords of the manor in the 17th century had been the Gores who judging by the inscriptions on their monuments in the church suffered miserably from child mortality. One touching memorial to six-year-old Charles Gore depicts a plump child kneeling at his prayers. No doubt with the best of intentions

Mr Neeld rebuilt the village, but in so-doing he may have swept away better things than he built as most of the village cottages now date from his time, and he may have demolished the house at Alderton owned Thomas Gore that his friend John Aubrey described as being 'of the fashion of Bradfield'.

Two miles west of Grittleton is Littleton Drew (831802), a small village that contains little of interest apart from a restored Perpendicular church and some damaged fragments of a 9th century Saxon cross.

Luckington (833838), a mile and a half north of Alderton, contains in Luckington Court a fine Queen Anne house, several good Georgian houses, and a heavily restored early-13th century church built by William de Colerne, Abbot of Malmesbury, that is dedicated to the Saints Mary and Ethelbert. The latter unusual dedication is not to the King Ethelbert who welcomed St Augustine to Kent but to the lesser-known boy King Ethelbert (779-794) of the East Angles who was beheaded by Offa of Mercia (d.796) for opposing him when he was expanding his territories by conquest. Hereford Cathedral and sixteen churches were dedicated to this St Ethelbert. Also at Luckington is Hancock's Well that was believed to have curative properties, and also in the parish at Brook End rises one of the head streams of the Bristol Avon.

In a fork between two minor roads on the county boundary a mile south-west of Luckington is the Giant's Cave Neolithic long barrow (821829). As this is the first of several chambered long barrows to be mentioned in this book it is appropriate to briefly describe the characteristics of this type of field-monument. The chambered long barrows that were constructed to be communal repositories of the Neolithic dead date from about 4000 to 2000 BC. They normally consisted of long wedge-shaped earthen mounds containing stone chambers to receive the interments that sometimes seem to be family related. The material for the mound was generally obtained from ditches dug along the long sides of the barrows which are usually between 100 and 300 feet long, 30 to 100 feet wide and about 4 to 12 feet high and they are normally orientated with their wider end to the east. Long barrows that lack stone chambers are naturally known as unchambered, but the usual Wessex type of long barrow of the chalk downlands had a gallery down its spine with transeptual side chambers off it, as at West Kennet near Avebury. The Giant's Grave is however of the distinctive Severn-Cotswold type, meaning that it is un-galleried with external cavern-like chambers along its sides. This form of long barrow with random perimeter external chambers may have evolved to overcome the problem that galleried barrows with their chambers in their predictable locations were so easily plundered.

Aubrey wrote of the Giant's Grave Barrow in his *Monumenta Britannica*: 'It is long and some oakes and other trees and boscage cover it. Here were accidentally discovered since the year 1646, certain small caves, about five or six in number. They were about four foot in height and seven or eight feet long . . . I saw them in 1659'. Today this barrow measures about 133 feet long, 85 feet wide, and about 8 feet high, and is of the false entrance type with side chambers. It has been greatly damaged by the removal of its stone for road-making and only a single side chamber now remains visible. Otherwise it remains much as Aubrey described it, still smothered with 'trees and boscage' now in the form of mature trees with shrub undergrowth.

Suggested Walks in the North-Wiltshire Cotswolds

Note: refer to General Notes relevant to all of the Suggested Walks in the General Introduction.

2A: The Fosse Way and Easton Grey (5 miles)

This is an entirely level rural walk in an area with many Roman associations.

– Note: there are no public houses along its route.

PARK on the Fosse Way [40-5] at 879855, a mile S of Easton Grey and about 3 miles W of Malmesbury. The Fosse Way is a byway open to traffic and must not be obstructed.

1: Walk ½ mile SW down the Fosse Way to point 874847 signposted on your right NE of Ladyswood.

2: Follow this sign by crossing the ditch by the sleeper bridge and following this path for a short distance W towards Sherston church to a timber pedestrian gate.

3: After passing through this gate immediately turn NW and pass to the right of a group of three poplar trees and a conifer standing in the middle of a field.

4: Beyond these trees pass through a gate and follow a green lane NW, passing left of a horse gallop, follow a hedgerow and then another lane running NW to the road junction at 866857.

5: Cross the junction and continue straight on NW down the road for about 200 yards towards Easton Town, and at 864858 turn right (NE) along the signposted footpath along the edge of Pinkney Park.

6: After passing through iron gates at the end of a stone wall on your left at 869865 turn left and follow the lane N to Park Farm at 868868.

7: At 868868 turn right towards Easton Grey as indicated by the signpost (on your left) and follow the footpath NE through Park Farm following on your right a stone wall.

7A : The directions in **7** above are consistent with the Ordnance Survey, but currently (September 2007) a signed diversion passes S of Park Farm.]

8: Continue NE along the footpath above the River Avon [96-7] passing left of a walled copse of trees and above Pinkney Mill (870870) to a stile at a tiny stream in the corner of a field at the end of a barbed wire fence on your left.

9: Cross the stile and stream and bear bear right away from the river passing right of a copse of trees to a stile a little left of a dead tree ahead in a distant hedgerow.

10: Cross this stile and then follow a post-and-rail fence to enter a road S of Easton Grey [105] through trees and a timber gate immediately S of the bridge (880873). At the road turn left and walk a short distance N towards the village.

11: Immediately after crossing Easton Grey road bridge turn right, walk about 100 yards up a minor road and when confronted by gates turn left and follow the signposted path E through a gap in a stone wall between two stone buildings and through a gate.

12: After about ¼ mile the footpath turns right from E to SE at a gap in a hedgerow.

13: Follow this hedgerow first to its left and then to its right and cross the Avon by a footbridge at the site of a derelict mill (887872) [44].

14: Continue SE to the Fosse Way crossing of the River Avon that is known known as White Walls (889871) [105].

15: From the crossing walk for about a mile SW along the Fosse Way back to the start point, crossing a minor road at 883862 and joining a minor road for the last ¼-mile

2B: Ashton Keynes and Cotswold Water Park (3½ miles, with a longer option)

This level walk with no hills passes through the interesting village of Ashton Keynes [65-70] and optionally visits parts of the Cotswold Water Park [72].

Note: there are several public houses in Ashton Keynes.

PARK at the car park (060933) beside Waterhay Bridge.

1: From the E end of the car park walk N past a metal gate and after walking a few yards N up a bridleway diverge left from the bridleway and follow the signpostedd Thames Path NW for half a mile between two lakes of the Cotswold Water Park [72].

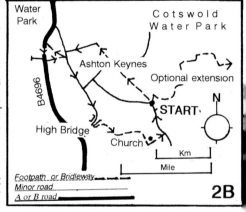

2: Pass through a gate into a small copse, enter a sports ground, and continue NW passing in front of a sports pavilion. Pass through a gate in the NW corner of the sports ground into a lane at Kent End at 053942.

3: Cross the road lane and follow the Thames Path signs NW through Kent End to the road at 050944.

4: Turn right then left and follow Back Street W to the NW corner of the village at 045953.

5: At the road turn left, walk for a few yards S down High Road, and at the remains of a stepped standing cross on your right opposite a cottage on your left turn right and walk NW along Church Walk beside the tiny stream of the River Thames to the former mill [69], now converted to a house ahead.

6: At a seat under a hedge in front of the former mill bear away right up the tree-lined footpath to the church, passing a dry-moated site on your left [67-8].

7: Continue W through the churchyard past the churchard cross that serves as a war memorial and the church [66-7], enter the B4696 and walk S (left) for about 300 yards down the road. Take grea care as the B4696 is often busy with gravel lorries.

8: At a pair of large gatepiers on your right (041942) a diversion may be made right through the gatepiers as far W as is desired along a footpath to see the derelict Manor House [68] and some of the flooded gravel pits of the vast Cotswold Water Park [72].

9: Return E to the B4696 and at 041942 carefully cross the busy road and continue E along a signposted footpath that follows a high fence past a waterworks, passes S of the former mill site into Church Walk, and rejoins High Road at the point where you left it earlier.

10: Here turn right and walk for ½ mile S down High Road through the centre of the village along a stream of the Thames spanned by many bridges on your right [66], and continue S out of the village as far as High Bridge (050931).

11: Immediately beyond High Bridge in the lay-by on your left look for a semi-concealed footpath that leaves the N end of the lay-by and enters a copse beside the Swill Brook.

12: In the copse turn right away from the stream, cross a stile, and follow the footpath signs first E along a slight causeway and then zig-zagging generally E along field paths signed with yellow arrows, crossing footbridges and passing through gates and over stiles.

13: After passing through a metal farm gate turn left, follow a hedgerow E, and pass through a small copse to the graveyard of Leigh old church [70-1] visible ahead at 058928.

14: From the churchyard walk a short distance SE, turn left round the end of a hedge, follow a lane NE to the road at 061930, and there turn left and follow the road N back to the start point.

POSSIBLE EXTENSION: More of the Cotswold Water Park [72] may be seen by following the Thames Path generally NE over its winding course between lakes as far as desired. It should however be noted that in dry seasons when the water level drops some of the lakes shown on the map become merely rush covered wetlands.'

2C: Cricklade and the Upper Thames (4½ miles, with a longer option)

This is a level walk from Cricklade [72-80] along a once navigable stretch of the Upper Thames [76]. The walk is linear returning by the outward route in order to avoid hazardous crossings of the A419, the only really safe crossing of this busy dual carriageway being that taken on both the outward and return walk under the bridge over the Thames at 108937.

– Note: there are many eating establishments and public houses in Cricklade.

PARK at one of the public car parks in Cricklade.

1: From a few yards S of St Mary's Church [77] towards the N end of Cricklade High Street walk E for about 300 yards along Abingdon Court Lane, take the lane on the left marked 'Cricklade Cricket Club' N to the Thames Path and follow that long distance path E to the bridge at 108937 by which the A419 Ermine Street [73] crosses the Thames.

2: Pass under the bridge and follow the S bank of the river NE for ¼ mile.

3: At 113941 cross the river by the footbridge and possibly make a short diversion N to visit Eysey (113943) [85-6].

4: Return S and at the river do not cross the footbridge, instead turn left and follow the N bank of the river E for ¾ mile to another footbridge

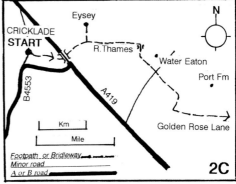

(124940) a short distance NW of Water Eaton.

5: If you return by the same route from this point the total walk will amount to 4½ miles, but the walk may be extended as far as is required by: –

(a) continuing NE along the footpath that follows the right bank of the Thames, or

(b) continuing along the footpath that runs SE, pass SW of Water Eaton Farm, and continues E along Golden Rose Lane which here is the county boundary passing S of Port Farm and along the S edge of Water Eaton Copse.

2D: King's Heath and Malmesbury (6 miles with a 4 mile option)

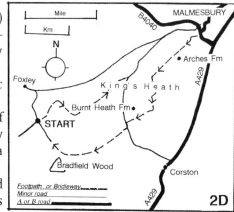

The historic King's Heath (Malmesbury Common) [94] and the ancient hilltop town of Malmesbury [86-93] are included in this walk which involves a fairly steep climb into Malmesbury.

– Note: there are many eating places and public houses in Malmesbury.

PARK near the road junction at 896853 a little S of Foxley at the SW end of King's Heath (Malmesbury Common) [94]. An alternative start point for a shorter 4 mile walk is suggested below.

1: Walk NE along footpath passing SE of a copse and a farm group and then NE down a drive towards Cowage Farm.

2: Before reaching Cowage Farm at 901857 turn right and walk SE passing left of an isolated house and on SE along the SW edge of Cowage Grove to its far corner.

3: There turn left and continue for a mile NE along the S edge of Cowage Grove and the SE edge of another wood (913859) and enter the road near the bend at 916861.

4: Continue straight on NE for a mile along the road passing N of Thornhill Farm and at 928872 shortly before the river bridge turn right out of the road and cross a stile beside the road on your left.

5: Follow the footpath E along the River Avon towards Malmesbury ahead on its hill [86].

6: Cross two footbridges (932873) on your left and walk E and then N up the hill by the steep lanes to enter the centre of the town through the site of the former Postern Gate a little W of the Market Cross [92-3] and near the abbey [90-1].

7: After if desired exploring the town, leave Malmesbury downhill by the same route but at the foot of the hill at Daniel's Well (931872) continue for a short distance S beside the river and at 931869 turn your back on the river and follow the footpath SW.

8: Pass N of Arches Farm on your left and S of a copse (924864) on your right to a lane S of Thornhill Farm.

9: Turn left, walk SE down this lane, and near its end at 923859 turn right out of the lane, walk S to 922854 and pass S of Burnt Heath Farm to the minor road at 916852.

10: Walk for a short distance S down this road and from 916850 turn right out of the road, continue SW for a mile to the N corner of the triangular Bradfield Wood (902844), and from there turn right and proceed NW through Gorsey Leaze (899847) to the start point.

Note: this walk may be reduced to about 4 miles by starting from the road W of Burnt Heath Farm and following a similar clockwise circuit.

3
The Mid-Wiltshire Cotswolds,
including Castle Combe and Biddestone

THE AREA THAT HAS BEEN IDENTIFIED as the middle region of the Wiltshire Cotswolds for the purposes of this book extends from the Wiltshire county boundary on its west to the A350 on its east. Its northern limit is the M4 motorway and it is bounded to its south by by the A4 running through the northern edges of Box and Corsham to Chippenham. As they lie mainly south of the A4 Box and Corsham are described in Chapter 4 (Bradford and the South), while Chippenham is excluded because it lies east of the A350. The precise extent of the mid-Wiltshire Cotswolds is shown on the map on page vi.

The Cotswold characteristics of this region were impressed upon me in the early-1960s when I was serving in the army and living in a camp near Antwerp in Belgium where a mural painting of Castle Combe on the mess wall was incorrectly entitled 'Castle Combe, Gloucestershire'.

For reasons of continuity the Fosse Way that in places borders and in others crosses this region was described earlier, in Chapter 2 pages 40-5.

The By Brook

THROUGH THE HEART of this region flows the beautiful By Brook tributary of the Bristol Avon that in its progression through Castle Combe and down the Weavern Valley provides one of the great delights of this district. Its old names of *Weaverne Brook* in 1623 and

Wavering Brook in 1862 were expressions of its meandering nature over much of its length. By Brook House (842769) at the south end of Castle Combe was recorded as *Bybrok* as early as 1545, and was so-named because it stands beside the brook, and the modern name of By Brook for the Weavern Brook seems to be a back-formation from the name of the house.

Clapper Bridge over Broadmead Brook

The By Brook and its headstream the even more secluded and equally beautiful Broadmead Brook geographically emulate on a much smaller scale the Bristol Avon by running first east, then south, and then roughly west. Broadmead Brook enters Wiltshire at Shire Hill (774764) west of West Kington, the By Brook enters the county west of Nettleton (786784), and their confluence takes place beneath the former castle site a little north-west of Castle Combe (at 836777). From there the combined streams flow south down a narrow tree-clad combe containing Castle Combe and then gradually swings south of west to flow through Box and join the Bristol Avon at Bathford.

The local artist Robin Tanner loved the valley of the Broadmead Brook and in his memoirs *Double Harness* (1987) described how, when he decided to illustrate his poem in which he lamented modern changes in agriculture, 'The setting that chose itself for the etching was that untouched country, the valley of Woodford Brake, a few miles away, near the old cobbled ford across Broadmead Brook which winds between Nettleton and Castle Combe'. The ancient clapper bridge (830774) beside this ford may in view of its close relationship to the Roman settlement at Nettleton Shrub (823769) be Roman in origin. Of it Robin Tanner also wrote in his memoirs:

Then, later that year [1972], 'The Clapper Bridge' saw the light. I had long wanted to commemorate the curious old bridge in the Weavern Valley which Heather [his wife] and I had crossed so often in our school days. I enjoyed

By Brook below Slaughterford

setting it among willows, with mounds of marsh marigolds and a bed of dog's mercury on the banks of the stream so aptly called the Wavering.

y Brook Valley from Rack Hill

After flowing under this clapper bridge the Broadmead Brook flows north-east past the site of the former Nettleton Mill (833776) and then, as already described, joins the By Brook above Castle Combe (at 836777) immediately south of the site of the former castle that provides the village with the first element of its name.

The scenery associated with the By Brook is varied. After rising in open country the brook flows from Castle Combe to Long Dean down a glorious narrow wooded gorge and then around Slaughterford it becomes a gentle meandering stream with open banks running through the pasture lands of the Weavern Valley. East of Colerne it expands and becomes a wider river, and then at Box, where it is sometimes known as Box Brook, it narrows and flows down another beautiful steep-shouldered stretch of valley. From Castle Combe to Box an excellent public right-of-way accompanies the By Brook, at first south through woods along the shoulder of Rack Hill. At Long Dean the path crosses the brook and after diverging a little away from it over open high ground between Long Dean and Ford it then follows the stream down the Weavern Valley past Corsham and through Box. Around Slaughterford the By Brook, like Tennyson's 'The Brook', 'winds about, and in and out' in its progress down the Weavern Valley through Slaughterford and along an interesting reach east of Colerne Park past Weavern Farm to Box.

Mention of the wooded nature of parts of the valley of the By Brook reminds me that I should mention that the most common trees in the Wiltshire Cotswolds are the beech and the oak, two species whose conflicting requirements dictate the positions in which they flourish. The beech, being shallow-rooted prefers shallow soils, will not tolerate waterlogging, and flourishes on well-drained upland wolds and on hangers (hanging woods) on steep hills or valley slopes. Some authorities insist that the beech is not native and was introduced, although in some places in Wiltshire it now regenerates itself. It has a potential life of over two hundred years after which it tends to succumb to parasitic fungi. The oak is in contrast with the beech a lowland tree that likes deep clays and

By Brook feeder stream near Weavern Farm

fertile soil and flourishes in river valleys where it will tolerate waterlogging. At two hundred and fifty years the oak is generally full-grown, but it can live on for centuries during which it can attain immense age and huge bulk. Aubrey mentioned that the oaks around his home at Easton Piercy near Kington St Michael were 'not inferior' to the especially fine oaks in Oaksey Park where there are still good oaks.

By Brook Valley from Lo[...]
Dean

The many former woollen mills shown on old maps along the three-mile stretch of the By Brook from Castle Combe to Slaughterford are a reminder of the considerable amount of industrial activity that once took place on this now essentially rural stretch of the By Brook. These were Nettleton Mill (actually on Broadmead Brook 833776), a mill under Colham Wood between Castle Combe and Long Dean (at 842761), two mills at Long Dean (851757 and 850756), and two more at Slaughterford (839738 and 843737). There were also more mills lower down the By Brook around Box and Colerne.

When a sudden increase in the demand for paper for printed books arose in the 17th century the water of the By Brook was found to be suitably pure for paper-making and the valley soon became a centre for this light industry that developed here because this district was conveniently situated for supplying the paper needs of Bristol and Bath. At this time several woollen mills on the By Brook were converted to paper-making, and the Rag Factory and Chaps Factory at Slaughterford were the last mills to make paper in Wiltshire. The Rag Factory was driven by a nine foot wide water-wheel which was ultimately replaced by a gas engine. It obtained its name because here rags were converted into a product known as 'stuff' that after being conveyed in large wheeled elm vats to Chaps Mill was there made into paper and paper bags. The last paper-making machinery was installed in Slaughterford Rag Factory by Bentley and Jackson of Bury in the 1890s.

More information on paper-making in this region was provided earlier, on page 37-8.

Castle Combe

N HIS *Cotswold Country* (1937) H. J. Massingham described Castle Combe as being 'sandwiched into the lower end of a wooded gully walled by the broad-backed hills', and indicated that he considered that it to be 'the first place among all the limestone villages I met between Bath and Tetbury'. Later A. E. Trueman, after in *Geology and Scenery in England and Wales* (1949) describing Castle Combe as 'The most interesting village in this valley', and as 'perhaps the most perfect village of the Cotswolds', continued:

> Some will hold that other villages are as beautiful but certainly none are more unspoilt. In this village every cottage is a picture, every view is delightful. The brook runs for some way through the village street, and the irregular grouping of the houses around the market cross, with the thickly wooded hill slopes, makes a scene in which no touch of modernity, unless it is a visiting car, seems to intrude.

By Brook Valley north of Ford.

Malmesbury may be the capital town of the Wiltshire Cotswolds but Castle Combe is its principal show village. Being a showpiece brings with it the disadvantage that it is on the tourist itinerary and consequently often becomes overcrowded. Enjoyment of the village can sometimes be marred by what the Wiltshire writer Richard Jefferies described as 'a thickness of people', and by the vehicular congestion arising from the many cars and coaches that bring the visitors here in the summer season. That this is not a new phenomenon is proved by Arthur Mee's 1939 description of Castle Combe in which he commented: 'Every motor coach for fifty miles knows its crumpled-up roofs'. Nevertheless Castle Combe must be seen but since overcrowding can inhibit full enjoyment of the village I tend to visit it out of season.

During the summer season it is however possible to escape the throng by walking out of the village along some of the many old tracks that radiate from Castle Combe and were once followed by packhorses bringing bales of wool down into the village. The path already mentioned south along the hills above the east side of the By Brook to the secluded hamlet of Long Dean (851757) and perhaps further on to Ford (840749) can be followed, as can the footpath west across the golf course past the site of the former castle (838778) on the hill north of the village, and then south-west along the Broadmead Brook to the Roman settlement on the Fosse Way (823769) south of Nettleton Shrub (see later, pages 139-44).

The first important person in the history of Castle Combe was Walter de Dunstanville who is commemorated by an armoured effigy in the church dating from 1270. He was a member of the family that built above the village the Norman castle (838778) that was apparently never a true motte and bailey castle but a square keep of modest dimensions set within a ringwork built within an Iron Age earthwork that seems to have rather inhibited its layout. By the early-14th century a deer park had been created beside the castle, according to a 1327 *Wiltshire inquisition post mortem* by Bartholomew de Badlesmere. This park cannot have been large as it was contained within the space between the castle and the village. Although he was a powerful Marcher Lord and joint Deputy Constable of England, little attention has been paid to the short-term ownership of Castle Combe by de Badlesmere. After acquiring Castle Combe in 1309 he in 1321 joined the rebellion of the barons against Edward II and in October of that year insulted Queen Isabella by refusing her entry to Leeds Castle in Kent. This provoked the usually lethargic Edward II, with an uncharacteristic flash of his father's great energy, to assault and capture Leeds Castle and hang de

Looking south through
Castle Combe Market C

Bridge at south end of Castle Combe.

Badlesmere for treason, unaware that within six years his queen would engineer his downfall and murder him in favour of her lover Mortimer. Most of de Badlesmere's forfeited lands, including Castle Combe, were bestowed upon Edward's favourites the Despensers, who did not long survive de Badlesmere.

About seventy years later the Scropes became lords of the manor of Castle Combe when three infant daughters of Sir Robert Tiptoft, Baron of Castle Combe (d. 1372), were made wards of Sir Richard Scrope, First Baron Scrope of Oldham (c. 1327-1403). He was a celebrated soldier and administrator and friend of Chaucer who made him the model for the knight of 'The Knight's Tale' in *The Canterbury Tales*. In 1394 Castle Combe was granted to Sir Richard, the eldest son of Sir William Scrope, Earl of Wiltshire (c. 1351-1399), who became Richard II's principal counsellor and chamberlain and in 1398 his Lord High Treasurer. With Richard II absent campaigning in Ireland the following year (1399) Sir William was the king's guardian of the realm when the exiled Henry Bolingbroke invaded the kingdom, nominally to recover his estates but in reality to claim the throne. Confronted by Bolingbroke's superior forces Sir William sought refuge in Bristol Castle where after withstanding a siege he surrendered and was summarily beheaded without trial by the warlike future Henry IV on 30 July 1399.

As Sir William Scrope had remained loyal to Richard II the Scropes must have been out of favour with the usurper Henry IV, but shortly before his death in 1403 Sir Richard Scrope improved their standing with the new Lancastrian royal house by declaring his support for the deposition of Richard II. Sir Richard's third son Sir Stephen Scrope (d. 1408) inherited Castle Combe and married a lady called Millicent (d. 1446). After his death the manor was in 1409 temporarily acquired by Sir John Fastolf (c. 1378-1459) when he married the widowed Lady Millicent Scrope. At her death in 1446 Sir John became 'by courtesy' for many years effective lord of Castle Combe. As Sir John Fastolf's name was adapted by Shakespeare for his character Falstaff in *Henry IV* and *The Merry Wives of Windsor* it is a matter of interest that Castle Combe is, in addition to its rather tenuous association with Chaucer mentioned above, also connected with Shakespeare. Falstaff was not in fact modelled on Fastolf but upon Sir John Oldcastle, 'the good Lord Cobham' (c. 1378-1417), another of Henry V's soldier companions who later led a Lollard rising for which he was condemned as a heretic and executed by being 'hanged and burnt hanging', which amounted to being slow-roasted alive. When Shakespeare wrote his plays many years later Oldcastle's descendants objected to the use of their name for such a comic character and Shakespeare, obliged to cast around for another name, for some unknown reason decided upon Falstaff.

Castle Combe church tower from Park

Sir John Fastolf of Castle Combe was in fact far from the corpulant, witty, jest-loving drunkard of Shakespeare's plays. He was an experienced and successful commander in Henry V's French Wars who became a prosperous landowner and in 1432-5 built for himself a fine castle at Caister-on-Sea in Norfolk. As early as 1415 he as a military man of some standing provided ten men-at-arms and thirty archers for the Agincourt campaign and himself fought at the battle. He was held in high esteem by a succession of monarchs from whom he obtained the privilege that the king's officers – then known as 'takers' – would not confiscate any oxen, sheep or horses belonging to his tenants. Sir John's high standing is also indicated by the fact that at his death in 1459 Edward IV redeemed from his executors jewels that Edward's father Richard of York, the father of Richard III, had pledged for a loan of £437 from Sir John.

Castle Combe Church and Cross

According to the *Letters and Papers Illustrative of the Wars of the English in France during the Reign of Henry the Sixth, King of England* (edited by Stevenson in 1861-81), Sir John Fastolf first established his military reputation in the Hundred Years War (1337-1453) as one of the leading English captains. An document written by Fastolf to Henry V's Royal Council survives in which he extolled the virtues of the military tactic known as *le chevauché* in which between June and November raiding parties of mounted men-at-arms and archers struck deep into French territory and undermined French morale by laying waste to harvests, burning houses and vineyards, driving off cattle, and taking away prisoners for ransom. Michael Drayton eulogised Fastolf in his *Poly-Olbion* (1598-1622), and during Jack Cade's Rebellion in 1450 Sir John as an elderly man of seventy-two recruited a band of 'old soldiers of Normandy' to defend his house at Southwark against the rebels. His

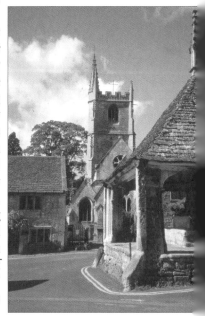

servants alleged that Sir John was 'cruel and vengeful' and 'without pity or mercy', and after the death of his wife the Lady Millicent he contrived to for many years exclude her Scrope son from his rightful inheritance of Castle Combe. He was however sufficiently popular for his secretary and steward at Castle Combe to collect materials for his biography, and his redeeming characteristics were an interest in literature and his munificence to the church.

During the time that he held Castle Combe manor Sir John Fastolf encouraged the local woollen industry and made the village renowned for both the weaving and the dyeing cloth, and is said to have promoted its products by clothing his soldiers in a livery of white and red cloth made at Castle Combe. He also encouraged clothiers to reside in the village

h end of Castle Combe

and build new houses, and also decreed that Castle Combe should have only one tavern in which no dicing would be allowed, which was surely an extremely un-Falstaffian action!

Castle Combe is fundamentally a one-street village with many of its gabled cottages built in the Cotswold-style with stone-slated roofs and stone-mullioned windows, lining the winding street, and standing directly off the back edge of the pavement. Opposite the church at the centre of the village stands a fine market cross that is square in plan with a pyramidal stone-slated roof supported on four substantial piers at its corners and a column at its centre. This column was apparently once an elaborately-carved free-standing preaching cross and it seems that when a covered market cross was required money was not available for an expensive stone vaulted cross of the Malmesbury type and the villagers improvised by building an open shelter around their existing cross, a solution that proved to be a singularly happy one.

From the market cross the houses flow, in the words of Massingham, 'like boulders in a mountain stream down the village street' to an arched stone road bridge. A short distance beyond this bridge is By Brook House, and then a stone bridge (841768) with a single parapet which allowed packhorses carrying bulky bales of wool easily to negotiate it. This bridge crosses the By Brook and leads to the footpath that runs south along the flank of the tree-clad Rack Hill, with splendid views into the tree-filled valley to its west, to the remote hamlet of Long Dean (851757). Rack Hill probably obtained its name from the frames known as tenter-racks upon which broadcloth was stretched taut to dry and has provided us with the expression to be 'on tenterhooks'.

A mile south-east of Castle Combe – certainly not the '2 miles' indicated on the finger-post at the packhorse bridge – is Long Dean that was described by Pevsner as: 'A pretty group of mill and C18 cottages in the combe'. Here were built water mills for cloth-making, although Aubrey tells us that in his day one of them became a paper mill when the demand for paper increased and a number of paper mills were opened in the valley of the By Brook. The paper mill at Long Dean was in 1635 owned by a Mr Wyld, and it continued to manufacture paper until 1860 when the last reference to it occurs. (For other paper mills in this district see page 38 for Slaughterford, and page 168 for Colerne).

Bridge at south end of Castle Combe.

After for centuries prospering by exporting the wool from the sheep that grazed on its surrounding hills Castle Combe in the 15th century followed the national trend and became a weaving village making cloth from the wool that it had previously exported. John Aubrey recorded that Castle Combe was in the 17th century also a market town when he wrote:

> The most celebrated faire in North Wiltshire for sheep is at Castle Combe, on St George's Day, whither sheep-masters doe come as far as from Northamptonshire. Here is a good crosse and market-house ; and heretofore was a staple of wooll . . . I have heard old men say long since that the market at Castle Combe was considerable at the time of the staple ; the market days is Munday. Now only some eggs and butter, etc.

A man who loved Castle Combe as intensely as did John Aubrey was the local artist and etcher Robin Tanner (1904-88) who lived for most of his life a few miles away at Kington Langley, a little east of the area covered by this book. In his memoirs *Double Harness* (1987) Robin memorably revealed his affection for the village when recalling making the sketches for his etching 'Christmas' (1928):

> One night of perfect moonlight, Heather [his wife] and I stood by the ancient market cross in Castle Combe, the village I used as my source, and drew the Flemish gables, the great barns, the inn, and the cross itself. I remember the snores of one of the sleepers coming from a mullioned and dripstoned window of a cottage nearby. It was an uncanny feeling, working through the small hours in that empty village where the moonlight lay in sheets of silver so bright and constant that we drew as easily as by day.

Despite its idyllic peaceful setting Castle Combe has not been without its troubles. In 1491 a man called Richard Lyllingston was sentenced by the ecclesiastical courts to be led around Castle Combe, Cricklade, Malmesbury, Chippenham and Salisbury bearing a bundle of faggots on his back, and was also made to confess his sins at these places for in the alehouse ridiculing the Castle Combe preacher. Three hundred years later a late-18th century poster tells us of a law and order measure that was taken at Castle Combe at a time prior to the formation of police forces when a single village constable was responsible for enforcing the law. Landowners then often combined to offer rewards for information leading to the conviction of criminals and this poster reveals number of property owners at Castle Combe, Grittleton, Nettleton, West Kington, and Yatton Keynell collaborating for this purpose. It is headed: 'Castle Combe Association for the Prevention of Robberies and Thefts and for the Protection of Persons and Property' and the highest reward offered was 5 guineas (£5.20p) for information leading to a conviction for: 'Murder, Burglary, Housebreaking, Shoplifting, Highway Robbery, or setting Fire to any Dwelling-House, Barn, or other Outhouse, or to any Mow or Stack of Corn, Grain, Hay, Wood or Fuel'. A footnote indicated that the contributors to the scheme met annually 'at the Salutation Foss House, in the parish of Castle Combe, on the last Thursday in October in every Year', the Salutation Inn being situated at The Gibb (838791).

Two miles north-west of Castle Combe are Nettleton (820781) and Burton (817795) which together really constitute one village with a shared church; this is St Mary's with its Perpendicular tower that stands on rising ground at Burton almost a mile north of Nettleton. Its Norman font suggests that an earlier church stood here but the present church is later and it contains a Georgian box-pews and a strange pseudo-Norman 14th century nave arcade that Pevsner described as 'puzzling'. These two places are not situated on the By Brook although two of its headstreams rise near them. Associated with Nettleton, although over a mile to its south, is the important Nettleton Shrub Roman settlement that is described later (pages 139-44).

West Kington and Bishop Latimer

OPPOSITE CASTLE COMBE and west of the Fosse Way are West Kington and Nettleton Shrub. Anyone who is interested in the development of English protestantism should visit the remote church at West Kington (813775) that lies about three miles west of Castle Combe near the western edge of Wiltshire for here is the pulpit from which Bishop Latimer (c.1495-1555), one of the first English protestant martyrs, as a humble parish priest preached reformation of the church.

Latimer's once-Norman but subsequently rebuilt church is perched on the summit of a high tree-clad hill above the pretty village of West Kington on the Broadmead Brook. The church with its impressive embattled and panelled tower in its imposing situation is best approached on foot from the south-west up the signposted footpath that runs north-east from a bend in the road at the north end of the village. This approach involves a short climb up a steep hill and crossing a stile and a field, but the church may alternatively be reached by car from Nettleton to its east passing through a farmyard. It is said that an underground passage once ran from this church west towards Marshfield.

Kington means 'tun or enclosure of the king' which suggests that it may have been a royal manor, and since Kington St Michael stands six miles east of West Kington with Kington Langley even further east it seems that this part of the Wiltshire Cotswolds may once have been a substantial royal estate. Hugh Latimer, who was rector of West Kington from 1530 until 1535, described the village in a letter as 'my little Bishoprick'. He would have known the ancient yew tree in the churchyard under which he traditionally liked to preach, he may have known the underground passage if it existed, and would have christened the village children at West Kington's Norman font. During the five years before he emerged on to the national scene he would from West Kington's 14th century pulpit have thundered reformation of the catholic church to a probably bemused congregation. I use the word 'thundered' as Latimer was because of his resonant speaking voice known as the mouthpiece of the English Reformation. John Aubrey, who would have seen it only about a hundred years after Latimer was here, described: 'a little scrubbed hollow oak called Latimer's Oak where he [Latimer] used to sit and walk in the Parsonage House'. From its close proximity to the church and the stone-flagged path and gate from the church leading to it Latimer's parsonage house may have been on the site of the much later large house north-east of the church. The 17th century Latimer's Farm (807771) towards the west end of the village can in its present form have had nothing to do with Hugh Latimer and may occupy former glebe lands or be so-named merely to perpetuate Latimer's name in the locality.

Hugh Latimer's father was a Leicestershire yeoman-farmer who fought in 1497 for Henry VII against the Cornish rebels at Blackheath. From his pulpit his son Hugh told his

Bishop Latimer's Pulpit

Church from West King

congregation how as a child he learned to draw the longbow and that man 'shall never shoot well unless brought up to it'. At Cambridge he took holy orders and became in his own words 'as obstinate a papist as any in England'. He continued in this belief until 1524 when he 'began to smell the word of God' and became a reforming churchman dedicated to reforming the existing church. Latimer was one of the divines appointed to investigate the legitimacy of Henry VIII's marriage to Catherine of Aragon who had been married to Henry's deceased elder brother Arthur, and as a reward for declaring in favour of the king he became one of Henry VIII's advisers. From his pulpit in 1532 he so enthusiastically glorified the king's marriage to Catherine of Aragon's protestant succcessor Anne Boleyn that Archbishop Cranmer warned him not to preach too long about it lest 'the King and Queen may wax weary, and so leave'. He was then appointed a chaplain to Anne Boleyn.

While at West Kington Latimer watched with interest pilgrims making their way along the Fosse Way less than a mile east of the village to the Cistercian abbey of Hailes near Winchcombe in Gloucestershire.

West Kington Church

In a letter to his fellow reformer Thomas Cromwell he wrote: 'I dwell within a mile of the Fosse Way, and you would wonder to see how they come in flocks out of the west country to many images . . . but chiefly to the Blood of Hailes'. This holy relic was a phial that had been deposited at Hailes centuries earlier by Edmund, Earl of Cornwall, and was alleged to contain some of the lord's blood. A few years later Latimer was as Bishop of Worcester instrumental in sending this supposed relic to London for destruction, accompanied by a letter stating that: 'we think, deem, and judge the substance and matter of the supposed Relic to be an unctuous gum coloured'.

In March 1532 while he was still at West Kington Latimer was censured and excommuni-cated by the conforming Archbishop Warham (c. 1450-1532) for his reforming ideas, but he retained the king's favour and in 1534 became a royal chaplain. Latimer's final break with Rome occurred in 1535, the year in which he left West Kington to become Bishop of Worcester, and from this time he took a leading part in the turbulent religious events in London. When Jane Seymour, the Wiltshire-born lady who had in 1537 succeeded Anne Boleyn as Henry VIII's third queen, gave birth to a son, Latimer wrote enthusiastically to Cromwell: 'Here is no less rejoicing at the birth of our Prince, whom we hungered for so long, than there was at the birth of John the Baptist'. Two years later Latimer preached two powerful sermons demanding Reformation of the church, and in April 1539 he was appointed to a committee set up by parliament at the king's instigation to investigate the increasing religious problem. This committee as the king probably intended became deadlocked and Henry VIII then responded by drafting the Six Articles in which he declared his religious conservatism by re-asserting catholic doctrines. This delayed progress of Reformation and when the Six Articles Act was in 1539 duly enacted by parliament Latimer and another bishop were sent to the Tower of London for resigning their bishoprics.

Latimer recognised that by selling the monasteries to his friends and associates Henry VIII was neglecting a great opportunity to endow the poor and provide them with education, and with Stanley Abbey near Calne in mind he unavailingly pleaded with the king to spare two or three monasteries in each county to maintain some contemplative religious life. For this he was in 1546 again sent to the Tower, but the following year Henry VIII died.

Henry's son Edward VI had been brought up by protestant tutors and when he succeeded as a young boy at the death of his father in 1547 he, aided and abetted by the Wiltshire-born Edward Seymour, Protector of the Realm during his nephew's minority, strongly promoted the protestant religion. In these propitious circumstances Latimer became closely associated with Archbishop Cranmer, Bishops Hooper and Ridley, and Protector Somerset as a reformer, and also supported the rights of the common man when at St Paul's Cross in January 1548 he denounced the acquisitiveness of the ruling classes in his controversial 'Sermon of the Plough', preaching that:

> ever since the prelates were made made lords and nobles, their plough standeth, there is no work done, the people starve. They hawk, they hunt, they card, they dice, their pastime in their prelacies with gallant gentlemen, with their dancing minions, and their fresh companions, so that ploughing is set aside.

Soon after delivering this sermon Latimer expressed to the boy king the hope that he would be 'brought up in learning and knowledge of God's word', and that he would 'shortly provide a remedy' and: 'choose a wife that is of God', but in 1553 Edward VI died aged only fifteen. The succession of the ardently catholic Mary then put a temporary end to reformation and placed Latimer in an extremely vulnerable position, but he resolutely refused to flee abroad and at the great disputation at Oxford in April 1554 he confronted the catholic spokesmen. For this he was imprisoned and was twice examined for heresy, and despite resigning his bishopric and restricting his activities to preaching and charitable works, as he persistantly advocated reformation he was tried and found guilty of heresy. When burnt as a heretic at Oxford in October 1555 he shared his stake with Bishop Ridley (c.1500-1555) who had been implicated in the abortive plot to secure the succession for the protestant

*The Burning of Bishops
Latimer and Ridley*

Lady Jane Grey. To the end Latimer tremained resolute in his beliefs and some time before they were burnt at the stake wrote to Ridley: 'Better it is to suffer what cruelty they will put upon us, than to incur God's high indignation. Wherefore, good my lord, be of good cheer in the Lord, with due consideration what he requireth of you, and what he doth promise you'. He died nobly exhorting his fellow sufferer: 'Be of good comfort, Master Ridley, and play the man. We shall this day light such a candle by God's grace in England as I trust shall never be put out'.

A Roman Settlement on the Fosse Way

L ITTLE OF THE ROMAN SETTLEMENT south of Nettleton Shrub at the Fosse Way crossing of the Broadmead Brook (at 823769) would have survived in Latimer's day, but he would have known its site because it is located at the nearest point of the Fosse Way to West Kington only about three-quarters of a mile from his church and it was therefore probably here that, after strolling through Parsonage Wood and down the combe of the Broadmead Brook along a footpath that may still be followed, he observed the pilgrims trudging along the Fosse Way on their way to Hailes Abbey that he described in his letter quoted above.

The Romans were adept at selecting choice sites and in choosing this one they excelled, as it is probably the most interesting Roman site in the Wiltshire Cotswolds. The shallow sheltered grassy combe has running down it a stream that flows in sufficient volume to have driven a Roman water mill, stone for building was to hand, and associated with the site was woodland that provided timber for both building and fuel. The fact that a statue of Diana, the Roman goddess of the chase was found here in 1911 suggests that the district also then provided good hunting.

At intervals along their roads often in rural locations and especially where water was available the Romans built shrines and temples at which they thanked their gods for preserving them from the dangers of the roads, and at this remote site on the Fosse Way they built a settlement that included a temple and a shrine and much more besides, but remains little-known despite being described by Webster and Dudley in *The Conquest of Roman Britain* (1965) as a 'remarkable site'.

Site of Nettleton Shrub Settlement looking west towards West Kington

It requires some imagination to today envisage this now remote and peaceful combe beside the old Roman road as it was in Roman times when it must have have buzzed with activity, for hidden beneath its turf lie the remains of one of the two known substantial Roman settlements in the Wiltshire Cotswolds, the other being White Walls further up the Fosse Way near Easton Grey.

Along their principal roads the Romans also set up staging-posts, and the spacing of these two settlements along the 28 mile stretch of the Fosse Way between Bath (*Aquae Sulis*) and Cirencester (*Corinium*) suggests that both may have been either *mutationes*, that were stations where horses could be changed and civilian travellers could lodge overnight, or *mansiones* that provided overnight lodgings for persons on official business. The Nettleton Shrub site is 9 miles from Bath while White Walls is 8 miles further on and 11 miles from Cirencester, all mileages which represent a comfortable day's walking. A short distance north of the point where the Fosse Way crosses Broadmead Brook at Nettleton Shrub a vertical stone outcrop in a tree covered bank on the north-west side of the road (at 824769) looks as though it may have been quarried for stone that may have been used for building and also perhaps for metalling the Fosse Way.

The Nettleton Shrub settlement does not appear to have been planned but appears to have grown in a haphazard way around the Fosse Way crossing of the Broadmead Brook. Although evidence for this suggestion is not entirely secure, the Romans seem to have first constructed a triangular military camp and then a settlement that extended over a large area and contained about twenty-four buildings that may have included overnight lodging-houses for travellers along the road, stables for remounts, and workshops. The settlement was enclosed within embankments, its northern edge being a now tree covered bank (at 822770) and its eastern edge the Fosse Way. To the south it extended for about 170 yards south of the present road bridge, and its western edge was a little west of an octagonal shrine that stood at about 822769. Its two principal buidings were this shrine and a simple rectangular temple measuring 64 feet by 24 feet, containing two cells, and built end-on into the bank at the north end of the site about 50 yards west of the Fosse Way. The northern inner and smaller cell contained against its north wall a sculpture of Diana and her hound that prompted Richmond in his *Roman Britain* (1955) to suggest that this sculpture made this temple 'plainly a hunters' meeting place'. Within this inner cell rose a spring that was channelled south into the southern cell then turned towards its west wall. The temple stood a little aside from the rest of the settlement buildings that were mostly located south of the brook which was overlooked by this building as it ran a few yards to its south, although the excavators found that the Romans canalised the brook into a straight line a little north of its present course with channels from it conveying running water south into the settlement.

The other significant building at Nettleton Shrub was the octagonal shrine (822769) that occupied the site of an earlier circular building that was destroyed by fire immediately south of the brook and towards the western edge of the settlement. It was subdivided by eight

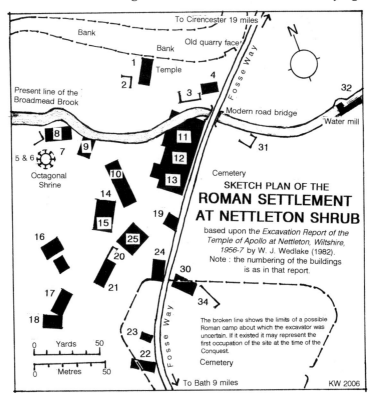

SKETCH PLAN OF THE
ROMAN SETTLEMENT
AT NETTLETON SHRUB

based upon the *Excavation Report of the Temple of Apollo at Nettleton, Wiltshire, 1956-7* by W. J. Wedlake (1982). Note : the numbering of the buildings is as in that report.

The broken line shows the limits of a possible Roman camp about which the excavator was uncertain. If it existed it may represent the first occupation of the site at the time of the Conquest.

radial walls into eight identical chambers around a central shrine and lined with painted plaster. Since it contained an inscription to Apollo this shrine has generally been assumed to have been a temple to that god, although Eric Wood in *The Collins Guide to Archaeology in Britain* (1963) suggested that it may have been an example of the type of Roman building known because of its plan form as a 'cartwheel' mausoleum. In the 4th century AD this shrine was adapted into a cruciform shape and decorated with saltire crosses, suggesting that christianity may have been practised here, as do some of the burials in the cemeteries at this site in that they were orientated east-west and contained none of the grave goods that are usual in pagan burials.

Although the Romans occasionally built stone bridges to cross large rivers, their crossings of small streams such as the Broadmead Brook were generally achieved by constructing timber bridges which are by their nature impermanent and leave few archaeological remains other than their masonry abutments in the banks of the streams. Here the former Roman crossing has been replaced by a brick bridge, but the fact that some Samian ware and three iron horseshoes were found 'well below the Medieval level' at the crossing indicates that the abutment of the present bridge could be Roman.

Fosse Bridge at Nettleton Shrub Roman site

The Romans harnessed water power for many purposes including grinding flour, sawing timber and cutting stone, and opposite this site a short distance east of the Fosse Way stood a water mill (823769). The excavators (see *Excavation of the Temple of Apollo at Nettleton Wiltshire 1956-7 to 1982*: W. J. Wedlake, 1982) also tentatively indicated that a possible first century AD triangular camp with rounded corners existed at the south end of this complex around Fosse Barn (823765). This may have been a temporary camp constructed soon after the initial conquest at the time when the Fosse Way was being built as a military frontier road.

This camp, for which it must be emphasised evidence is by the excavator's admission rather tentative, is believed to have stood slightly across the Fosse Way and may have been abandoned as the conquest advanced, possibly leaving behind a settlement that had originated as a vicus, a civilian settlement dependant upon the camp.

Prolonged use of this site is suggested by its many Romano-British finds that cover the entire Roman period and especially the 3rd and 4th centuries. The settlement was abandoned in about the early-5th century and in Medieval times its derelict and by then no doubt roofless buildings were used as stock pens for cattle and sheep.

Pevsner writing in 1963 indicated that from this site came: 'A sculpted relief of Mercury [the Roman god of commerce and travellers], a candlestick in the form of a cockerell, a stone relief of the goddess Diana [a woodland deity associated with hunting and fertility] and her dog, and quantities of Samian and coarse wares'. The existence of the sculpture of Diana (now in Bristol Museum) suggests that the temple served as a wayside shrine for hunters, and if this was the case this is the only known countryside shrine situated in a valley in Wessex.

Lacking a name of its own this settlement is generally referred to as Nettleton Shrub. Very little survives to be seen today in this little shallow grassy combe with its bubbling little stream, and yet it is well worth visiting for its atmosphere that is redolent of the distant past and evokes that indefinable feeling of melancholy that is often felt at places that were once inhabited but have long had their life withdrawn.

Before leaving this archaeological site I must emphasise that it stands on private agricultural ground and should not be entered. It is however overlooked from the Fosse Way that is here a public byway to its south-east, and from the Fosse Way a public footpath runs roughly west along the north shoulder of the combe to West Kington.

A mile and a half as the crow flies south-west of Nettleton Shrub is the Roman villa site on Truckle Hill (836762) that was probably associated with the Nettleton Shrub settlement. A stone coffin was found here in about 1800 and after more coffins were turned up this hilltop became known as the Coffin Ground. Excavation in 1859-60 revealed the former existence of a large rectangular Roman villa measuring overall 180 feet by 36 feet and containing sixteen rooms, hypocausts, tesselated floors, a separate bath house, and a hexagonal building containing a well 68 feet deep, all within a walled enclosure. Its situation in this exposed position on the top of Truckle Hill and a little east of Fosse Way has led me to speculate that this site may have originally been, in the first phase of the Roman Conquest, one of a series of signal signal stations behind the Fosse Way frontier (see pages 170-3).

The fate of their villas after the Romans left Britain in about AD 410 is a matter for speculation. As alien marauders approached some villas seen to have been abandoned intact by their occupants who, presumably intending to return, retired for safety into the neighbouring towns, in this case Bath or Cirencester. The fact that two human skeletons were discovered in its well suggests that the Truckle Hill villa came to a violent end. Some elements from it were later built into the former Truckle Hill Barn (834759) about 300 yards south-west of the villa site that has now been converted into a house also called Truckle Hill Barn.

Both the Nettleton Shrub site and Truckle Hill are accessible. A footpath follows the north edge of the Nettleton Shrub settlement leaves the Fosse Way (at 823769) and runs a little north of west up the combe through Parsonage Wood and across Broadmead Brook to West Kington. The site may also be reached by a rather longer walk along the public footpath across the golf course, past the former castle site at the north end of Castle Combe, and south-west along Broadmead Brook to the Fosse Way past the interesting clapper bridge (830773) that, as it is only half a mile from the Nettleton Shrub site and is associated with an ancient hollow-way that runs south-east from the bridge up the hill towards Shrub House Farm (837766), may be Roman.

As at Nettleton Shrub nothing tangible survives to be seen on Truckle Hill but the site of the barn and villa may be reached by walking a little over a mile up the metalled track which runs east from a point (817753) a short distance north of North Wraxall church, or alternatively by a half mile walk along the zig-zag woodland footpath that runs from a point (838762) on the road near Shrub House Farm, at first downhill north-west and then uphill south and west. This path passes close to the the villa site which is a short distance north-east of the house on the site of Truckle Hill Barn.

Lugbury Long Barrow

A LITTLE MORE THAN A MILE north-east of Nettleton Shrub stands an archaeological field-monument that predates by many centuries that Roman site. This is Lugbury (831786) Neolithic chambered long barrow that is reached from the Fosse Way by a quarter-mile walk west along a footpath that follows the north edge of a wood. The barrow stands islanded in a field about ten yards north of the footpath. *The Place-Names of Wiltshire* (1939) fails to explain its name that may commemorate the Celtic god Lug whose name is well-known both on the Continent and in Britain as a place-name element and also appears in the Celtic festival of *Lugnasadh*.

Most chalkland long barrows in Wiltshire and elsewhere contain an axial passage way with side chambers off it rather like the transepts in a church, but Lugbury is an example of a different pattern of long barrow known as the Severn-Cotswold type that was described earlier (page 120). It measures about 200 feet by 80 feet by 6 feet high and is orientated east-west. The three large standing stones that form a dramatic false entrance at its east end explain it being named 'Three Stones' on the 1773 map of Wiltshire. Colt Hoare's excavation in 1821 discovered a crouched primary burial near its east end, and along its south side four now-covered limestone chambers that contained about thirty skeletons. The barrow also contains a large capstone measuring about 12 feet by 6 feet.

Anyone intending to visit Lugbury should be aware that when I last visited the barrow in October 2006 it was quite overgrown and its huge standing false portal stones were so much shrouded with briars and shrubs that I was unable to photograph it for this book.

Kington St Michael and John Aubrey of Easton Piercy

SINCE WEST KINGTON is about seven miles to its west and Kington Langley is almost two miles to its east, Kington St Michael (903774) may have been at the centre of a large hunting estate of the Anglo-Saxon kings until Ethelred II gave it to Glastonbury Abbey in AD 987. As it was the birthplace of the 17th century pioneer biographer and antiquarian John Aubrey, and of his antiquarian successor John Britton, Kington St Michael is for me one of the special places of the Wiltshire Cotswolds.

After the Abbot of Glastonbury was hanged for not co-operating with the Dissolution of the Monasteries, the manor and the Benedictine Priory of St Mary at Kington was bought in 1543 for £804 by an

...gton St Michael Church

opportunistic agent of Glastonbury Abbey called Nicholas Snell, allegedly with money belonging to the abbey. The priory had been founded by the Empress Maud before 1155 but at the Dissolution there were only three nuns at the priory, two of whom were described as being 'incontinent' that in those days meant lacking in self-restraint in sexual matters. It stood on the site of Priory Farm (894778) where several coffins have been found.

After acquiring the manor and the priory Nicholas Snell emparked West Field that lay probably west of the church (around 899773) and according to Aubrey then 'shutt the people out of the park and took away their allotments'. Aubrey's references here and elsewhere 'Kington Parke' and the 'Parke of Kington St Michael' suggest that its new owner – who prospered, became an MP, and was knighted – may here have created a deer park. Sir Charles Snell (presumably the son of Nicholas) according to Aubrey sold up much of his inheritance including the manor of Yatton Keynell and the farm at Easton Piercy to invest in a ship called the *Angel Gabriel* for the expedition to Guiana led by Raleigh in 1595 in an attempt to recover the fortune that he had lost on his Virginia plantation. A few years before this Kington St Michael in 1582 suffered a visitation of the plague during which the Church Registers registered the deaths of eighteen villagers.

John Aubrey

The birthplace of John Aubrey (1626-97), whose sometimes scurrilous lives of his contemporaries were published as *Brief Lives* long after his death, was at Lower Easton Piercy (891774) about a mile west of Kington St Michael. Aubrey was a complicated multi-talented man who displayed a compelling curiosity about everything. His interests absorbed so much of his time and energy that he neglected both his business and his literary activities and so lost the substantial fortune that he inherited. His short biographies of his contemporaries establish Aubrey as being one of the earliest biographers and a delightful Wiltshire personality who has never received outside his native county the recognition that he deserves. This was emphasised when Mr Oliver Lawson Dick wrote in 1949 'of the extraordinary neglect of this man of genius'. Aubrey was also an intriguing Wiltshire character and a pioneer biographer and antiquary. His importance to archaeology was emphasised by the archaeologist O. G. S. Crawford when he described him in *Archaeology in the Field* (1953) as 'the effective founder of British field archaeology, and a good deal more than that as well'. Crawford also pointed out that '*Brief Lives* marks the first essays at modern biography', that Aubrey 'was an acute observer and careful recorder' and that he was 'blessed with an attractive style and a knack of vivid portraiture'. Edward Thomas, who knew Aubrey's writings almost verbatim, aptly summarised his character and writings when he described him in 1913

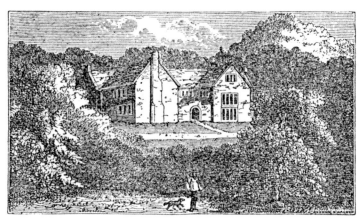

ubrey's birthplace, Lower Easton Piercy

as: 'a gossip whose odds and ends about men, things, and places, are now better than most full-dress literature'.

John Aubrey's immediate ancestors were Wiltshire people, although his paternal family had formerly been in Herefordshire. His maternal great-grandfather Thomas Lyte had lived in an earlier farm on the site of Easton Piercy Manor Farm (886777), but sold up and built himself a new house in which John Aubrey was born, over half a mile down the lane towards Kington St Michael near Lower Easton Piercy Farm (892774). This house is now gone and its precise location is uncertain, but surviving sketches made by Aubrey show it surrounded by oak trees of which he wrote: 'the oaks at Easton Piers (once mine) were, for their number, not inferior to the oaks in Oaksey Park'.

Aubrey's paternal grandfather William Aubrey (1529-95) was a doctor-at-law at the court of Elizabeth who called him 'her little doctor'. John's parents were Richard Aubrey whose mother came from the Wiltshire family of Danvers, and Deborah, the heiress of a London alderman Isaac Lyte who built the attractive Cotswold style Lyte Almshouses at Kington St Michael. Deborah was fifteen when she married Aubrey's father and only sixteen when John was born. He proved to be a sickly child but he survived his lonely childhood growing up: 'in a kind of Parke far from Neighbours and no child to converse withall'. The 'parke' was Nicholas Snell's park which occupied the open area between Priory Farm and Kington St Michael church. After early local schooling at the churches of Yatton Keynell and Leigh Delamere, Aubrey went to the fashionable Blandford School in Dorset and then in 1642 to Trinity College at Oxford. His university education was however interrupted when the royalists made Oxford their Civil War headquarters causing Aubrey, despite his royalist sympathies, to leave and spend much of the war at his father's farm at Broad Chalke in south Wiltshire.

By the time he was eighteen Aubrey had developed the

te Almshouses, Kington St Michael

antiquarian interests that he retained for the rest of his life and these were intensified in January 1649 when he visited the Marlborough Downs and saw for the first time the prehistoric landscape around Avebury. We know that when he went to Oxford Aubrey had developed social aspirations and become a man of fashion from his friend Anthony Wood who recalled how Aubrey 'came to town with his man and two horses' in 'sparkish garb', and 'spent high'. Subsequently he travelled extensively about the country on horseback, pursuing his historical and antiquarian interests and, being rather accident-prone, he sometimes fell from his horse as on the occasion when he reported having 'a very dangerous fall' from his 'Uncle's Nag'.

At his father's death in 1652 Aubrey as the eldest son inherited substantial estates which he no doubt hoped would support his new life-style, but these estates were encumbered and he seems to have been extravagant and inept in handling his business affairs, probably because he was pre-occupied with his researching and writing. Even in these activities he was slapdash and by his own admission put things together 'tumultuously' and consistently failed to see through projects that he started. Being by nature a muddler and being easily distracted from properly managing his estates he progressively lost them, and despite never marrying also became embroiled in disputes with several prospective brides which further aggravated his financial position and ultimately ruined him, leaving him dependant upon his friends. His biographer Anthony Powell aptly described him as 'a Wiltshire squire fallen on evil days', but despite his many financial problems Aubrey was both clever and industrious in the subjects that interested him.

In his home district Aubrey was well-connected being directly related through his paternal grandmother with the Danvers family of Dauntsey, and he became a friend of Colonel Sir James Long of Draycot, these being the two families who had been involved in a mysterious murder at Corsham that I shall refer to later (page 207). As an ardent royalist he was after the Restoration in 1660, that occurred when he was thirty-four, personally acquainted with Charles II and his brother James, Duke of York who became James II, and he was also a founder member of the Royal Society where he associated with some of the great intellects of his time, men of the calibre of Newton, Hobbes, Wren and Hooke.

Aubrey's uncompromising frankness about his apparently interminable financial, matrimonial and literary problems is an endearing characteristic, as is his quaint language. One cannot help sympathising with him over his recurrent problems, and it is a testament to his personality that his friends stood by him in his adversity, especially Colonel Sir James Long of Draycot Park who supported him in his later years, as did Lady Long after her husband's death. Aubrey died at Oxford on his way to visit Draycot Park and was buried in St Mary's Church at

Oxford where the register for 1697 reads: 'JOHN AUBERY A Stranger was Buryed June 7th'.

John Britton

A LESS IMPORTANT TOPOGRAPHER than Aubrey who shared Aubrey's lack of recognition was John Britton (1771-1857) who was born at Kington St Michael only about a mile from Aubrey's birthplace seventy four years after Aubrey's death. When a stained glass window was in the 19th century dedicated in Kington St Michael church to the memory of Aubrey and Britton, the Canon Jackson drew attention to how the two men were : 'born as to time within 146 years; as to distance within a mile of each other'. Britton was the eldest son of a baker, maltster, shopkeeper and farmer at Kington St Michael where his birthplace has like Aubrey's been destroyed.

John Britton grew up enjoying the normal pursuits of a country lad at a time when Kington St Michael remained a self-sufficient rural community. He received only a rudimentary education at schools at Foscote, Yatton Keynell, Draycot Cerne and Chippenham, but his letters in his later life reveal his sensitivity over the fact that he lacked a proper education and also suggest that he suffered from a sense of inferiority that made him a little vain about his undoubted achievements. In his early teens Britton often stayed with his grandfather at Maidford (892845)

John Britton

immediately east of Norton at the south-west end of Malmesbury Common but when he was thirteen he was summoned home to help in the family business of baking, delivering bread, and working on the farm. This life did not appeal to him and when he was sixteen he left home and went by coach with his maternal Uncle Hillier to London 'at a speed of about five miles an hour'.

In London his uncle tied him by a six-year apprenticeship to a wine merchant but he abandoned his apprenticeship and for a time acted in the theatre. He then met a publisher called Wheble who suggested that he should collaborate with Edward Brayley (1773-1854) in writing *The Beauties of Wiltshire* and when undertaking his researches he consulted Aubrey's manuscripts at Oxford. He was amiably received at Bowood by Lord Lansdowne and later regarded this meeting as marking the start of his writing career. He did not get on with Colt Hoare and regarded him as a rival. We do not know where Britton learned to draw, but the first two volumes of *The Beauties of Wiltshire*

(1801) included many drawings by him. The third volume appeared belatedly in 1825. Britton was then commissioned to write *The Beauties of England and Wales* (1803-1814) in twenty-five volumes, and his *The Cathedral Antiquities of Great Britain* came out intermittently until he was sixty-four. During the rest of his long life Britton continued to write on archaeology and architecture, his *Life of Aubrey* appeared in 1845, and he also edited Aubrey's *Natural History of Wiltshire*.

In his later years from about 1853 Britton became a driving force on the committee that founded the Wiltshire Archaeological and Natural History Society and his papers, books and drawings formed the nucleus of that society's original library at Devizes. He died in 1857 and was buried in Norwood Cemetery in London where his grave is marked with an eleven foot high monolith (illustrated in the *Wiltshire Archaeological Magazine*, Volume 4 facing page 391) that was deliberately left unwrought to simulate the stones of Stonehenge.

As recently as 1937 a street in Clerkenwell was named Britton Street in recognition of his work on London topography but in his native county Britton has received rather less recognition. The site of his birthplace in Kington St Michael is now occupied by the village hall which has built into its wall an almost indecipherable inscribed stone that was presumably salvaged from his home when it was demolished. There is also a later plaque in the south gable of the village hall.

The stained glass window in memory of Aubrey and Britton mentioned above was installed in 1857 at the east end of the south aisle of Kington St Michael church, and the Royal Institute of British Architects funded an inscription on brass to Britton's memory in Salisbury Cathedral.

The influence of Britton's drawings on architectural style in the

John Britton's birthplace Kington St Michael

19th century was recognised by Kenneth Clark who wrote in his authoritative *The Gothic Revival* (1928):

> The man who popularised engravings of Gothic by publishing them cheaply and in great numbers was John Britton . . . Britton deserved his success. His text was painstaking and his illustrations . . . achieved an accuracy and detail never before attempted. Though Britton's volumes were a commercial venture, they did not merely feed a craze; they gave the average cultivated man a far truer idea of Gothic forms than he had hitherto had, so that after their publication the old fantastic parodies of Gothic were no longer possible. Britton killed Ruins and Rococo.

Aubrey's Countryside

THE AREA SOUTH of the M4 motorway and east of Castle Combe was the native countryside of John Aubrey who was born and spent his lonely childhood at Lower Easton Piercy (891774). Although he died more than three hundred years ago anyone who is familiar with Aubrey's writings will find this district redolent of this 17th century Wiltshireman, and when wandering in this district I am constantly reminded of the former presence in this area of this gossipy and generally much underrated writer and historian whose special pride in being a Wiltshireman is revealed in his description of Thomas Hobbes as 'our Wiltshire philosopher' who: 'though he left his native country at fourteen, and lived so long, yet sometimes one might find a little touch of our pronounciation'.

Aubrey recorded his lifelong interest in the history and topography of his native county in his notoriously disordered papers. That he recognised his lack of method we know from his admission that he wrote things down 'tumultuously', and his memorable mention that things often went 'Kim-Kam' with him, this being an archaic expression meaning 'wholly awry', used by Shakespeare in *Coriolanus*. Fortunately Aubrey's papers were put into some order and published by John Britton and Canon Jackson in the 19th century, and they tell us much about this part of Wiltshire as it was soon after the Reformation of the church in the 1540s.

Since he lived at Broad Chalke in south Wiltshire and also here at Kington St Michael towards the north of Wiltshire Aubrey was familiar with most of the county. From his lonely childhood at Kington St Michael he demonstrated consuming curiosity about everything around him, later in his life he recorded in writing his recollections of his childhood spent in this area, and in his preface to his Wiltshire Antiquities left us his description of this region as it was immediately before it was enclosed:

This country was then a lovely 'campania', as that about Sherston and Cotswold. My grandfather Lyte did remember when all between Cromhall's [west of Easton Piercy where the names Cromhall Farm and Cromhall Lane survive] and Castle Combe was so, when Easton [Piercy], Yatton [Keynell] and [Castle] Combe did intercommon together. In my remembrance much has been enclosed, and every year more and more is taken in . . . So likewise in his remembrance was all between Kington St Michael and Draycot Cerne common field.

His immediate neighbourhood was Easton Piercy where the site of a former chapel marked (at 886777) immediately north of Easton Piercy Farm on old maps suggests that Easton Piercy may once have been a village although it is now reduced to three farms strung out along Cromhall Lane that runs west out of Kington St Michael to Yatton Keynell. These farms are from west to east Upper Easton Piercy Farm (882776), Easton Piercy Farm (886777) and Lower Easton Piercy Farm (891774). Easton Piercy Farm survives as a fine example of a multi-gabled Cotwsold style stone-built and stone-slated farmhouse whose extensive farm buildings are at the time of writing (2006) being sensitively reconstructed into dwellings. Lower Easton Piercy Farm is also being reconstructed, although the present house is a successor to the house in which Aubrey was born, being built much later beside the little stream which Aubrey knew. After rising near Fowlswick a little over a mile from Lower Easton Piercy, this stream flows north-east past the site of Aubrey's birthplace and south of Priory Farm before turning east and crossing the north end of Kington St Michael. As a boy Aubrey would have wandered south-west along this brook towards called Fowlswick Farm (882758), an old moated house that once belonged to Malmesbury Abbey and was in 1303 owned by John Burel of Kington Langley. It was described by Aubrey as an 'ancient house with a faire mote about it', and

Lower Swinley Farm

it was either built or greatly enlarged by Abbot William of Colerne.
Fowlswick is now the headquarters of a storage company.

At the road junction (901778) where Cromhall Lane and the road
to Stanton St Quintin leave the village at north end of Kington St Michael
the First Series 2½-inch Ordnance Survey map (Sheet 97) marks 'Cross
(Site of)'. This cross is absent from both the 1773 map by Andrews and
Dury and the first edition Ordnance Survey, but John Aubrey knew of it
and recorded that here was held: 'a little market for fish, eggs, butter and
such small gear'.

About a mile north-east of the site of this cross, towards Stanton
St Quintin and immediately south of the M4 motorway beside the A429
is Lower Swinley Farm (913790). Canon Jackson established that this
farm was once held under Glastonbury Abbey by the Fitzurse family, one
of whom led the four knights who murdered Becket in the cathedral at at
Canterbury. Swinley was then owned by the Estcourts some of whom
described themselves as being 'of Swinley' and are buried at nearby
Kington St Michael. Later Swinley was held by the Hungerfords who
let it to the Coller family, and the initials over the front door are those of
William Coller. The farm was later bought by Mr Neeld of Grittleton (see
pages 118-19)

*Priory Farm, Kington St
Michael*

Although the monasteries had been swept away as part of the
Reformation almost a hundred years
before he was born, Aubrey early in life
developed a nostalgic affection for the
monastic life and left us a recollection of
the nunnery that once occupied the site of
the present Priory Farm (895778) when he
recorded the memories of a local man
known as 'Old Jacques'. This man
recalled to Aubrey seeing 'from his House
the Nuns of the Priory of St Mary (juxta
Kington) come into the Nymph-Hay with
their Rocks [cleft sticks used in hand
spinning] and Wheels to spin, and with
their Sowing Work'. The interesting name
Nymph-Hay is believed to be a 17th century corruption of 'Minchinhay'
meaning 'nuns' field', a nymph being a semi-divine maiden. Regardless
of the fact that womens' religious houses were in the 17th century
sometimes so impoverished that their inmates often lived on the verge
of starvation, Aubrey considered this to be 'a fine way of breeding-up
young women'. Although now a typical 16th century Cotswold
farmhouse set among a cluster of barns and dry-stone walls with its stone
gatepiers crowned with large spherical stone ball-finials that feature so
often in the Wiltshire Cotswolds, Priory Farm incorporates some
remnants of the former nunnery. The 'Nymph-Hay' (896777) that lies

across the minor road east of Priory Farm is now by agreement with its owner open to the public. It has been extensively planted by The Woodland Trust with hazel coppice and is crossed by a public footpath that runs east from Priory Farm to Kington St Michael, crossing on its way the stream by a little unparapeted footbridge.

Aubrey also reminisced about his childhood journeys to his first schools at Yatton Keynell and Leigh Delamere, although his accounts are characteristically contradictory. After describing how going to Yatton Keynell involved 'a five mile walk', he as an afterthought confessed that he 'had a fine little horse and commonly rode'. His walk, or ride, to Yatton Keynell from Lower Easton Piercy in fact involved a journey of only about a mile and a half each way, west along Cromhall Lane and then south to Yatton Keynell (866764), or he may have followed the surviving fieldpath that passes a little south of Grove Farm. To attend his next school at Leigh Delamere (884793) Aubrey probably followed the direct route amounting to a long mile, north from Easton Piercy along the lane past Easton Piercy Farm and Little Spinney, which becomes a footpath before crossing the M4 motorway by a bridge at Leigh Delamere.

Being slightly north of the M4 Leigh Delamere stands just outside

Footbridge in the Nymph Hay, Kington St Michael

the area that I have defined for the mid-Wiltshire Cotswolds, but for convenience I shall deal with it here. Long after Aubrey's time a resident of Leigh Delamere was Major Vince's wife who left her husband to live with the radical Wiltshire politician 'Orator' Hunt (1773-1835). The son of a prosperous Wiltshire farmer from near Upavon, Hunt against his father's advice married the daughter of the landlord of the Bear Inn at Devizes but after a few years ran off with the wife of his friend Major Vince and became a radical colleague of Cobbett who when Hunt stood for parliament destroyed his prospects by describing him as the man 'who rides about the country with a whore, the wife of another man, having deserted his own'. Hunt earned his nickname of 'Orator' Hunt by being a fine public speaker and with Cobbett absent abroad he was the principal speaker at the 1819 Peterloo Massacre in Manchester. At the age of fifty-seven he in 1830 succeeded in being elected to parliament but soon lost his seat and then lived by manufacturing blacking, a circumstance that prompted a man called Gale who was the village carpenter of Leigh Delamere to indelicately enquire of Major Vince whether his wife was still living with 'Hunt the blacking man'. The major's reply is not recorded but presumably Gale got no more work from Major Vince!

Gale was presumably related to the Gales who were squires at Bolehyde Manor (893757), a gem of a house at the north end of Allington merely a mile and a half south of Easton Piercy and the same distance from Kington St Michael. It was once moated and Aubrey tells us that in 1275 it was the home of Thomas de Bolehide. The name of this house has undergone many variant spellings including *Bolhides* in 1606 and *Bulhyde* in 1636, but I have chosen to use the spelling 'Bolehyde' used on both the old and the current Ordnance Survey maps, although Pevsner emulated *The Place-Names of Wiltshire* (1939) by calling it 'Bulidge' and described the house as being mainly of the 17th century but with a Medieval wall and 'two oblong pavilions of Elizabethan date framing the original approach'. One of these pavilions has a cellar that is said to have been used as a cell for local offenders. At the Reformation Bolehyde was together with Kingston St Michael acquired by the Snells who in 1635 sold it to the Gales, the yeoman family who were then renting it. For generations it continued to be the home of the Gales and was the scene of an amusing episode when Sadler Gale, having apparently decided to emulate the aeronautical escapade of the monk Elmer of Malmesbury described earlier (on page 88) summoned the local people to watch the event that was amusingly recorded by the Rev. Francis Kilvert (1840-79) in his diary entry for 4 March 1875:

> Old William also told the story of how old Squire Sadler Gale of Bulwich House at Allington made himself wings and flew off the garden wall. "Watch I flee!" he cried to the people. Then he dashed down into the horsepond.

Sadler Gale died in 1841 and is buried beside the path to Kington St Michael church.

A short distance south of Bolehyde is Allington that was given by King Stephen to a French priory and was later transferred to Monkton Farleigh Priory. Here a large barn (at 894752) with its ancient windows walled-up is all that remains of the former home of Sir Gilbert Prynne.

Francis Kilvert, who was quoted above, was a local man who like Aubrey before him and Robin Tanner after him profoundly loved the countryside of north-west Wiltshire. He was born in Hardenhuish rectory at the north-west edge of Chippenham and spent much of his life in this district, passing the remainder at Clyro in Wales where he is buried. He led the quiet life of a Victorian country clergyman assiduously writing up his diary that caused a sensation when it was discovered and published in the late 1930s, about sixty years after he died as a comparatively young man. Kilvert expressed his feelings for this countryside in this evocative diary entry for 31 August 1874:

> I love to wander on these soft mournful autumn days, alone among the quiet peaceful solitary meadows, tracing out the ancient footpaths and mossy overgrown stiles between farm and hamlet, village and town, musing of the many feet that have trodden these ancient and now well nigh deserted and almost forgotten ways and walking in the footsteps of the generations that have gone before and passed away.

Yatton Keynell and Thomas Stumpe

SINCE YATTON KEYNELL (867764) stands only about a mile and a half south-west of Easton Piercy and two miles east of Castle Combe, it is an important place in John Aubrey's countryside, and he attended a school held in its church. Listed as *Church Eaton* in Domesday, Yatton became a grange of Stanley Abbey east of Chippenham After obtaining the patronage of the village the Keynell family appended their name to it. Aubrey wrote in his autobiographical notes: 'In 1633 I entered into my grammar at the Latin school at Yatton Keynell, in the church, where the curate, Mr Hart, taught the elder boys Virgil, Ovid, Cicero, etc.'. By attending Yatton school Aubrey emulated his grandfather who could recall seeing in a south window of the chancel many heraldic escutcheons which were lost when the window was blocked with masonry. Aubrey tells us that in his time a paper mill at Yatton Keynell manufactured brown paper but this mill was in fact at Long Dean (851757), in Yatton Keynell parish and south of Castle Combe. This we know because Aubrey also wrote: 'the trough of the paper mill at Long-deane in the parish of Yatton Keynell, in 1636, was made of oak from Langley Burrell'.

A short distance along the road that runs south-west from Yatton Keynell church to West Yatton is a fine Cotswold-style manor house (at 864763) with an interesting early-Renaissance north-east front that illustrates how the

Yatton Keynell Church

North-east front of Yatton Keynell Manor House

Gothic style of architecture persisted in this region. This facade provides a perfect example of how the local masons, while tentatively attempting to adopt the new Renaissance style that they did not properly understand, added to an earlier building a facade that is quirkily attractive because it is not constrained within any strict stylistic rules. The old vernacular Tudor-Gothic style was half-abandoned and half-assimilated classical detail was grafted on to a design that was despite being symmetrical fundamentally earlier in style. The new facade is flat-fronted with three-gables capped by tiny ball-finials on posts, the roof is traditionally stone-slated, and the first floor windows are traditional and of three lights with stone mullions and transomes, while the ground floor windows to the outer bays are of four lights. The central bay has a projecting two-storeyed porch with an unusual flat ogee pediment that is swept up and capped with a single ball finial, and the porch has a flat Tudor arch. This facade was built in 1659, some time after Aubrey left Yatton Keynell school although he would have known it as an adult.

So far as I am aware Aubrey never mentioned a deer park at Yatton Keynell, although the place-name Park Farm (866779) almost a mile north of the village suggests that a park once existed here, particularly as it was *le Parkmede* in the 1354 *Additional Charters* at a time when the word 'park' was almost invariably an indicator of the former existence of a deer park. On this evidence Professor L.V. Cantor listed Yatton Keynell as a 'possible' park in his *The Medieval Deer Parks of England* (1983), but the evidence is minimal. It is possible that a park was created over this still open area, possibly as a short-lived 'out-park' to augment the very restricted 'home park' that was squeezed between the castle and the village at Castle Combe a mile and a half to its west. Multiple deer parks were quite usual associated with Medieval castles, but an alternative explanation is that Castle Combe Park once extended as far east as Park Farm.

Aubrey's extreme credulity is revealed in a story that he told of Mr Hart, the curate of Yatton Keynell, whom he recorded saw in 1633-4 when returning home 'innumerable quantities of pigmies making all manner of strange noises', but were it not for John Aubrey we would know nothing of the much more credible adventurous life of one of his schoolfellows at Yatton Keynell. Thomas Stumpe was the son of the vicar of Yatton Keynell and a great-grandson of William Stumpe, the prosperous Malmesbury clothier. Yatton Keynell Church has a very fine panelled and battlemented tower and according to Aubrey Thomas Stumpe was: 'a boy of a most daring spirit' who 'woulde climbe towers and trees most dangerously ; nay, he would walke on the battlements of the towers there [Yatton]'. Aubrey tells us that: 'He had too much spirit to be a scholar', and when he was sixteen in about 1633 Thomas Stumpe went with his uncle on a voyage during which four or five of the men when stranded in Guyana were seized by savages who killed and ate some of them. Thomas was saved by the intercession of their queen and lived with the natives until about 1637 when he escaped by swimming out to a passing Portuguese ship. As this ship was sailing off Cornwall he swam ashore and begged his way home to Yatton Keynell where surprisingly no one recognised him except for the village carpenter. He ultimately convinced his family of his identity and the last that Aubrey tells us is that he continued to live an adventurous life and in 1642 was an infantry captain in the royalist army. We hear no more of Captain Stumpe, but his existence is confirmed by a memorial stone in the vestry of Malmesbury Abbey that reveals that he lived the latter part of his life at Malmesbury and there died and was buried aged 79 in April 1698, the year after Aubrey died in 1697.

Yatton Keynell Church Tower

Ford, North Wraxall, Slaughterford, and Bury Camp

IN THIS AGE OF HEAVY MOTOR TRAFFIC any small village that is bisected by a busy A-road inevitably loses some of its appeal and that sadly is the case at Ford (841748) that stands on the busy A420 which was formerly the main coach road from Calne and Chippenham to Bristol. This village has generally been ignored by topographical writers although Pevsner had some good words for it when he recognised at Ford 'several worthwhile houses with gables and mullioned windows'. The church that was rebuilt in 1823 has a good stained glass window by Morris and Company. Through Ford runs the By Brook on its way south from Castle Combe to Slaughterford, and set back from the road at a bend in the A420 almost a mile east of Ford is an interesting limestone rock face that is best seen in winter as in summer it becomes smothered with plants.

Aubrey suggested that near Ford: 'St Oswald was slain by Penda [of Mercia] on the great down east of Marshfield in Gloucestershire, from whence it is called St Oswald's Down'. Oswald (c.604-42) was the christian king of Northumbria who founded the Lindisfarne bishopric. According to the *Anglo-Saxon Chronicle* he was killed at a place called *Maserfeld* that is generally but inconclusively said to be Oswestry, although as Oswald had established his lordship over Wessex it is possible that Aubrey was correct by siting this battle at Marshfield that was according to Bede *Maserfelth*, was *Meresfelde* in Domesday, and *Maresfeld* in 1221. Aubrey's 'great down east of Marshfield' may have been the now unnamed promontory three miles east of Marshfield on which stands the Iron Age hillfort called Bury Camp (818740), or alternatively Colerne Down (833737) above Slaughterford. The authors of *The Place-Names of Wiltshire* (1939) positively derive the name Slaughterford from the Old English 'sloe thorn or bush' prefixed to 'ford', but the name is suggestive of a battle and traditions that a battle was fought in the neighbourhood have persisted. Following the battle described by Aubrey the resolutely pagan Penda became the anti-hero of Bede's *Ecclesiastical History* for mutilating Oswald's body, and by so-doing promoting the widespread cult of St Oswald the martyr.

Two miles west of Ford is North Wraxall (819749) that straddles in a steep-sided coombe a stream that enters the By Brook at Ford. The largely Norman and Early English church on the north side of the coombe has a 13th century tower with a saddleback roof – that is a short length of pitched roof used to cap a tower. There was in the Wiltshire Cotswolds a fashion for roofing church towers with these oddly attractive saddleback roofs rather than the more usual spires or lead-flat roofs. They were especially popular towards the south end of the Wiltshire Cotswolds where examples exist at South Wraxall, Holt, Winsley, Staverton and Monkton Farleigh, all within about three miles of Bradford on Avon. This outlying example at North Wraxall may be explained by the presence here of the Methuen clothier family of Bradford and Corsham who acquired it when Paul Methuen (d. 1795) married the heiress of Sir George Cobb. It is possible that the Methuens, who built the Methuen mortuary chapel in the church in 1793, may also have added the saddleback roof with which they may have been familiar around Bradford.

From North Wraxall came a man who played a part in the events that led up to the Wars of the Roses between the rival houses of York and

Ford from North Farm

Lancaster. Thomas Young (d.1476) – sometimes Yonge – was the MP for Bristol, the Chief Justice of the Court of Common Pleas, and a dedicated Yorkist with large law practices in both London and the south-west of England. With the ineffective and then childless Lancastrian Henry VI showing symptoms of the mental instability that he had inherited from the French royal family through his mother Catherine of Valois, Young in June 1451 boldly presented to the House of Commons a petition from his Bristol constituents suggesting that the Yorkist Richard Duke of York (1411-60) should be made heir presumptive to the throne. This was regarded by the Lancastrians as so treasonable that Young was sent to the Tower. After being released in April 1452 he sought redress on the grounds that MPs enjoyed freedom of speech but then appears to have dropped his claim. His advocacy probably encouraged Richard of York to make his

Cottages at Slaughterfor

bid for the throne that brought on the bloody civil war during which, after York was killed at Wakefield in 1460, two of his sons pursued the Yorkist claim and successively usurped the throne as Edward IV and Richard III. Young's contribution to the Yorkist cause was in 1471 recognised when Edward IV rewarded him with a knighthood.

Writing in 1685 John Aubrey tells us that sanfoin, a highly nutritious plant that was introduced from the Low Countries and became extensively sown to enhance soil fertility, was introduced into this area

Slaughterford Church

in about 1650 by a North Wraxall farmer called Nicholas Hall who had moved here from Dundry in Somerset. Sanfoin was also used as cattle-feed – Culpeper described it as: 'a singular feed for cattel . . . to cause them yo give great store of milk' – and the fields of sanfoin with its pink flowers would once have been a distinctive feature of the Wiltshire Cotswold scene in June and July.

The charming small village of Slaughterford (840738) stands aside from main roads on the meandering By Brook half a mile south of Ford. Its church, that stands unusually in a field towards its northern end, stood for two hundred years in ruins after having allegedly been plundered by passing parliamentary soldiers during the English Civil War. On the 1773 map it was 'Church in Ruins', but in the mid-19th century it was restored by its vicar the Rev. Mr Clarke. At Slaughterford some of the woollen factories on the By Brook were adapted for making paper, as described earlier (pages 37-8).

Opposite Slaughterford, at the western edge of the plateau that stands above the eastern edge of the Weavern Valley of the By Brook, is

a little-known archaeological habitation site known as Guy's Rift (845737). Since the site is aside from all public rights-of-way and therefore not accessible I have been obliged to compile this description from old published sources and have not seen its present condition. It consisted of a 75 foot high vertical rift in an oolitic cliff face near a place formerly known as Cloud Quarry east of Slaughterford, and was discovered by the landowner in 1922. When excavated in 1925 the skeletal remains of the four adults and three children were found, which would be of little interest were it not for the fact that associated pottery sherds proved this to be one of the few recognised Iron Age sites in this region. It is situated a mile and a half west of Bury Camp (818740) that is the only Iron Age hillfort in the Wiltshire Cotswolds other than the earthwork upon which the Norman castle at Castle Combe was built. These three Iron Age sites – Guy's Rift, Bury Camp and Castle Combe hillfort – are all situated high above the Valley of the By Brook.

Bury Camp is the only surviving unaltered Iron Age hillfort in the Wiltshire Cotswolds (see plan on page 5). It a roughly triangular promontory hillfort situated within a mile of the Fosse

Slaughterford village and church

Way and fortifying a now wooded spur one and a half miles west of Slaughterford. The fort encloses 22 acres and was built in about 350 BC, but it for some reason appears to have been abandoned by the 2nd century BC, long before the Roman Conquest. Where the hillside is steep on its north-west and east sides the fortification is univallate (single-banked), but on its potentially weaker south-west side it is bivallate. No public footpaths approach the hillfort other than one that passes north-south through the woods a little to its east. Aubrey described 'Burywood camp' as:

. . . a camp, double works ; ergo not Roman but British: very large, and the graffes [ditches] are very deep, notwithstanding the rock. It hath an aperture, west towards Colerne down. It stands on a kind of promontory, and every side is well secured by a precipice. A pretty clear little stream runs on the rock, and gravel in each bottom.

Almost a mile east of Bury Camp the ridge is crossed by a defensive dyke (833743) with a ditch on its east side which implies that it served as a defensive dyke to Bury Camp from the east, as was noticed by Aubrey who described it as: 'a rampart with a graffe [ditch] eastward, but no camp ; it was to obstruct the enemy's coming'. The dyke abuts the minor road from Ford to Colerne.

Biddestone and its surroundings

I N AN UPLAND SITUATION on the limestone plateau about two miles east of Slaughterford is Biddestone (863735), a village that being smaller, situated on flatter ground, and lacking a river, is geographically less dramatic than is Castle Combe in its steep wooded coombe, but gains over its better-known neighbour by being less frequented by tourists. Here Cotswold-style stone houses, barns, cottages and inns cluster casually around a flat green with a large spring-fed village pond. A building known locally as The Barracks is said to have accommodated parliamentary troops on their way to Bristol, presumably the night before they are traditionally said to have wrecked Slaughterford Church.

Until 1884 Biddestone consisted of the two parishes of Biddestone St Peter and Biddestone St Nicholas and had two churches of which only

Biddestone Green

Biddestone Green

St Nicholas survives. It stands away from the green at the west end of the village and has a Norman south porch, an attractive small spired bell-cote perched on the gable above the chancel arch, and inside a Georgian gallery and a Norman font. An epitaph on its south wall dated 1736 reflects the hard life of the 18th century rural poor by informing us that Edward Davis was:

> Peacable with his neighbours,
> And loving to his wife,
> Kind unto his children,
> And painfull was his Life.

A few yards west of the church on the north side of the road that runs steeply down from Biddestone Church to Slaughterford is a Cotswold-type slabbed stile that leads into a stone-walled field. Another similar stile exists on the south side of the village pond, and a short distance east of the church stands an interesting small circular open timber-framed well-house of indeterminate date with a conical stone-slated roof. Pevsner omitted to mention it in his Wiltshire volume of *The Buildings of England* in 1963 possibly because he assumed it to be modern, although Robin Tanner drew it for *Wiltshire Village* before 1939. It was some time before I realised that this attractive little structure resembled the open timber-framed and braced conical-roofed well-head that was built in the late 1860s at William Morris's Red House in Kent. This led me to suspect that the Biddestone well-house was an Arts and Crafts building inspired by its influential Kentish predecessor and dating probably from about 1900-1910 and after searching through some old maps I found it shown on the 1921 25-inch

Biddestone Church

Ordnance Survey map. The well-head was also mentioned as: 'an interesting well-cover' in Walters's *A Complete Guide to Wiltshire* (1920), but I was unable to find a copy of the 1900 map. This pre-1920 date raises the interesting questions who locally could have provided such a design at this date, and could one of the Gloucestershire-based Arts and Crafts designers such as Ernest Gimson or F. L. Griggs have designed it?

Biddestone's other church of St Peter stood (at 867733) east of the road junction and a little east of its surviving manor house on the north side of the road that runs east past Sheldon to Chippenham. The church was finally destroyed in 1840, but Aubrey recorded that even in his time in the 17th century it was 'lamentably ruined' and used as a barn. Its ruinous state seems to have upset Aubrey who wrote of his dislike of Biddestone for its drift into non-conformity:

Biddestone Bellcote

> heretofore nothing but religious houses, now nothing but Quakers and fanatics. A sour woodsere country and inclines people to contemplation so that the Bible and ease (for it is now all up with dairy grazing and cloathing) set their witts a running and reforming.

Aubrey also informs us from what sounds like bitter experience that: 'At the George Inn [at Biddestone] the beere that is brewed of the well there is diuretique'. It is interesting to speculate why the George Inn was co-called in pre-Hanoverian times since the name was then unusual, although Edward IV's brother who was executed by drowning in a butt of malmsey was George, Duke of Clarence.

Being south of Biddestone beside the site of the now-demolished church on the Chippenham road, Biddestone Manor House (867733) must often be missed by those who come to Biddestone from the north. It is a fine Cotswold-style stone-built house with gabled fronts, mullioned

Wellhead at Biddestone

windows, and a stone-tiled roof, standing among numerous outbuildings including barns and a gazebo, most of which probably date from the 17th-century when the house was sold in 1626 by Sir Gilbert Prynne of Allington to William Mountjoy who was a little later obliged to pay a fine to Charles I for refusing an unwanted knighthood. After the adjacent church was demolished its site was absorbed into the manor house garden.

On Barrow Hill on the south side of the A420 a mile and a half north-east of Biddestone is Lanhill, a Neolithic chambered long barrow (878748) that has suffered much vandalism probably due to

its accessible position beside the main road. Originally 185 feet long by 90 feet wide and 12 feet high, it is orientated east-west and had at its east end dry-stone walls forming a funnelled false entrance. These were removed in 1909 presumably to obtain stone for building or roadworks. This barrow is of the chambered Severn-Cotswold type (see page 120) and contained three burial chambers of which only one survives as an accessible chamber on its south side. It measures 4 feet wide by 8 feet deep, has a corbelled roof, and was found to contain eleven burials.

The former 13th century Sheldon Manor (888741) about two miles east of Biddestone was in 1231 granted to Sir William de Godarville and

Biddestone Manor from west

at his death in 1249 it went to Sir Geoffrey de Gascelin. In 1424 Sir Walter Hungerford bought Sheldon and let it out but the spendthrift Sir Edward Hungerford sold the manor in 1684 when gambling away the Hungerford fortune. Sheldon is now a largely 17th-century house with an outsize 13th-century porch that has been claimed to be the oldest domestic architecture in Wiltshire. Its scale and the quality of its pointed arch and two-light traceried Gothic window persuaded the usually restrained Sir Nikolaus Pevsner to describe it as 'astonishing'. It may once have fronted a much larger house. Attached to the current house is a chapel dating from about 1450, the house also has a barn and a granary, and earthworks to its west indicate the former existence of a settlement that may have housed family retainers when the house was larger.

Midway between Biddestone and Sheldon Manor is Starveall Farm (879734) that for almost twenty years of her fifty-year widowhood (from 1932-52) was the home of Helen Thomas, the wife of the poet Edward Thomas who was killed in action in 1917 in the Great War. Helen shared Starveall, that she always called 'Starwell', with the farmer Harold Tucker and his wife Adeline. As the posthumous standing of her husband as a poet grew Helen was visted at 'Starwell' by many celebrities from the worlds of art and literature. Shortly before her death at the age of almost ninety-five in 2005 Myfanwy Thomas, the 'daughter the younger' of her father's poem, told me how her mother had attracted to 'Starwell' a wide circle of intellectual friends, and also recalled how from 'Starwell' Helen went for long walks often in the company of her friends, one of whom was Robin Tanner who as a local man had found Starveall as a suitable home for Helen when she decided to leave London to live in her husband's favourite county of Wiltshire. Myfanwy often stayed at Starveall and in

Biddestone Manor group from south

her memoirs recalled her mother's 'full rich life at Starwell Farm' and the occasion when Helen, returning home bearing as usual armfuls of wild flowers, was delighted to be greeted by the local roadman: 'There be you again, sprack as a daisy' – 'sprack' being a Wiltshire word meaning sprightly or active.

An interesting local feature is the number of 'well' names in this area that presumably arise because here was once a holy well, one of those water sources that after achieving a reputation for being curative of ilnesses became sanctified. As they provided pure underground water that was a necessity of life such water sources were often dedicated by Celtic peoples to their gods who were believed to inhabit springs and wells. Holy wells remain numerous in Celtic areas like Cornwall and Ireland and some survive elsewhere, although as Celtic and christian beliefs became merged during the Middle Ages names of saints were often substituted for the original dedications to pagan water deities. A law passed in 1018 that forbade the worship of trees, stones and wells was generally disregarded, and some holy wells were in Medieval times furnished with wellhouses and chapels. After the influence of the saints diminished after the Reformation people continued to visit their holy wells, but there is no national record of such wells and although many are now virtually lost it is believed that they still number from two to three thousand in England, the most celebrated being St Winifrede's at Holywell in North Wales that is annually visited by 30,000 visitors.

Andrews and Dury in 1773 marked nothing significant in the area around Starveall Farm although the first Ordnance Survey marked 'Holy Well' (at 880727) beside a little stream near Middlehill Farm and nearly half a mile south of Starveall. Aubrey, who frequently recorded his interest in ancient wells and springs, visited in his words this 'Holy Well in the parish of Chippenham, near Sheldon', and took samples of its water for analysis. The First Series 1: 25 000 Ordnance Survey map nominated this well as 'Holy Well' but it is now omitted from the modern maps. Helen Thomas always called Starveall Farm 'Starwell', presumably because tiny fossilised starfish are found in the well's water. The existence nearby of Stowell Farm (880724) with its well element is also of interest, and we also find Robin Tanner reminding us in *Wiltshire*

Village (1939) that: 'A century later John Aubrey, a native of these parts, was testing the waters of Starwell and Holy Well for their medicinal properties', and adding the comment that: 'The field in which it [the well] lies has been nicknamed Starveall on account of the poverty of the soil'. The site of this well is not accessible to the public but it is overlooked from the public road near the line of electricity pylons to its east.

Colerne and games on Colerne Down

ANYONE APPROACHING COLERNE from the south, particularly when toiling on foot up the hill, will become very much aware that Colerne is a hilltop settlement. It stands at 500 feet (152 metres) above sea level and the 15th century tower of its largely 14th century church (821711) is a landmark for miles around. The derivation of the name Colerne is uncertain, but hilltop villages are often of early foundation and have sometimes been continuously inhabited from Romano-British times. This may be the case here since Colerne stands only a short distance from the Fosse Way and is associated with a number of Roman sites. In 1838 a twelve-roomed Roman villa was discovered (at 811718) half a mile from the Fosse Way on the plateau that was taken over by the airfield north-west of Colerne. When this villa was excavated in 1854 hypocausts and tesselated floors were found, one of which incorporated a representation of a charioteer driving a four-horse chariot with the inscription 'SERVIVUS SEVERUS'. The Saxons generally founded their settlements in valleys beside rivers and well away from Roman roads along which enemies might approach. They often ignored existing upland settlements, although Seebohm in *The English Village Community* (1926) provided convincing evidence of continuity in some upland villages from Roman right through Anglo-Saxon times.

Colerne from Box Hill

Aubrey knew Colerne which is only about seven miles from his birthplace at Lower Easton Piercy, and of its church wrote: 'Here is a most noble prospect, a stately high well built tower, which, when the bells, which are new cast, ring, shakes much. A very fair church, but nothing of antiquity left . . . ' . Built into the internal wall of the church are two fragments of an Anglo-Saxon cross shaft found during reconstruction of the church. Pevsner considered these to be parts of: 'one of the best C9 crosses in the West Country', although they could be remnants of one of the crosses set up at the stops made by the body of St Aldhelm on its way for burial from Doulting, where he died in AD 709, to Malmesbury. If so these fragments are rather older than Pevsner believed.

In early-Medieval times the manor of Colerne was held with their manor of Castle Combe by the de Dunstanvilles. The manor house towards the east end of the village has a 1689 datestone and Lucknam Park (821729) in its extensive grounds one mile north of the village is late-Georgian. Cloth-weaving took place in the Colerne area that in the 17th and 18th centuries emulated Slaughterford by becoming a centre for the manufacture of paper when a number of woollen mills towards the edge of the parish on the By Brook and Doncombe Brook were converted to papermaking.

Colerne on its hill from south

Among the local celebrities are William de Colerne (d.1296) who became an Abbot of Malmesbury and musy presumably have come from Colerne, and another ecclesiastic the learned scholar William Grocyn (1449-1519) who was born here the son of a Winchester College tenant. After going to New College at Oxford in 1465 he learnt Greek and became the first public teacher in Greek at Oxford. He then held various ecclesiastical appointments and after travelling to Florence to improve his Italian and Greek contributed much to the early Tudor revival in learning. Upon returning to Oxford he took as pupils Sir Thomas More and the great Dutch humanist Erasmus who lodged in his house and wrote of him: 'Who does not marvel at such a perfect round of learning as is in Grocyn'. Grocyn with Colet and More, all friends of Erasmus, by their revival of learning and their study of Greek and the Classics hoped to influence a moderate reform of the old-established English church, and cannot possibly have anticipated that their work would within fifty years utterly revolutionise their church.

Traditions of hilltop sports exists at a number of sites in Wiltshire and two miles north of Colerne is Colerne Down (832737), that is in fact much nearer Slaughterford than Colerne. Of it John Aubrey wrote:

Colerne down is the place so famous and frequented for stool-ball playing. The turf is very fine, and the rock is within an inch and a half of the surface, which gives the ball so quick a rebound. They smite the ball with a staff, commonly made of withy about three and a half feet long. A stool-ball is of about four inches diameter, stuffed very hard with quills, sewed into sole leather, and hard as a stone. I do not hear it is used but hereabout and in Gloucestershire adjacent.

According to *The Pocket Oxford Dictionary* (1961) Stool ball is an 'old game of cricket or rounders kind still played esp. in Essex', although Aubrey's description of the game played at Colerne Down suggests that by devising their own 17th century amusements the residents of the remote countryside around Colerne may have invented a precursor of the the game of golf.

Colerne Park

NORTH-EAST OF COLERNE and about a mile and a half from the village is Colerne Park (837726) that now consists of a largely wooded hill above the By Brook. At its southern end near Monk's Wood is Euridge Manor Farm (832721) – the name means 'Yew-tree ridge' – where Aubrey tells us: 'At Eweridge in the parish of Colerne' yew trees grew 'indifferently plentifull'. In the valley of the By Brook below Euridge is Weavern Farm (840719). The *Wilts Inquisitions post mortem 1242-1326* mention in 1311 200 acres of parkland at Colerne, but despite its 'park' name Colerne Park seems unlikely to have ever been a deer park, although Arthur Mee in *The King's England: Wiltshire* (1939) categorically stated that: 'At Euridge Farm . . . once lived Sir Walter Raleigh'. Raleigh is known to have been associated with deer parks as a ranger, and is also known to have sometimes visited South Wraxall only five miles south of Euridge, but I have been unable to confirm Mee's assertion and mention it merely in case he had some authority for making it.

The existence of Monk's Park at the south end of Colerne Park suggests that the locally born William of Colerne, who was Abbot of Malmesbury from 1260 until 1296, could at this time when senior ecclesiastics owned deer parks have created a possibly short-lived monastic park in his home parish. On 18 September 1633 the writer of the *Progress Notes of*

Colerne Church

Warden Woodward recorded: 'I rode again about 3 a clocke to see the parke [Colerne], about 20 acres of wood that hath some good trees in it'. It seems that by 1633 Colerne Park had been reduced in area tenfold in the three hundred years since the aforementioned 1311 record. Many ash trees around Colerne were according to John Aubrey in the 17th century destroyed by the local people who barked them to make boxes in which they sent strawberries gathered from the local woods to market. Colerne Park is not marked by name on Andrews and Dury in 1773 although the wood shown by them is of much the same configuration as it is today, except that it at then extended as far north-west as the Thickwood to Slaughterford road.

No public access enters Colerne Park other than a right-of-way that runs from near Euridge Manor Farm south-east across its southern end down to to the By Brook. It may however be viewed at a distance from the lane which runs southwards from Slaughterford towards Weavern Farm down the east side of By Brook.

Some Roman Signal Stations?

IN DOING THE FIELDWORK for this book the possibility that a line of Roman signal stations might have existed behind the Fosse Way was first suggested to me by the cluster of eroded mounds, one large and two small (at 835733), beside the road that descends from Thickwood to Slaughterford two miles west of the Fosse Way and a short distance south-east of Colerne Down at the north-west edge of Colerne Park. The largest mound is designated by the Ordnance Survey 'tumulus' and was described in the *Victoria County History for Wiltshire* (Volume 1, Part 1, page 167) as a bowl barrow 24 paces in diameter and 9 feet high 'surrounded by large and deep ditch'. It is described as 'flat topped' with a flat area about 25 feet in diameter, but the fact of particular interest is that a scatter of sculptured stone and Roman pottery sherds found around the mound suggests that it was either of Roman origin or was for some reason a Roman adaptation of a Bronze Age barrow. Aubrey in his *Topographical Collections for Wiltshire* wrote: 'At Colerne Park, above Slaughterford, they tell me their is a single works camp: i.e. Roman, which see', and his use of the term 'works camp' suggests that more than three hundred years ago Aubrey saw something substantial that was Roman and perhaps a military installation. This, together with the presence of the Roman sherds and pottery, set me speculating about whether this mound could be the base of a Roman signal station associated with the nearby Fosse Way when it was the temporary Roman frontier, perhaps with a signal tower on its flat top and accommodation for its operatives. If this were the case it would have been one of a series.

It is recognised that the Romans often built chains of signal stations behind their frontiers and the Ordnance Survey in its *Field Archaeology in Great Britain* (1973) indicated that: 'The known pattern of [Roman] signal stations suggest many more remain to be spotted'. The Fosse Way as explained earlier (on pages 41-2) was during the Roman Conquest a frontier zone, and the probability that signal stations are to be expected associated with the Fosse Way was advanced by the eminent field archaeologist O. G. S. Crawford when he wrote in *Archaeology in the Field* (1953):

> To an early stage in the conquest must belong some of the signal-stations .
> . . recent excavations at Willoughby-on-the-Wolds have revealed what may
> be the remains of one such on the Foss-way, which is exactly where a line of
> signal-stations would most be expected . . .

Roman signal stations were built in chains on high points and obviously within sight of each other to relay messages over long distances, just as were semaphore stations in Napoleonic times. Crawford described these signal stations as being: 'round, ditched platforms about fifty feet in diameter' and indicated that they are to be expected 'a mile or two apart'. The Greek Polybius (c.204-122 BC) described a Roman method of signalling using light signals but other methods of signalling were later developed and the later Roman military writer Vegetius (flourished about 400 AD) mentioned the use of fire, smoke, and semaphore for signalling. Crawford suggested that: 'signalling was by means of lighted torches fixed to posts thrust through an aperture, and also by beacons such as those carved on Trajan's column in Rome'. Roman signal stations so far recognised in Britain have generally consisted of wooden towers about ten feet square erected on mounds with four heavy corner posts. At least one authority suggests that by making them broad-based and stepping them back at intervals as they rose the Romans were capable of constructing signal towers to a height of about a hundred feet, a fact that could compensate for them not necessarily being sited at the most elevated natural situations. In high towers this buttressing effect would have created a fairly large structure at ground level, although it seems unlikely that such structures would have been permanently occupied because of the inherent danger of fire caused by combustibles falling from the beacons. The Romans also sometimes used much less elaborate signal stations known as beacon stances consisting of simple flat-topped earthen mounds as beacons, much like the mound in Colerne Park. Behind the Antonine Wall four pairs of such beacon stances were used to signal back to the rear of the frontier.

Signal stations generally dated from the 1st century AD, the century of conquest during which the country remained hostile, and the

Colerne Park site in its elevated position only two miles behind the Fosse Way frontier is in an appropriate situation for a signal station. If it was a signal station it is interesting to speculate where were the other signal stations associated with it.

A Roman site discovered the 1950s in a high situation beside Ashley Barn about 500 yards south of Euridge Manor Farm (at 833716) about a mile south of the Colerne Park site is another possible candidate as a signal station. This site is on a south-facing slope but a signal tower that provided more height could have been built up the hill near Euridge Farm on the ridge that the name of the farm recognises. Excavation at this site (see *WAM* 93: 218-232) revealed that it consisted of a large courtyard building associated with other buildings which could have been barrack blocks or Roman buildings of later date. Finds and numismatic evidence suggested that 'the site was occupied from the latter part of the 1st century AD or the 2nd century' (*Excavation Report*) – in other words the period of the conquest. A signal station here could after pacification have become the villa that it is now generally assumed to have been, but it may be significant that the excavator expressed doubts about it being a villa and concluded his report by stating that it was only 'a possible Romano-British villa' and, very interestingly, that it lacked the 'fragments usually diagnostic of villas'.

Both the Colerne Park and the Euridge Farm sites are at high points between the National Grid northing lines 83 and 84, and another Roman site on the Fosse Way west of Grittleton (at 843800) – that was significantly suggested to be a possible signal station by L. V. Grinsell in *The Archaeology of Wessex* (1958: 259) – stands very near this north-south line. If such a chain of Roman signal stations existed more examples are to be be expected at other high points along this line, and appropriate possible locations exist on the high promontory west of Ford near Mount Scylla Farm (at about 836747), and at the former prehistoric site (838778) on the hill above Castle Combe. *The Place-Names of Wiltshire* (1939) fails to explain the unusual name of Mount Scylla Farm although Scylla was a classical deity, and the building of the Medieval castle could have destroyed any signs of Roman work on the former Iron Age site of the castle. Another elevated site along this line is on Truckle Hill where the villa site (at 836761) could originally have been a signal station at the time of the Roman Conquest and only become a villa when peace was established.

My own inclination is to be extremely sceptical about most alignment theories, and the existence of these recognised Roman sites almost in alignment behind the Fosse Way frontier (see map) is only speculative, but it is interesting particularly as the spacing is appropriate

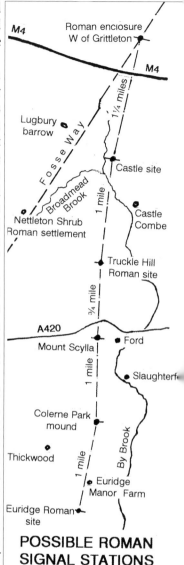

POSSIBLE ROMAN SIGNAL STATIONS
east of the Fosse Way

for signal stations. The distance from Euridge Farm to the Colerne Park site is approximately one mile, as is the distance from the Colerne Park mound to Mount Scylla. From there to the Truckle Hill site is only three-quarters of a mile, and it is then a mile from Truckle Hill to the castle site at Castle Combe and a mile and a quarter from the castle site to the Roman enclosure on the Fosse Way west of Grittleton. All of these distances are well within Crawford's criteria for visual signalling of 'one or two miles', and it is relevant to note that a chain of ten recognised Roman signal stations in Perthshire extended over eight miles at average intervals of a little less than a mile.

My theory that these sites are possible signal stations is I believe entirely original and has not been discussed with any archaeological authority. It would however be interesting to find by excavation whether any large post holes of signal towers exist at any of these six suggested sites, although their absence would not necessarily destroy the theory because the sites may have been signal stations of the beacon stance type consisting simply of mounds without towers.

Ditteridge, Cheney Court and Sir John Cheyney

I N DELIGHTFUL REMOTE COUNTRYSIDE between the limestone Colerne plateau and the By Brook at Box are Ditteridge, Middlehill, Alcombe and Cheney Court. Ditteridge (817695) is a tiny village with an interesting small church that despite restoration in 1860 preserves a number of Norman features in its doors and windows. From the hillside at this southern edge of the limestone plateau around Colerne emerge a number of springs and a little over quarter of a mile south-west of

Ditteridge Church

Ditteridge is Middlehill (813691) where a spa presumably inspired by the success of Bath was opened in the late-18th century. A well was sunk in 1783 and by 1786 a William Falconer was publicising the spa. The failure of the enterprise in 1818 may be due to its proximity to Bath, but a pump room and a possible former boarding house for visitors survive in Spa House (817690). West of Middlehill the Jacobean Cotswold-style three-storeyed Cole's Farm dates from 1645 and was once the dower house to Cheney Court, and to its west is Alcombe Manor (809694), a much modernised house in an attractive combe that incorporates a few Medieval fragments. .

Cole's Farm

Throughout the south of England the name Cheney frequently occurs as a proprietorial place-name indicating former ownership by the family of Cheyney (or Cheney). At Ditteridge it occurs in Cheney Court (817694), a three-gabled Jacobean house with many strangely disposed mullioned windows and a single-storey gabled porch with a later shell-headed doorway and classically styled stone-balustered balustrades. This house was the dower house to the Spekes of Hazelbury (see pages 200-1) that stands on the other side of Box a mile and a half to its south-east. The Spekes built the present Cheney Court in 1530 and reconstructed it in Jacobean times. A local tradition asserts that during the Civil War Charles I's Queen Henrietta Maria hid at Cheney Court and was concealed in one of its barns when parliamentary troopers descended upon the house that becamefor a time a hotel but is now the offices of a commercial company and as such is strictly private.

An earlier house on the site of the present house was in 1431 owned by Sir Edmund Cheyney and later in 1478 by John Cheyney (d.1499), a

man who was very active during the Wars of the Roses and deserves more attention than he has received for a military exploit that fundamentally changed the course of English history. Like many Lancastrians Cheyney, who was reputed to be a very large man, acknowledged the problems arising from Henry VI's madness which had prompted the Yorkist Edward IV to opportunistically usurp him. Cheyney then served and was well-regarded by Edward IV. He served Edward, first as an esquire of the body and then

Alcombe

from 1479 until Edward's unexpected early death in 1483 as his Master of Horse. He was however unable to accept Richard III's usurpation and probable responsibility for the murder of his nephews, Edward IV's sons. The fact that one of the conspirators who attempted to snatch the little princes from their imprisonment in the Tower of London in 1483 was John Smith, a groom who had served under John Cheyney at Court, suggests that Cheyney may have been involved in this failed rescue attempt that probably sealed the fate of the little princes. Their subsequent disappearance provoked many of the Wiltshire Lancastrian landowners into the 1483 rebellion that was in Wiltshire led jointly by John Cheyney and Walter Hungerford. When it failed Cheyney and his brothers, together with a number of other disaffected Lancastrians, fled abroad and joined the exiled Henry Tudor who after the the Duke of Buckingham's execution at Salisbury during the rebellion became the leading Lancastrian claimant to the throne. When Henry Tudor invaded England in 1485 Cheyney accompanied him as one of his principal military

approach to Cheney Court

supporters and was knighted on the Welsh beach where the Lancastrians landed. The decisive battle then took place at Bosworth, where when battle was joined a large number of Richard's army decided not to engage. With the battle going against him Richard then charged across the battlefield with a small body of mounted attendants in a desperate attempt to kill Henry Tudor and settle for once and all the future of the throne. He very nearly succeeded as after personally killing Henry's standard bearer Sir William Brandon, who would inevitably have been beside Henry, Richard was at the vital moment confronted by the huge mounted figure of Sir John Cheyney whom he succeeded in unseating. Henry Tudor was a political intriguer rather than a soldier and had the warlike Richard III reached Henry he would almost certainly have have killed him, but after Cheyney had checked his charge Richard was dragged from his horse and slaughtered on the ground by foot soldiers.

By his defence of Henry Tudor Sir John Cheyney effectively secured his accession to the throne as the first of the mighty dynasty of

Tudors. Cheyney survived the battle and led the courser of state at Henry's coronation as Henry VII, and after fighting at the final Yorkist defeat at Stoke in 1487 he became a baron. At his death without an heir in 1499 being a Wiltshire landowner owning estates at Falstone and Southwick as well as at Ditteridge, Cheyney was buried in Salisbury Cathedral. When when his tomb was opened during Wyatt's reconstruction of Salisbury Cathedral his reputation for having been a large man was confirmed as his thigh bone was found to be twenty-one inches long.

Hartham Park

THIS HOUSE STANDS in private grounds in open countryside a mile and a half east of Colerne Park and a mile south of Biddestone. The name Hartham is derived from from *heorot* (hart or deer) and *ham* (enclosure) meaning literally 'deer enclosure' and the name park appended to a Domesday name meaning 'deer enclosure' strongly implies that Hartham may once have been one of the many lost Medieval Wiltshire deer parks. Such parks were often associated with castles and Hartham's credentials as a possible former deer park would gain credence if the 'Castle Mound' marked on the early Ordnance Survey maps (at 857724) was indeed a castle site but there is considerable doubt about this as no surviving evidence of an associated bailey or ringwork exists at Hartham.

Being merely about twelve feet high with a flat top, this mound may have been the base of a small temporary timber adulterine castle built at the time of Stephen and Matilda, but it could equally be one of the 'mounts' that were created in the 17th and 18th centuries as viewpoints for overlooking estates, sometimes as bases for gazebos. These have often been mistaken for castle 'mottes' and we know from Andrew's and Dury's 1773 map that the grounds of Hartham Park were in the 18th century extensively landscaped. This suggests that the Hartham mound was probably a garden feature and it is now re-designated 'Mound' by the Ordnance Survey. John Aubrey mentions at Hartham 'The Conigre' (meaning rabbit warren) but no park, and if such a park ever existed the 18th century landscaping would probably have obliterated all signs of it.

In 1756 the Bath coach road was re-routed past Hartham Park from the Cross Keys at the edge of Corsham to Box. We know its route from a plan of the Bath roads dated about 1790 which shows it running from Cross Keys (872713) west past the church (864715) and Hillgreen Lodge (857714), running slightly north of Pickwick Lodge (through 852713), and swinging south-west then south to the present A4 at Rudloe (843703). The reason for this diversion is not obvious but it must have been a sound one as it was implemented in the face of objections by a number of landowners. Most of this route is no longer a public right-of-way.

Throughout the 17th and 18th centuries the Ducketts of Calstone Wellington were at Hartham and were probably among the objectors to the re-routing of the coach road across their park. John Duckett was High Sheriff of Wiltshire in 1628 and in 1773 Andrews and Dury showed 'Wm Duckett Esq' in occupation. This family often provided the MPs for Calne, and during the Civil War. John Duckett of Hartham was in 1630 fined £28 in the Knighthood Compositions for Wiltshire which was one of the stratagems by which Charles I without the sanction of parliament illegally raised revenue.

The present house at Hartham Park was designed in 1790-95 for Lady James by the renowned architect James Wyatt (1746-1813) who designed Fonthill House and died when travelling in Wiltshire as a consequence of not wearing a hat! When he was returning from a site visit somewhere near Beckhampton about sixteen miles east of Hartham Wyatt's coach jolted and his bare head struck the ceiling of his coach so violently that he died from his injuries. Hartham Park was extensively extended in about 1858 and again 1888 in a style that is sympathetic to Wyatt's originl building, and a chapel was also added in the grounds in 1862.

The grounds of Hartham Park are strictly private and the area is lacking in public footpaths, although a road that runs north out of the A4 from Corsham (at 868711) past Hartham Park to Biddestone follows its eastern boundary, and Weavern Lane, a driveable cul-de-sac minor road that runs south-west from Biddestone Church, passes to its north-west.

uggested Walks in the
id-Wiltshire Cotswolds

e: refer to General Notes relevant to all of the Suggested
ks in the General Introduction.

: Castle Combe and the Broadmead
ook (5¼ miles)

; walk passes through the village of Castle Combe [129-35], emote hamlet of Long Dean [134], and along the secluded ey of the Broadmead Brook [126-7]. It involves one steep b out of Ford.

ote: there are public houses on this walk at Castle Combe at Ford (by a short diversion).

RK at the signposted car park at Upper Castle Combe

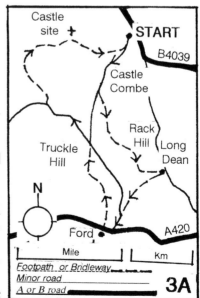

near the B4039 at 845777.

1: Walk for ¾ mile S downhill through the village [133] past the market cross [133] and continue through past the public toilets and over the road bridge, and continue as far as the footbridge on yo left at 841768.

2: Cross the By Brook [133] by this bridge, turn right, and follow the Macmillan Way footpath sign 'Long Dean' for a mile, first S uphill and then SE along the hillside over Rack Hill to Long Dean ham (851757) [134].

3: There turn right, cross a footbridge and follow the footpath SW uphill beside a wall on your left.

4: When the path emerges on to an open hillside (at 847755) follow the contours SW along the hills to a stile beside the road at 845750.

5: Cross this stile, turn left, and follow the minor road SW down to the A420 at Ford [158].

6: Walk a short distance W along the A420. (The public house stands a short distance S of the A⁴ down a side road at 841748 S of the church).

7: At a bus shelter (843748) on the N side of the A420 turn N up Park Lane and after a short distanc the end of the lane cross the high stile on your left.

8: Bear away right and walk N along the grass track above the stream keeping near the stream to ens that you do not miss the footbridge across the stream at 843754. Cross this bridge, continue N up a ste hill through a wood, then continue N along the hillside and descend to a road junction at 839762.

9: From here a short option is to return N along the road to Castle Combe, but for the full walk fr this road junction walk NW along the road past Shrub Farm and where the road bends left (at 8337 turn right up a footpath and follow it NW down to a clapper bridge at 830773 [126].

10: Cross this bridge, turn right, and follow Broadmead Brook NE, and at the former Nettleton Mil 833776 turn right through a semi-concealed pass-gate and continue E following the signed footpa across the golf course passing S of the former castle site and crossing the bridge at 837776.

11: From the bridge continue SE and as you near the Manor House Hotel gates fork left away from hotel, follow the footpath S ignoring a long flight of steps on your left, and continue along the footp with a wall on your right to a point overlooking the church.

12: Where the path divides at 841773 take the left branch uphill, pass left of a football pitch, conti E through some stone gatepiers by a former school, and rejoin the outward route at the road a l downhill from the start point at the car park.'

3B: Biddestone and Slaughterford (5½ miles)

The fine villages of Biddestone [162-7] and Slaughterford [161] are included in this walk that also twice crosses the beautiful valley of the By Brook [125-8]. The walk involves a climb up Colerne Down and negotiating a long slow rise from the By Brook to finish back at Biddestone.
— Note: the only public houses on this walk are at Biddestone.

PARK in Biddestone (863735).

1: Walk W past public toilets on your left and the church (862736) on you right and a little beyond the church take the right fork in the road and walk for a mile down hill to a T-junction (843734).

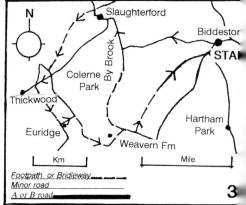

3

There turn right, walk N into Slaughterford [161], and there turn left and then right keeping N of the
idge to the church (840740) which stands aside from the road in a field.

At the telephone box (838740) NW of the church walk SW down an unmarked footpath that runs
st some cottages and under some power lines to the By Brook [125-8] that is crossed by a footbridge
836739.

From the footbridge cross a stile on your left and then take a footpath SW up a double hedgerow.

At the end of the hedgerow continue SW under some overhead lines and join the grassed track over
lerne Down [168-9].

A rather obscure footpath will take you SW to Hall Farm (832732), but if this is missed an alternative
blic footpath may be followed W past some cottages at 831735 and then S to Hall Farm.

Walk SW past Hall Farm (832732) for about 150 yards and at the road turn left and at a crossing at
1729 turn right and walk SW down the road towards Thickwood.

At 827727 before reaching Thickwood turn left from the road and walk for a mile SE from the road
wn a signposted footpath to Euridge Manor Farm (833721).

At the farm turn NE (left) along the road and at the edge of Colerne Park (835723) [169-70] leave the
d by turning right and walking SE down the footpath that follows the the edge of Colerne Park, swing
nd pass S of Weavern Farm, and cross the By Brook by a footbridge (842718).

•: From the bridge continue NE for about 300 yards uphill to the lane at 843720 and there turn right
1 walk E along the lane for almost ¼ mile.

: At 846719 walk the remaining 2½ miles back to Biddestone by following the unmarked footpath
your left through a gate with a large stone as a step, walking NE up a long slope passing a copse on
ir right (at 848723) continue NE and through gates enter a tarmacadamed road that takes you back
3iddestone near the church.

⁀: Nettleton Shrub and West Kington (4½ miles)

is rural walk crosses a clapper bridge across the
admead Brook [126-7], passes the little-known
man settlement at Nettleton Shrub [139-44], and
ts West Kington [135-9] where the protestant martyr
hop Latimer was vicar. It involves gentle uphill
king to West Kington, a steep climb to visit the
rch, and another towards the end of the walk from
Broadmead Brook to the start point.

Jote: there are no public houses on this walk.

.RK in the lay-by ¾ mile S of Castle Combe at road
ction (839761) .

Valk NW for ½ mile up the road past Shrub Farm.
Vhere the road bends left (at 833767) turn right and
d left along a footpath that becomes a hollow-way

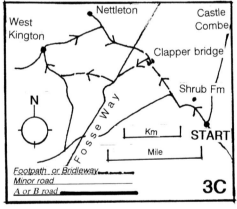

almost ½ mile down to the clapper bridge [126] on Broadmead Brook [126-7] at 830773.

Cross this bridge, turn left, and walk for almost ½ mile SW along a field edge and a hillside, keeping
htly above the brook, to the Fosse Way [40-5] and there walk a short distance SW to the site of
tleton Shrub Roman settlement [139-44] on the Fosse Way at 823769.

rom here walk for ½ mile W along the S edge of a tree-capped mound above Broadmead Brook and
ugh woods to a minor road at 814771.

5: Continue NW up the road to West Kington [135-9] and there (812714) turn right across the road brid and at the bend in the road at 812775 leave the road and walk straight on N up the steep path to Hu Latimer's West Kington church [136] crossing a field on your right at the top of the path.

6: From the church walk first N and then E round the N side of Church Farm and then for ½ mile sligh N of E along the road to a road junction (822778) at the SE end of Nettleton.

7: There turn right and follow the road SE to the Fosse Way at 827775.

8 Cross the Fosse Way, walk on SE down the footpath to the clapper bridge, and then follow the outwa route back to the start point.

3D: A Short Walk in John Aubrey's Countryside (2½ miles)

This short walk starts from Kington St Michael [145-8], visits some of the immediate countryside known to John Aubrey, and offers a short diversion to see the site of his his birthplace at Lower Easton Piercy [146-7]. The walk is basically level on generally good surfaces with only slight hills. I would have liked to offer a longer walk from Yatton Keynell to Kington St Michael across the fields, and did reconnoitre one, but because of difficulties experienced with obstructions reluctantly decided that it was not feasible.

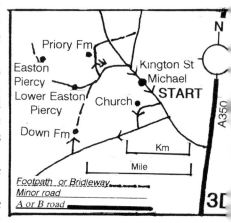

PARK in Kington St Michael and see the Lyte Almhouses [147] and the church.

1: After visiting the church (that is in my experience seldom open), from the church gate walk SW from Stubbs Lane to 902768 on the minor road from Fowlswick Farm to the S end of Kington St Michael

2: Walk SW down that road for ¾ mile and shortly after passing on your left Heywood Farm at 892 turn right up the signposted path to Down Farm.

3: Walk for ¾ mile up this path past Down Farm passing a little E of Lower Easton Piercy and j Cromhall Lane at 895775.

4: A ¼ mile diversion (each way) may be taken from this point W along Cromhall Lane to see the (892774) at Lower Easton Piercy [146-7] of Aubrey's birthplace, now replaced by a later farm that at the time of writing (2006) being converted into a dwelling.

5: Return E along Cromhall Lane and at 896776 turn N up the metalled lane to Priory Farm (8957 [153-4] on the site of St Mary's Priory.

6: Where the stone-walled lane bends right opposite the farm (895778) pass through a gate on your r into the Nymph Hay [154] that is now a public open space, and walk a little S of E down a path, cro little bridge across the stream (897777), and continue E through a recreation field and pass throug gate (899778) to the crossroads at the N end of Kington St Michael [153].

7: Walk SE down the main street passing on your right the Lyte Almshouses [147].

4
Bradford and the South,
including Box and Corsham

THIS THE FINAL TOPOGRAPHICAL CHAPTER covers the largest and most densely populated of the three districts into which this book is divided. Its northern boundary is the A4 from which it extends south to the Kennet and Avon Canal that is its southern boundary, its western limit is the county boundary from the A4 south as far as Freshford, and its east is the A350 from Chippenham to Semington, all as shown on the map on page vi. Because they lie principally south of the A4 Box and Corsham are described in this chapter, as are a number of historic small villages and towards its southern edge the historic town of Bradford on Avon, the interesting hamlet of Avoncliff, and two important waterways in the Lower Bristol Avon and the Kennet and Avon Canal. Of these southern Wiltshire Cotswolds the writers of the *Little Guide* to Wiltshire wrote:

> . . . the wooded heights are very charming, ; but as the neighbourhood of Bath is approached, the deep winding valleys with the hanging woods that clothe the slopes of the downs are exceedingly attractive, while the glorious panoramic views from rich elevations, like that of Monkton Farleigh, make the district a particularly attractive one.

As it is so distant from the Gloucestershire Cotswolds it might be assumed that this district would demonstrate few Cotswold characteristics. This is not the case because the ready availability of its deep beds of oolitic freestone and surface deposits of cornbrash rubble have ensured that many of the stone-built buildings of this district so closely resemble the buildings of the Cotswolds that the area has sometimes been confused with Gloucestershire.

Communications

ACROSS THIS SOUTHERN END of the Wiltshire Cotswolds run four historic lines of communication that jointly exemplify much of the history of the development of travel in England. These are the Roman western road to Bath, the Great West coach road to Bath, the Kennet and Avon Canal, and the Great Western Railway from London to Bristol, all of which will now be described in the chronological order in which they were constructed, the first being:

The Roman Western Road to Bath

BEING UNACCUSTOMED to the cold English climate the Romans were naturally attracted to the natural hot springs of Bath that soon became a Romano-British recreational centre called *Aquae Sulis* served by a road that ran west from the Roman commercial capital of *Londinium* and after passing south of Lacock entered region covered by this book about two miles north of Melksham (at 914672). It then continued westwards to Bath across the high limestone plateau south of Corsham and Box. I. D. Margary in his *Roman Roads in Britain* (1955) pointed out that this road is 'strikingly seen from . . . the top of Bewley Common [above Lacock] running straight across country to Ashley Wood above Bath', and drew attention to the fact that it forded the River Avon 'at a point called Lydford [919673]'. Margary also mentioned how today 'only hedgerows with a parish boundary and traces of the ridge

*Roman Road looking ec
from south of Five Ways*

can be seen, these being clear to the east of the Whitley-Chapel Knapp road', and how 'At Neston Park the agger is again very conspicuous, 45 feet wide and 2 feet high'. Unfortunately this Roman western road provides few opportunities to be explored as, unlike most Roman roads, practically none of it today survives as public rights-of-way in this region.

Before leaving this Roman road it is necessary to discuss the line that the historic post-Roman linear earthwork known as Wansdyke was formerly believed to have followed across this region. Early in the 19th century Colt Hoare suggested that Wansdyke in this district coincided with the Roman road, and this suggestion for long held sway virtually unchallenged after the Ordnance Survey showed Wansdyke coinciding with the Roman road for about ten miles from Bowden Hill to Kingsdown, although by labelling it 'ROMAN ROAD & Wansdyke (course of)' half acknowledging that few signs of it survived on the ground. When discussing Wansdyke in *Archaeology in the Field* (1953) the eminent archaeologist O. G. S. Crawford accepted Colt Hoare's theory but acknowledged that the assumption that Wansdyke coincided with the Roman road needed 'clarifying by excavation'.

In most of its course across the chalk downlands of mid-Wiltshire Wansdyke survives as a stupendous linear earthwork that follows meandering lines over the hills. These characteristics utterly conflict with Colt Hoare's belief that for about ten miles the dyke suddenly changed character and slavishly followed a dead straight Roman road, and had become so slight that it had disappeared without trace. The instance where Crawford saw Wansdyke 'plainly visible' coinciding with the Roman road immediately east of the B3353 road (at 890670 north of Whitley) by no means proves that it continued beyond that point and raises the question, did Wansdyke ever exist over this stretch? In sounding this doubt I find that I am supported by L. V. Grinsell who in *The Archaeology of Wessex* (1958) concluded that Wansdyke was not continuous and that there was a 'considerable gap' between West Wansdyke in Somerset and East Wansdyke in the Marlborough Downs, and by the fact that the Ordnance Survey has now dropped all reference to Wansdyke along this line.

Medieval and Tudor roads were so poor that in winter they became virtually impassible and most heavy freight was carried by barges over a system of navigable rivers. From Roman times until the 18th century practically no major roads were engineered in England and because river transportation was unacceptably slow the poor state of the trackways became an obstacle to the development of prosperity during the industrial revolution in England. The Roman roads had by then become a mere shadowy network of ancient derelict ways whose surfaces had had been quarried for building stone, and in the 18th century the need for road improvements began to be addressed. Initial reactions were to enforce wider wheel treads on vehicles and to effectively limit the weight of laden vehicles by restricting the number of draught animals that were permitted to draw the lumbering carts and coaches of that time. After these measures proved ineffective and faster 'flying' coaches were developed the demand for better roads began to be met by the construction of new roads with much-improved running surfaces. An unforeseen effect of these improvements was that they contributed to depopulating the countryside as was pointed out by Arthur Young when he wrote in his *Farmers' Letters* (1771): 'But now! the country fellow, one hundred miles from London, jumps on a coach box in the morning, and for eight or ten shillings gets to town by night!'.

The communications of England were during the industrial revolution between about 1700 and 1850 revolutionised by three immensely significant new introductions in turnpike roads, canals, and railways. Examples of all three created towards the southern end of the Wiltshire Cotswolds will now be described.

The Bath Coach Road

FROM ABOUT 1700 Bath was reinstated to being the recreational bathing place that it had been in Roman times, and for over a hundred years until about 1840 people from many classes of society travelled the Bath Road, particularly after the invention of four-wheeled sprung coaches solved the age-old problem of conveying entire families including the young and the infirm in comfort. People of quite limited

Bath Mail Coach

means then travelled by coach to Bath where they indulged in the many pleasurable activities that the city offered, and as early as 1706-7 an Act for the repair of the Bath roads described Bath as: 'a place of very great resort from all parts of the Kingdom of Great Britain and from foreign parts, for the use of the baths'.

Travellers from London to Bath followed the Great West coach road that adopted a much less direct route than was followed by the Roman western road described above. From Beckhampton the coach road ran west to Lacock and then at first followed the indirect Medieval route past Gastard (884685) and Neston (861683), over Kingsdown (812671) and

ue Vein Turnpike Cottage

down into Bath. Its line was however subsequently often altered. In 1745 the Chippenham Turnpike Trust re-routed their New Bath Road through Chippenham and Pickwick to the north of Corsham, and by promoting it as the best and shortest route for coaches made the Old Bath Road effectively redundant. For about ten years the usual way to Bath remained past Chapel Plaister and over Kingsdown but in spite of objections from some local landowners another route was negotiated in 1756 that by going from the Cross Keys Inn (872713) across Hartham Park, down to Box, and then through Batheaston, avoided the hazardous descent of Kingsdown.

Whether Charles Dickens (1812-70), who as a young reporter was sent to Bath in 1835, took the idea for the name of his *Pickwick Papers* (1837) from Pickwick at Corsham or from Moses Pickwick of the famous Bath coach firm is not clear. Subsequently a Pickwick newsagent named his shop Pickwick Papers!

After the middle of the 18th century an alternative low-level route was opened through Devizes and Melksham, and the line was then re-routed through Atworth and Blue Vein and over Kingsdown, but this route too was altered when a road was made from east of Blue Vein north-east to Box, again by-passing the descent of Kingsdown.

The demise of the Bath coach road was heralded in July 1829 when a steam road carriage was driven by its inventor Sir Goldsworthy Gurney (1793-1875) at an average speed of about fifteen miles per hour from London to Bath and back via Devizes and Melksham . At Melksham it was bombarded with stones by a gang of roughs hired by coach postilions concerned about the threat to their livelihoods that steam posed, an apprehension that was entirely justified as this steam carriage heralded the advent of the railways and the end of coach travel along the Bath road. The Chippenham Turnpike Trust was to the delight of the local people wound up in 1835, the toll-houses at Pickwick, Cross Keys and Blue Vein were sold for £50 each, and that at Box was demolished as it obstructed the main street.

Among the historic relics that survive along former turnpike roads are original milestones and direction posts, the latter being sometimes known as 'parsons' because they pointed the direction but did not follow it themselves! Tollhouses are also known as turnpike cottages as the original barrier was a hinged pike that formed a bar to traffic across the road. The milestones of the Bath Trust consisted of cast iron plates bolted to stones with hands as pointers and the distances 'To the Guildhall at Bath' precisely indicated in miles and furlongs. Tollhouses such as the surviving example at Blue Vein (see page 185) are often characterised by splayed fronts with windows in the splays facing down the road to observe oncoming traffic. A side-effect of the introduction of faster coaches was that the dust created such a problem that the turnpike trusts levied higher tolls and watered their roads using wayside pumps. A complete set of these pumps once existed along the Bath Road from Hounslow to Bath, although I am not aware of any surviving examples in this district.

The western Bath coach road has now been superseded for through traffic by the M4 motorway.

The Kennet and Avon Canal

A S THIS CANAL has been designated the southern limit of the area covered by this book it is literally peripheral to my subject, but it is of such immense historical and topographical interest that it is extremely relevant to a book devoted to *Exploring Historic Wiltshire*.

From early times rivers were used to transport of heavy and bulky goods by barge, but these navigable waterways tended to silt up and required much dredging and bank maintenance. With the expansion of trade early in the 18th century the inadequacies of the navigable river system was exposed and this led to schemes for constructing man-made waterways. The commercial success of the canal built by the Duke of Bridgewater in Lancashire between 1759 and 1776 initiated the Canal Age and one of the network of canals that was then constructed throughout England was the Kennet and Avon that was built to provide a waterway across southern England linking London to Bristol by joining the Thames at Reading to the River Avon at Bath. Until the coming of the railways it for about forty years admirably fulfilled this need.

The idea for a man-made waterway across southern England was not new. An early-17th century proposal for a much shorter canal was supported by John Aubrey but nothing came of the idea until 1789 when Robert Whitworth suggested a canal taking a line through Hungerford, Marlborough and Calne. The great engineer John Rennie (1761-1821) then investigated the proposal and in 1793 suggested a route farther south and it was decided to proceed along this line. Work started in 1794 but was held up by engineering problems and financial constraints imposed by the Napoleonic Wars, but when the canal finally opened in 1810 it proved to be of immediate benefit to the trade of this region, particularly the stone trade as stone was such a heavy material to transport long distances over bad roads. The cost of carrrying heavy materials now fell dramatically and coal also benefitted, as did the trasportation of bulky bales of wool which led to the construction by 1822 of 'a handsome and commodius wharf at Bradford'.

Because the canal was constructed primarily for freight traffic its passenger use prior to the introduction of the railways has tended to go unnoticed. In 1833 the canal company bought a wrought-iron boat of Scottish construction for use as a passenger boat and between 16 July and 21 September 1833 the 'Scotch Boat' as it became known, containing first and second-class cabins and a string band, carried many passengers between Bath and Bradford, a journey that took less than an hour and a half. After the coming of the railways passenger traffic on the canal became largely recreational and my mother, who was born at Bradford on Avon in 1896, could recall Sunday school outings on the canal. She also remembered seeing, at the time when the Old Court at Avoncliff was used as a military hospital during the Great War, during the summer months of 1917-18 a horse-drawn narrow-boat called the *Bittern* carrying wounded soldiers on canal outings into Bradford.

Some of the canalside public houses such as the Canal Tavern, The Barge, and The Beehive, all of these at Bradford and standing beside or in close proximity to the canal, may have once provided for the users of the working canal, and some may have originated as beer houses catering for the navvies who built the canal.

The arrival of the railways in the mid-19th century sounded the death knell of the canals and by 1852 the Kennet and Avon was failing to compete with the railway. Its directors considered competing by

Bradford Wharf

constructing railways along its towpaths and petitioned parliament to that effect, but when that idea failed they sold the canal to the Great Western Railway Company which deliberately ran down the canal traffic. The Second World War finally killed off canal trade and after the canals were nationalised in 1948 the Kennet and Avon gradually became derelict and after the last through passage was made in 1951 it soon became impassible and even in places dry. It was saved when local enthusiasts formed the Kennet and Avon Canal Preservation Trust that working with the Canal Preservation Trust and the British Waterways Board restored the canal that now provides a fine navigable recreational route for boats, and excellent walking and cycling along its towpaths.

The Canal enters the area of this book at Semington Bridge (900611) and its total length from here to the Somerset boundary at Dundas Aqueduct in the Limpley Stoke Valley amounts to approximately ten miles over which the entire towpath may be walked. From Semington Bridge the canal runs west through open fields and after passing south of Whaddon through the south edge of Bradford on Avon where Bradford Wharf (825603) was constructed

Canal looking west oppos Bradford Tithe Barn

with a dry dock for repairing barges to enable the Bradford cloth trade to make use of the canal. From Bradford it continues its now tree-lined way past Barton Farm to Avoncliff along a hillside above the level of the parallel River Avon. To ensure that it held water the canal bed was 'puddled' with wet clay and its is said that herds of cattle were driven along it to trample and compact the puddling before the canal was filled with water. During the construction of the hillside stretch between Bradford and Avoncliff a seven-acre landslip occurred.

At Avoncliff the canal crosses the river over the imposing Avoncliff Aqueduct (804600) that was intended to be east of Avoncliff but was moved to its present position at the instigation of the canal's engineer Rennie. No one was prepared to tender for the foundations of this aqueduct and the coffer dams below water level were installed by a direct labour force which may explain the sagging of the structure that

Avoncliff Aqueduct

necessitated repairs that were inappropriately effected in brick. At the inside of the bend where the canal turns north to cross the aqueduct a standing stone bollard (at 805559) is scored with grooves made by tow ropes. Beyond Avoncliff the canal continues just within Wiltshire past Freshford. During its period of neglect the clay puddling between Avoncliff and Winsley Bridge failed in October 1954 and the canal was drained because it was feared that it would flood the railway. This stretch then remained dry for many years and I can remember walking along the bed of the canal from Avoncliff almost to Limpley Stoke when the canal bed was being concreted by its restorers in the 1970s.

Opposite Limpley Stoke (783609) the canal swings right and runs north along the west edge of Conkwell Wood and across the neck of a salient of Wiltshire that extends west to Midford. After about a mile it turns sharply west and crosses Dundas Aqueduct (784626) into Somerset, the Avon being here the county boundary. This aqueduct was like Avoncliff Aqueduct also moved during the construction of the canal from its planned position opposite the south end of Conkwell Wood to its present position almost a mile further north.

The canal near Dundas Aqueduct in 1962

The canal passes through much beautiful and tranquil countryside and its towpaths, that provide access to many interesting historical canal features, can also be incorporated with other rights-of-way into walks over much of the surrounding countryside. Canalside attractions east to west along the ten-mile reach of the canal covered by this book include a former wharf at Semington Bridge (901610), a small single-arched stone aqueduct over Summerham Brook west of Semington (897609), Hilperton Wharf between Staverton and Hilperton (now on the outskirts of Trowbridge at 860603), the Biss Aqueduct (855594) that carries the canal over the River Biss, Bradford Wharf (825603) at the south edge of the town, and the magnificent classical stone-built aqueducts that carry the canal across the River Avon. These are the Avoncliff Aqueduct (804600) and the Dundas Aqueduct (784626) near Limpley Stoke. The latter, that is named after Charles Dundas the first director of the canal company, is easily reached down a footpath from a lay-by on the A36 (at 783626).

The canal companies sometimes used tramways to fill any gaps where construction was difficult and also to link sources of heavy material with their canals, and topography of the Kennet and Avon in some places allowed stone from hilltop quarries to be lowered down gravity tramways to the canal. Such a tramway was opened from the quarry at Murhill (796605) in 1803 down which trundled stone-laden wagons to the canalside, the tramway being operated on the gravity principle by which the laden trucks as they descended raised the empty trucks back up to the quarry.. A little north of Murhill a quarry that operated on the same principle had in 1801 been opened by the Canal Company from a quarry at Conkwell to the canal beside Dundas Aqueduct, but when it was realised that the Conkwell stone was poor and the Murhill stone was found to be more satisfactory this tramway was superceded by the Murhill tramway. Another probably later stone tramway ran north from the quarries at Westwood downhill to Avoncliff and after passing east of the Old Court crossed the aqueduct along the west side of the canal and then turned west to a loading point (at 802601) where the stone was transferred to the canal barges to be transported away.

Canal at Dundas Aquedu

Dundas Aqueduct

The Great Western Railway

Mention of these tramways for transporting stone to the canal provides an appropriate introduction to the subject of the railways that were developed from them. Tramways using horse or man-drawn trucks were used in collieries as early as the reign of Charles I. Stationary steam engines were then developed for industrial use during the 18th century and the railway age was born in about 1830 when the mobile steam engine was invented. The network of railways that was then rapidly built throughout the country included the Great Western Railway that linked London to Bristol. It became affectionately known as 'God's Wonderful Railway' and soon consigned the stagecoaches on the western coach road to oblivion. The railway company also bought-out and soon virtually abandoned the Kennet and Avon Canal, although it might with advantage have been retained to carry very heavy goods.

The Kennet and Avon Canal had benefitted from the services of a very fine engineer in the Scottish-born John Rennie, but the Great Western Railway appointed an even greater engineer in Isambard Kingdom Brunel (1806-59) who had as a young man designed the Clifton Suspension Bridge at Bristol (1826-28) – which owing to lack of funds was only completed after his death – and the Bristol Floating Harbour (1830-31). In 1833 at the age of only twenty-seven he was appointed engineer to the GWR and in that capacity designed the tunnels, bridges, and viaducts along the line, including Box Tunnel that was commenced when he was thirty. While designing the GWR Brunel had his vision of extending his railway by steamship across the Atlantic and he ultimately designed three great steamships, the *Great Western* (1838), the *Great Britain* (1845), and the *Great Eastern* (1853-8) before dying in 1859, aged only 53 and worn out by overwork. While recognising the genius of Brunel the immense contribution to the GWR of the company's brilliant locomotive designer and superintendent Sir Daniel Gooch (1816-89) should not be overlooked.

Parliament required the railway developers to observe high standards of safety and provisions for the poor in the form of third-class transportation at a cost of only a penny a mile, but as the latter were not a paying proposition the railway companies deliberately made conditions spartan for third class passengers by carrying them in in unroofed open trucks without seats. They also derisively referred to them as 'goods passengers', and ran as few third-class trucks as possible.

Because it offered greater stability and potential for faster speeds Brunel decided to build the GWR to the wide gauge of 7 feet, although most railways had been and were still being built to a 4ft 8½ inch gauge which meant that where the gauges met all goods had to be transferred and passengers were obliged to change trains. This inevitably led to a 'gauge war' and despite the broad gauge emphatically winning competitive trials parliament ultimately decreed that the narrow gauge should be standard, their reasons being that it was cheaper to narrow rather than widen the gauge and that six times as much line had already been built to narrow gauge as to broad gauge. After experimenting for some time with a third rail that allowed mixed gauge operation the GWR in 1892 changed over to narrow gauge, it is said in a single weekend.

The route followed by the original main GWR line across north-west Wiltshire was from Chippenham south-west through Thingley

Junction (902705) and then south of Corsham and through Box Tunnel to Bath. The other GWR line that crosses the Wiltshire Cotswolds from Swindon to Bristol south of Malmesbury was built much later in 1903.

By May 1841 the only incomplete section of the main line from London to Bristol was the section from Chippenham to Bath which had involved much deep cutting and tunnelling through the limestone of Box Hill. The greatest engineering undertaking on the Bath line was the Box Tunnel that was built with an elaborate classically styled western portal which is best seen from the A4 (at 828688). The decision to tunnel for almost two miles through Box Hill had attracted great opposition when the GWR was proposed, but six permanent air shafts each 28 feet in diameter and one 300 feet deep from rail level to the surface were commenced in September 1836 and were completed by late

Box Tunnel West Portal

1837. Contracts were then placed for the tunnelling, one with George Burne of Herne Bay for three-quarters of the tunnel through clay and inferior oolite to be brick-lined, while the remaining unlined half-mile through solid limestone at the eastern end of the tunnel was allocated to Brewer of Box and Lewis of Bath. The tunnelling was supervised by Brunel's assistant Wiliam Glennie and its construction necessitated the use every week of a ton of gunpowder and a ton of candles, a hazardous combination of materials that may partly explain why a hundred workers lost their lives during construction of the tunnel. When informed that between September 1839 and June 1841 131 navvies had been taken to Bath hospital with bad injuries from the GWR workings Brunel commented that he considered this to be a 'small cost considering the very heavy works and the immense amount of powder involved'. The excavated material was lifted up the shafts in large buckets motivated by horse-gins on the surface, and in these buckets Brunel and his directors were periodically lowered to inspect the works – except for one who excused himself because his wife had forbidden it! The western end of the tunnel was lined with bricks brought on horse-drawn carts from a brickyard near Chippenham. The tunnel works became flooded in 1837 and 1838 and when the work fell behind schedule Brunel bolstered his workforce to 4000 men and 300 horses. When the tunnel was completed almost a year late in June 1841 its estimated cost of £6½ million had been doubled, but the stone excavated for the tunnel was used to construct the railway works and village at New Swindon, and was found to be of such good quality that new stone mines were opened at Corsham to exploit it.

Box railway station stood a short distance north-east of the A4 north of Ashley (at 815686) and where the A4 crosses the railway were loading sidings. The importance of the railway in the transportation of stone is illustrated by Sheet 31/86 of the First Series 1:25 000 Ordnance Survey map of about 1948 that shows the stone quarries south of Corsham linked to the railway by several miles of stone tramways. It must be emphasised that these lines were tramways and not steam-driven railways.

From London to Chippenham the GWR was so level that it became known as 'Brunel's billiard table', but the gradient of 1 in 100 through the tunnel caused Brunel some anxiety prior to the opening as it was severe for railway engines of the time. No real problems were however experienced and in June 1841 the first train passed through the tunnel laden with many passengers including the directors of the railway company, although the prospect of passing through Box Tunnel was too much for some early passengers who decided to by-pass it by taking the coach from Corsham to Box.

By providing cheap transportation of heavy building materials railways undermined vernacular styles of building that had always used local materials, as described by W. G. Hoskins in *The Making of the English Landscape* in 1955:

> What happened in Middlesex eventually happened all over England, and as Midland bricks and Welsh slates – and later more unspeakable materials like asbestos and corrugated iron – flooded into every corner of provincial England, the ancient local materials that fitted their own regions so well, for they came out of their very soil, disappeared one by one . . . All regional styles and all local materials were exterminated . . .

Box Hill from the railway tunnel west of Box

Within a few years of the opening in 1841 of the GWR through traffic on the Bath road had virtually ceased, its coaching inns and relay stables

were closed down, and travelling from London and the east to Bristol and Bath across the Wiltshire Cotswolds had been changed for ever.

Box and its Roman Villa

*East end of Box looking e
towards Box F*

T HE LARGE VILLAGE OF BOX (824684) in its beautiful undulating countryside six miles east of Bath is an interesting place of great historical interest. Beside its church are the remains of a large Roman villa, the village was on the line of the former Bath coach road and has several former coaching inns, and around Box are the ancient mines and quarries that since Anglo-Saxon and probably Roman times have been a principal source of the famous Bath stone. Through Box runs Brunel's Great Western Railway, and nearby is the famous railway tunnel that bears the name of the village (see earlier, page 192). When to these attractions are added its situation in the valley of the By Brook with picturesque hills rising to its north and south, and the existence nearby of such attractive places as Hazelbury, Chapel Plaister, Kingsdown, Ditteridge and Colerne, readers may appreciate why I find Box to be a much underrated place that I always enjoy visiting.

Most of its buildings scramble up the hill south of the By Brook that is here sometimes known as the Box Brook. In 1181 the village was called *la Boxe* and Aubrey's suggestion that 'in all probability it took its name from the Box-trees which grew there naturally, but are now worne-out' has been vindicated as the name is now recognised to be derived from the Old English *box* meaning box tree. The stone for building Box came from several local quarries and at Box Hill the Quarryman's Arms public house (836694) stands on the steep hillside among former quarrymens' cottages on a network of lanes (for information on the Box stone quarries see pages 31-6).

The towered and spired Box Church is largely 14th century but has in its north wall a classical stone pedimented doorcase dating from 1713. In its churchyard are a number of the fine limestone table tombs and headstones that feature in so many Cotswold graveyards and are as much monuments to their masons' art as to those they commemorate. One small pyramidal tombstone is said to commemorate a man who was determined to thwart his wife's threat to dance on his grave!

Across the lane from the church is the site of a large Roman villa described in an article in *The Gentleman's Magazine* for 1831 that was subsequently reprinted in Volume 26 of *Wiltshire Archaeological Magazine*. The Romans would have been attracted to this site by the

Box tombs in Box Churchyard

spring that still gushes out of the limestone rock and cascades through a garden gate down to the By Brook at a point where the stream flows swiftly and dippers are sometimes seen. Long after the Romans had left Monkton Farleigh Priory owned Box and the prior rebuilt the church and constructed on the villa site a Medieval water mill whose mill house was later incorporated into the adjacent house called The Wilderness in whose garden the spring rises. This spring is presumably the well described by Aubrey as the 'medecinall well in the street at Box, near Bathe, which has been used ever since 1670'.

Box Roman villa was large and L-shaped in plan with legs measuring 174 feet east to west and 216 feet north to south. It was built of limestone rubble rather than of freestone, and when excavated in 1881-2 was found to have contained many rooms, some with hypocausts, at least one with a mosaic floor, and one with a small sunken bath. Some painted plaster was found, together with some carved Roman capitals and a sculpture of a huntsman suggesting that this part of Wiltshire may have been popular with the Romans for hunting.

Box Church from the north

During the Interregnum the authorities decided to get rid of the the vicar of Box, the Rev. Walter Bushnell. It was alleged that he had been guilty of drinking and gambling, and he boldly defended himself, but the puritans prevailed and he was replaced by a man called John Stern. The people however did not much like their puritan minister and in 1658, the year of Cromwell's death, he was harangued in his pulpit by his parishioners who were no doubt pleased to see the Rev. Bushnell reinstated at the Restoration in 1660, although he died in 1664.

The Bear and the Queen's Head at Box were coaching inns that once served travellers on the Bath Road, and the 18th century lock-up beside the

By Brook opposite Box Roman Villa

Queen's Head is one of the 'blind houses' that are found in many west Wiltshire towns and villages. A short distance to its east is the 17th century Manor Farmhouse and its attached barn, now rather incongruously at the centre of the busy village. South-west of Box Andrews and Dury in 1773 show south-east of Ashley 'Box Mad House' (at 817677) that is now Kingsdown House and is divided into eight dwellings.

Box Blind House

The association of Box with the poet Coleridge will be described later (on pages 196-9) but a lesser literary association of the village is as the burial place of Henrietta Maria Bowdler (1754-1830) who with her brother Thomas Bowdler (1754-1825) edited a ten-volume *Family Shakespeare* (1818) in which 'those words and expressions are omitted that cannot with propriety be read aloud in a family'. The degree of Henrietta's contribution to the book is unclear, although she is generally regarded as the principal author. The popularity of their book encouraged the Bowdlers to make a similar assault on Gibbon's *Decline and Fall of the Roman Empire*, but they became ridiculed for their prudery and their surname provided us with the word 'bowdlerism'.

Coleridge at Box

A MORE IMPORTANT LITERARY ASSOCIATION of Box is with the poet Samuel Taylor Coleridge (1772-1834) who collaborated with Wordsworth on their *Lyrical Ballads* that instigated the early-19th century Romantic Revival in poetry and influenced similar revivals in the other arts. Coleridge was associated with a number places in Wiltshire, one of these being the hamlet of Ashley beside the coach road immediately west of Box (at 814684).

After abandoning family life because of his opium addiction Coleridge regularly sought out benefactors willing to take him in as a

Coleridge

lodger-patient. His drinking and drug-taking made him such a difficult house guest that he was described by Wordsworth as 'an absolute nuisance who rotted his guts out by intemperence'. After having resided for some time with the Wordsworths, when suffering from a drug-related illness he was in 1807 received into the home of a Bristol lawyer called John Morgan who admired his work and believed that he could help him over his addiction. The two men became like brothers and Coleridge admired his benefactor's wife Mary. He was also evidently attracted to her unmarried younger sister Charlotte Brent who lived with the family, and under the influence of opium imagined himself married to both ladies. After returning to London he wrote a long poem 'To Two Sisters, A Wanderer's Farewell', but he continued to maintain a close friendship with the Morgans and when in 1812 they moved into a London house he shared it with them until March 1813 when Morgan was taken ill after his investments failed due to wartime inflation. By October he was bankrupt and had fled to Ireland to escape his creditors.

The London house was sold and with Mary Morgan and her sister Charlotte practically destitute Coleridge assumed an entirely new role as provider for the family. Being such a brilliant talker that a landlord had once provided him with free accommodation merely in order to enjoy his conversation, he undertook a lecture tour in Bristol to raise funds for the Morgans and then, with Mr Morgan still absent in Ireland, proposed a trip west to find cheap accommodation for the family. On 29 November 1813 he together with Mary and Charlotte set out on a four-day journey by post-chaise along the London to Bath coach road. At Ashley, that was then known as Ashley Green, they found lodgings in a cottage with a Box grocer called Mrs Smith as their landlady.

At this time the coach road left the present A4 a little west of Box cemetery and followed the line of the minor road that loops slightly to its south through Ashley as is confirmed by the surviving milestones. It has often been alleged that Coleridge hurriedly left his lodgings at Box

Ashley trees and Manor House

when he found that his grocer landlord was storing explosives under his bed, but I am rather sceptical about this, as the excavation of Box Tunnel that provided one of the principal local demands for explosives only began in 1840, several years after Coleridge died and twenty-seven years after this 1813 visit. Explosives may however have been used in the local stone-quarrying.

The real explanation for Coleridge's hurried departure from the cottage at Ashley was that some untoward event occurred. He suddenly left late on Sunday 5 December and, having missed the last coach, in heavy rain carried his portmanteau of books into Bath. This would have been along the old route, now a minor road, a little south of the A4 through Ashley along the shoulder of Kingsdown and down to the present A4 at Box Bridge. We may imagine Coleridge finding from the surviving milestone at Ashley (813684) that he was committed to a five-mile walk in the rain into Bath. It seems that he may in a drunken or opium-related condition have attempted to take some advantage of the destitute ladies who were now so dependent on him.

At Bath he booked into the Greyhound Inn and there went through a spiritual crisis during which he re-affirmed his christian beliefs, acknowledged his drug addiction, and admitted that he had behaved badly towards Mary and Charlotte. The quarrel was however patched up and after the Morgan family moved to Ashley on a more permanent basis Coleridge was in June and July 1814 making regular weekend visits and in September became in his own words: 'joint tenant with Mr Morgan of a sweet little cottage at Ashley, half a mile from Box, on the Bath road'. Some buildings that Coleridge would have known at Ashley are Ashley Farm beside the coach road and Ashley Manor House that stands a short distance up the steep lane called Doctor's Hill that becomes a track called Wormcliffe Lane as it runs south past Sheylor's

Bath Road Milestone at Ashley

Ashley Farm

Ashley Manor House

Farm (811677). I have been unable to find a cottage of an appropriate age to have been Coleridge's lodgings, and suspect that it has been demolished or rebuilt.

Chapel Plaister and Hazelbury Manor

ONE OF THE DUTIES of abbeys and monasteries was to provide hospitality for wayfarers and prior to the Dissolution of the monasteries they built hospices that provided facilities for travellers. This was mentioned by Aubrey when he wrote that for people on pilgrimages: 'In the roads hither were several houses of entertainment built purposely for them', and he specifically nominated Chapel Plaister (840678), a mile east of Box, as being a hospice for Glastonbury pilgrims. 'Plaister' means play space or village green and this hospice stands beside a large green open space on the pilgrim route from Malmesbury to Glastonbury. It was built towards the end of the Gothic period in about 1460, less than a hundred years before the Dissolution and seems originally to have consisted of a chapel, a dormitory, and a priest's room all on one floor, but the building was subsequently widened and a first floor was created with external steps to the upper level. Two miles south of Chapel Plaister and a little south of that Roman road another hospice formerly existed near South Wraxall Manor House (page 217-18), as did another on the hill at Bradford on Avon (page 254).

The first mention of Chapel Plaister appears in a licence issued by Bishop Robert Wyvill of Salisbury to the vicar of Hazelbury entitling him to preach in the 'chapel of Pleistede in his parish of Hazelbury'. At the Reformation in about 1540 many hospices became secular inns as seems to have occurred here as Aubrey tells us that in his time in the 17th century Chapel Plaister was an alehouse. In 1790 the Bell Inn seems to have occupied the adjoining building and continued to

Chapel Plaister Hospice from south

be an inn until at least about 1850. An old print shows it with its inn sign casually hanging from a branch of a tree.

Chapel Plaister in 1790

In the time of Queen Anne Chapel Plaister was a private dwelling and it then became successively a bakery, a lumber room and, at the time when highwaymen were preying upon travellers using the western road, a hideaway for the notorious Wiltshire highwayman Tom Baxter (alias Poulter) who was hanged at Salisbury. Highwaymen at that time regularly worked the Bath Road and the London innkeeper and writer Ned Ward (1667-1731) described in *A Step to Bath* (1700) how at Marlborough on his way by coach to Bath he was warned that 'a party of Light Horse [Highwaymen] lay hidden, perchance to ease us of our

South front of Hazelbury Manor House

Rhino', 'Rhino' being 17th century slang for valuables. In 1893 Chapel Plaister reverted to ecclesiastical use as a result of the exertions of the Rev. Spooner.

Beside a footpath a few hundred yards south-east of Chapel Plaister is the monument to the African explorer John Hanning Speke who here met a violent death when out shooting (see pages 207-9).

Between Chapel Plaister and Box is Hazelbury Manor (836684), once a seat of the Spekes, that dates partly from the 15th century although Pevsner, after drawing attention to its 'most spectacular features',pointed out that Hazelbury was

Hazelbury in 1790

partly reconstructed in the 20th century and that it contains features brought in from elsewhere. A 1630 estate map marks the enclosure around the house extending east as far as the B3109 and designates it 'Hiselburie Warren' indicating that it was once a rabbit or hare warren. Hazelbury also formerly had a church associated with it in a field immediately to its north-west where stone coffins have been found.

Although public rights-of-way pass Hazelbury the nearest public road is the B3109 from Bradford to Corsham from which Hazelbury may be reached by a 600 yard walk each way from a lay-by a little north of Chapel Plaister (at 841683).

Corsham

BY REFERRING TO IT as a 'tounelet' Leland reflected the fact that in his time Corsham was too large for a village and rather small for a town. It has now gradually expanded over such a large area that it is now undeniably a town, of which Sir Nikolaus Pevsner wrote: 'Corsham has no match in Wiltshire for wealth of good houses. There are in fact no bad ones, and there are a few of really high merit'.

Corsham lies three miles east of Box and like Box lies mainly south of the former Bath coach road that is now the A4. Its 'wealth of good houses' mentioned by Pevsner are too numerous to describe here and a leisurely town stroll is recommended to see them, making sure not to miss the multi-gabled Flemish cottages in the High Street that are built in a style that would not look of place in such a Cotswold show-place as Chipping Campden.

In Anglo-Saxon times Edward the Confessor gave the manor of Corsham to his brother-in-law Earl Tostig of Northumbria (c. 1025-1066) who became a traitor and died fighting with the Danish invaders at

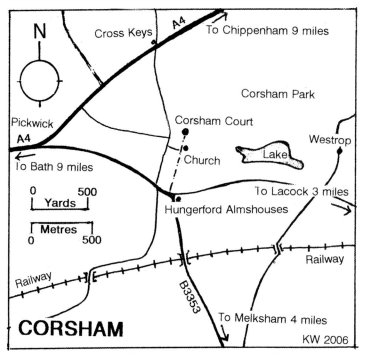

Stamford Bridge against his elder brother King Harold. Corsham then reverted to the Crown and was many years later granted by Henry III to his younger brother Richard Plantagenet, the Earl of Cornwall (1209-72) (see later, pages 204-5). Richard in a grant to his Corsham tenants mentions two parks, one being the home park beside the present Corsham Court and the other an out-park near Hudswell in the west of Corsham where the name Park Road survives today in a now built-up area.

Flemish Cottages, Corsham

Leland in 1542 mentioned the ruinous condition of the manor house at Corsham and ten years later Corsham was granted by Queen Elizabeth to her favourite godson Sir Christopher Hatton (1540-91) who soon sold it to Thomas Smyth, a local man who was known as 'Customer' Smyth. This son of a Corsham yeoman, after going to London and marrying the heiress of Sir Andrew Judde, became one of the great entrepreneurs of the Elizabethan age. At that time custom receipts were farmed out to individuals and Smyth was from 1557 the collector of the lucrative customs dues of the port of London. After 1579 he then made more money out of tin and copper-mining, but he was alleged to be corrupt which may explain why he was never knighted. Having made a vast fortune he acquired a great deal of property in Kent and some in his home town of Corsham.

Corsham Court from its Park

The Wiltshire Cotswolds contain a number of small to medium-sized manor houses of exceptional architectural quality but they lack any mansion house of the national importance of Longleat, Wilton or Stourhead elsewhere in Wiltshire. Corsham Court might have been such a house had it not lost some of its architectural validity because successive architects have extended and often obliterated the work of their predecessors. 'Customer' Smyth, after in 1582 replacing the ruin described by Leland with an Elizabethan house, sold the manor in 1602 to Sir Edward Hungerford (d.1648) and the Hungerfords then retained Corsham for it many years until they sold it to the Thynnes of Longleat who in turn sold it in 1745 to the Bradford on Avon clothier Paul Methuen whose family still own it. In 1761-64 Methuen altered the house employing the landscape designer 'Capability' Brown (1716-83) as his architect. He added a picture gallery to the east front of Smyth's Elizabethan house and on the west front a library that became a breakfast room. Henry Keene (1726-76) in 1759-64 rebuilt the north front for Paul Methuen, and from 1800 John Nash (1752-1835) in partnership with Humphrey Repton (1752-1818) rebuilt Keene's north front in the Gothic style. In 1844-50 most of Nash and Repton's work was remodelled by an architect called Bellamy and it was these successive makeovers that prompted Pevsner to write of Corsham Court that 'little of the outside and hardly anything of the inside is Elizabethan'. The house is however open to the public and is well worth visiting for its situation in a fine park, its fine collection of paintings, and its superb rococo plasterwork executed by Thomas Stocking senior (1722-1808) of Bristol during

Corsham Court through gate to its south

'Capability' Brown's reconstruction. His work at Corsham was Stocking's most important commission and for it between 1763 and 1766 he was paid £570 by Paul Methuen for plastering the state rooms, the library, and the coffered ceiling of the long gallery.

The south front of Corsham Court may be seen from near the church through a large triple-arched rusticated baroque gateway that is aligned with a tree avenue that runs south to an even bigger gateway at the road at the east end of Corsham. Practically all signs of the former Medieval deer park east of Corsham Court were destroyed by the landscaping by 'Capability' Brown in 1760-65 and Humphrey Repton in 1799, but the present park may be explored along its public rights-of-way, one of which runs from Corsham churchyard north-east past the west end of the lake. Corsham's former West Park at the other end of the town has been obliterated by modern building that makes it impossible to imagine a deer park ever having existed here.

The most celebrated members of the Methuen family were John Methuen (d. 1706) and Paul Sandford Methuen, the 3rd Baron Methuen (1845-1932). After 'England's oldest ally' Portugal, which had imported a great deal of English cloth, but in the late-17th century developed its own cloth industry the clothier John Methuen was sent to Portugal to negotiate the Methuen Treaty (1703) by which in return for preferential duties on port wine admitted into England English cloth was re-admitted into Portugal. Paul Sandford Methuen, the 3rd Baron Methuen, was the British general who won several battles during the Boer War and became commander-in-chief in South Africa 1908-12, governor of Natal from 1909 to 1915, and then governor of Malta and of the Tower of London.

A more important person associated with Corsham was Richard Plantagenet (1209-72), a son of King John and younger brother of Henry III. For most of the 13th century Richard, who was named after his uncle Richard I, held Corsham. During the misrule of Henry he frequently arbitrated between King Henry and his barons, and he achieved the distinction of being the only Englishman to become King of the Romans

– that is king of the Holy Roman Empire, the title by which the rulers of Germany had become known since Otto I had been crowned Emperor of the Holy Roman Empire in AD 963.

The Hungerford Almshouses

OPPOSITE THE SOUTH GATES of Corsham Park at the east end of Corsham are the 17th century Hungerford Almshouses and Free School (873701) which commemorate the Hungerfords who once owned Corsham where the parish church has the Hungerford arms carved on its porch and the remains of some old glass with the Hungerford sickle and a wheatsheaf badge in one of its windows. Their presence at Corsham appears to date from June 1483 when the Yorkist usurper Richard III granted the keepership of 'West and Home Park within the Lordship of Corsham for the term of his life' to a Hungerford, probably in an attempt to enlist the support of that family which during the Wars of the Roses had generally supported the House of Lancaster. The Hungerfords then made a number of advantageous marriages to rich heiresses, and further enhanced their prosperity by assisting Thomas Cromwell in his suppression of the monasteries. They lost Corsham when the family fortunes were dissipated by the spendthrift Sir Edward Hungerford (1632-1711) who, after gaining a reputation as an archer, in 1661 became lieutenant-colonel and in 1682 colonel of the Regiment of Archers. After being made a Knight of the Bath at the Restoration he lived recklessly and after gambling away the immense Hungerford fortunes became known as 'the spendthrift'. On one occasion he was said on the bowling green to have cried 'Here goes Rowden' as he delivered the bowl by which he lost the manor of Rowden at Chippenham that had been owned by the Hungerfords since 1484. Besides losing thirty manors

The Hungerford Almshouses

in 1669 he also lost his London town house Hungerford House, on this occasion by fire rather than by gambling. Sir Edward was obliged to sell Corsham but in an attempt to salvage something of his fortune he founded as a speculation Hungerford Market on the site of his ruined London house that is now occupied by Charing Cross Station, with beside it Hungerford Bridge that perpetuates the family name in London.

This man's parents Sir Edward and Lady Margaret lived in Corsham Court after their wedding in 1621, and forty years after her husband's death Corsham Almshouses and Free School were built in 1688 by Dame Margaret Hungerford as one of the last of the many Hungerford gifts to the people of Wiltshire before the Hungerford fortunes were finally lost. This large L-shaped almshouse consists of six dwellings for old people, a cloister, a master's house, and a free school with a schoolroom that still contains its original furnishings. It's north facade on the minor road to Lacock is like so many Cotswold style almshouses traditionally multi-gabled, but its west entrance front is in a style that is transitional between Tudor and Classical. The building is stone-slated with a cupola and a gabled projecting porch with above it a large cartouche of the Halliday arms of Lady Margaret. The

The Hungerford Almshouses, detail of porc

doorcase incorporates a pair of debased Ionic columns aptly described by Pevsner as 'bulgy', and some of its windows are flat-arched and latticed in the Tudor style. A comparison between these almshouses and the slightly later Hall's Almshouse at Bradford is made on pages 249-50.

Outer Corsham

CORSHAM NOW EXTENDS over a large area and several places loosely associated with it are of historical interest. At Lower Pickwick on the A4 former Bath coach road is Pickwick Manor (863705), a fine 17th century manor house described by Pevsner as 'unusually impressive' with a 14th century wing with cross windows. A mile and a half east of Corsham Court the charming hamlet of Easton (890706) contains a number of good stone cottages and the 18th century Easton House that belonged to the Longs before it was bought by Lord Methuen.

At the west edge of the stone-quarrying district a mile south-east of Corsham is the district that gave its name of Monk's Park to the Bath freestone quarried nearby. An exquisite little 17th century congregational chapel known as Monk's (876686) in Monk's Lane was originally built by the Quakers. It contains its original pews and elevated pulpit and galleries intact. Externally it has a stone-slated roof with its eaves swept up in a gentle 'eyebrow' curve over a three-light segmental-headed window above a central door that is flanked on each side by a single

Monk's Chapel, near Corsham

window. Over the central window under the curved eaves is carved the following text from *Ecclesiastes* 5:

KEEP THY FOOT WHEN THOU GOEST TO THE HOUSE OF GOD

In 1594 at some unknown location in or about Corsham Sir Henry Long was murdered by Sir Charles Danvers (1568-1603) and Sir Henry Danvers (1569-1644) accompanied by a gang of their retainers. The story was related by John Aubrey and by Canon Jackson in volume 1 of the *Wiltshire Archaeological Magazine*, but the reason for the murder and why the perpetrators were pardoned remain a mystery. Charles Danvers was executed in 1601 for his part in the Essex rebellion but Henry Danvers prospered under James I and became First Baron Danvers of Dauntsey.

Speke's death in Neston Park

TWO HUNDRED AND SEVENTY YEARS after the murder at Corsham just described another violent death occurred near Corsham when Captain John Hanning Speke (1827-64), who had claimed to have discovered the source of the River Nile, died violently when shooting partridges near Neston Park (862672).

The source of the River Nile had for long been a matter for intense speculation that reached its zenith in Victorian times when central Africa was being opened up, and in 1857 Captain Speke was appointed to assist the more experienced Richard Burton (1829-90) on an expedition in search of the Nile source. The two men were dissimilar in character and in intellect and during the expedition Speke grew to resent Burton's leadership. While the latter lay sick in camp Speke went out alone and returned claiming to have discovered that Lake Victoria Nyansa was the principal source of the Nile. This claim failed to convince Burton who disputed Speke's findings and they quarrelled. We cannot now know whether Burton's arose from genuine disbelief or the prospect of having the prestigious discovery snatched from him. Speke after returning to England ahead of Burton in 1859 voiced criticisms of his colleague and after returning to Africa with another companion claimed he had by further exploration confirmed his conclusions. To settle the acrimonious dispute a public debate was arranged by the British Association for the Advancement of Science at Bath on 16 September 1864, to be attended by Burton, Speke and Dr Livingstone, who was inclined to support Speke.

Burton was much the senior of the two men and was also an intellectual and a brilliant public speaker. After being expelled from Oxford University he had served in the Indian army and become an explorer, an oriental scholar, and a brilliant linguist who had mastered many languages and also achieved some notoriety by translating and publishing erotic oriental literature. Being much less sophisticated and not at his best in public debate, Speke would have been very much aware of Burton's reputation as in the words of his biographer 'a brawler in his youth and a literary brawler in maturity', and must have been anxious about the forthcoming debate. While staying with his Fuller relatives at Neston Park on the eve of the debate he went out shooting partridges accompanied by his cousin Mr George Fuller and a gamekeeper called Daniel Davis. They worked their

way west to a point between Wadswick and Wormwood Farm where long stretches of dry-stone wall range across the countryside. There, when he was clambering over a wall, Speke's Lancaster shotgun discharged one of its barrels into his chest and, after pleading : 'Don't move me', he died within about fifteen minutes. His body was taken for burial to his ancestral home at Dowlish Wake near Ilminster in Somerset and at the precise spot where he died (at 843673 a short distance north of Wormwood Farm up the footpath that runs north out of the A365) the incident is commemorated by a railed monument with the following inscription :'

HERE THE DISTINGUISHED AND ENTERPRISING
AFRICAN TRAVELLER, CAPTAIN JOHN HANNING SPEKE,
LOST HIS LIFE IN AN ACCIDENTAL EXPLOSION OF HIS
GUN, SEPTEMBER 15, 1864.

The question inevitably arises was Speke's death accidental? Burton had once commented on the extreme care with which Speke handled firearms and how he invariably ensured that no loaded gun was ever allowed to 'look at' anyone. Despite this and the improbability that a such an experienced soldier and sportsman would have been careless when handling a firearm, the coroner at the inquest held in Neston Park returned a verdict of 'Accidental death by explosion of a gun'. It was however widely believed that Speke had taken his own life. When told of the circumstances of his death Burton was heard to say : 'By God, he's killed himself!', and he later wrote : 'The charitable say that he shot himself, the uncharitable that I shot him'.

Burton outlived Speke by twenty-six years and was still living in 1875 when the American explorer Stanley after circumnavigating Lake Victoria Nyanza by boat confirmed Speke's opinion that this lake was the source of the Nile. This was generally accepted until 2006 when three reputable explorers claimed to have found the Nile's source in a National Park in Rwanda about 150 miles west of Lake Victoria. It appears that Burton after all may have been justified in disputing Speke's claim.

Atworth and Wick Farm

LESS THAN A MILE SOUTH of Neston Park lies Atworth (862660), a linear village that is strung out along the A365 Melksham to Box road with its older part down a lane that branches west out of that road to Bradford on Avon. Off this lane stands Atworth's modern church (859658) that was built in 1832 to the design of the Bath

architect H. E. Goodridge and linked
to the retained Perpendicular tower of
its predecessor. Near the church on the
east side of the road to Bradford stands
an elegant early-18th century five-bay
manor house (861657) with segmental
headed windows and panelled gatepiers that are now bereft of their
finials. In front of Atworth school a
small sheep market was held in the
early-19th century at which the sheep
were penned behind the school in the
field called The Pennings.

　　　In a field north-west of Atworth and a little south of the Roman
road to Bath a schoolboy in the 1930s picked up a Roman coin in a field.
His schoolmaster realised its significance and an excavation in 1937-8
revealed an L-shaped corridor type Roman villa (at 856664 beside the
A365) dating from four distinct periods. Loose *tesserae* were found but
no tesselated floors or hypocausts and of the many coins found on the
site only two were dated after AD 360. It was concluded that in about
AD 350-400 the villa's bath suite was dismantled and adapted to some
farming usage, probably for grain drying.

　　　In the rather unfrequented area three miles north-east of Atworth,
between Gastard and Lacock and immediately west of the railway line,
stands Wick Farm (902679) that was described in old deeds as a 'mannor
or reputed mannor'. In its farmyard stands a circular dovecote that
apparently confirms the farm's former status as a manor house as

Dovecot at Wick Farm

dovecotes were a seigneurial privilige. They were often built
circular in plan to allow the 'potence', a pair of ladders
bracketed off a heavy central spindle, to rotate round the
inside of the wall to facilitate easy removal of the edible baby
pigeons, known as 'squabs', from the nesting apertures. The
Wick Farm dovecot has at some time been converted to other
uses by the insertion of a door opposite its tiny original 15th
century access door.

　　　Wick was in early times a secondary manor to Lacock
known as 'Carlo's Wick' and associated with Hazelbury
Manor five miles to its west. Of the Wick estate Domesday
indicates that : 'Carlo held all the before-mentioned lands in
the time of King Edward'. In 1282 Wick was owned by
Reginald Croc II who obtained it by marrying Joan, a
daughter of Richard of Wick. Some evidence suggests that
Reginald was a member of the household of Edward I's queen

...worth Church

Elcanor of Castile. Wick then remained with the Crocs (who became the Crokes) until 1475 when the Croke heiress Anne married John Bonham of Lacock and the Bonhams then lived at Wick and Hazelbury. The *Feet of Fines* show them at Hazelbury in 1475 with Alice Croke who may have been Anne's mother. John Bonham's Will was proved in 1503, but after the 16th century Wick declined in status and in the reign of Elizabeth Sir Henry Sharington of Lacock purchased Wick from a later John Bonham. A 1685 document of settlement describes Wick as: 'the mannor, or reputed mannor, messuage, tenement, and farme, with the appurtenances commonly knowne by the name of Charles Weake, alias Weeke, alias Weake Farme, situate and being in Laycocke, etc'.

Andrews and Dury on their 1773 map show a short distance east of Wick Farm a now much-reduced square woodland (910675) that was landscaped with straight rides and designated 'The Fair Sister' and 'Inwood'. Its otherwise oddly isolated position suggests that this landscaped area may have been associated with Wick when it was a more important house, particularly as the formal style of the layout suggests a 17th or very early-18th century date rather than the late-18th century when landscaping had generally become informal.

Monkton Farleigh

THIS UPLAND VILLAGE (at 806653) derives its name meaning 'monks' fern clearing' from having been the site of one of the alien priories that were founded by the Anglo-Norman magnates in England, generally in the 13th century. They became known as alien priories because they were allied to priories in Continental homelands of their Norman founders.

Roman presence in Monkton Farleigh parish was established in 1826 by the discovery in Warleigh Wood (at 802633) of evidence,

Monkton Farleigh Church and Rectory

including a pot of Roman coins, of a Romano-British settlement. The
village contains a 13th century church that was remodelled in 1844, and
a large elaborately-glazed 19th century Gothick rectory north of the
church. On the county boundary about a mile north-west of Monkton
Farleigh is a substantial square tower known as Brown's Folly (794662)
that was built overlooking the valley of the Avon in about 1840 allegedly
for surveying purposes by a local quarry owner Mr Wade Brown, but
the principal building of interest at Monkton Farleigh is its former
Clunaic priory and the manor house that now occupies its site. The priory
was founded in 1125 and was made dependant upon the Abbey of Cluny
in Burgundy, its founder being Maud, a daughter of Edward Earl of
Salisbury and the wife of Humphrey de Bohun II, the Lord of nearby
Trowbridge Castle. Their son Humphrey de Bohun III later endowed and
enlarged the priory (for more information on the de Bohuns see Oaksey,
page 57).

Monkton Farleigh Cond
Hou

During the Hundred Years War (1337-1453) with France alien
monasteries were unpopular with the English monarchs because they
remitted revenue from English estates to the enemy. Many were then
confiscated but some Clunaic priories escaped by transferring their
allegiance to the oldest Clunaic house in England at Lewes. By this means
Monkton Farleigh Priory survived until the Dissolution, although in a
probable attempt at confiscation it was taken into the king's ownership
in 1294 it and may have escaped because in 1276 all of its monks were
English. In 1409 the priory was held jointly by Lord Stourton and Sir
Walter Hungerford, possibly on behalf of the Crown in another attempt
at confiscation although the monarch at that time was Henry IV whose
queen was Mary de Bohun, one of the two de Bohun heiresses.

At the Dissolution of the monasteries in the 1540s Thomas
Cromwell's agent Layton implied misbehaviour by the monks by
describing Monkton Farleigh Priory as 'a very stews'. He also indicated
that the priory had been 'gyven to the Earl of Hertford' (that was Edward
Seymour who became Protector Somerset), and from Bristol he sent to
Cromwell some 'strange things' confiscated from Monkton Farleigh
including : 'Mary Magdelen's girdle wrapped and covered with silver,
which girdle Matilda the Empress, one of the founders of Farley, gave
unto them, as says the holy father of Farley'. By 1540 the the buildings
of the priory had probably been demolished by Hertford for its materials
and its site was used as a rabbit warren, but in 1550 Hertford exchanged
it with the Bishop of Salisbury for property elsewhere. Some ecclesiastical
rebuilding may then have taken place as in 1571 Bishop Jewel of Salisbury
(1522-71), a leading churchman of his age and an early advocate of
English protestantism, died at Monkton Farleigh a few days after
preaching at Lacock.

Manor House, east j

The priory must then have finally fallen into lay hands as a manor house was built on the site incorporating a few parts of the priory and retaining the 14th century Monks' Conduit House with its steeply pitched stone-slabbed roof. This tiny building survives a short distance west of the manor house (at 803656) standing over the spring that had supplied water to the priory. It may be approached along a footpath that runs west past a farm at the bend in the road (806657) at the north-west corner of the village.

The manor house was extended in the 17th century and in the 18th century its east front facing down the long beech avenue towards South Wraxall was given a new facade in a style that superficially appears to

Avenue looking east

be Georgian-Palladian and was attributed by the *Wiltshire Victoria County History* to John Wood of Bath. Having spent almost sixty years studying history of architecture, fifty years studying English Palladianism, and practising as an architect for many years during which I worked on buildings designed by John Wood, I believe this attribution to be on stylistic grounds unlikely. John Wood was essentially a strict

Palladian who designed in strict conformity with the buildings and published design manuals (the *Quattro Libri* or *Four Books of Architecture*) of the Italian architect Andrea Palladio. Many features of this east front of Monkton Farleigh Manor House are distinctly un-Palladian and no work at Monkton Farleigh is attributed to either of the John Woods by H. M. Colvin in his definitive *Biographical Dictionary of English Architects, 1660-1840* (1954).

The writers of the *Victoria County History* do not quote their authority, but if they found evidence of Wood having worked at Monkton Farleigh it does not preclude the possibility that any work that he did there was subsequently altered. The Victorians were never bound by strict Palladian principles, they often debased architectural styles of earlier periods. The east facade of Monkton Farleigh Manor House seems to me to be eminently Victorian and Professor Pevsner also expressed this opinion when he described it as being apparently 'an Early Victorian remodelling of an Early Georgian front'. '

South Wraxall

THE ATTRACTIVE stone-built village of South Wraxall (833647) may be reached by walking a mile and a half from Monkton Farleigh along the footpath that runs east down the tree-lined avenue from Monkton Farleigh. South Wraxall was *Wroxhal* in 1227 and *Suthwroxhall* in 1468. From the 15th century most of the manor was owned by the Longs, a family with a history that is complicated because they were so numerous and they owned many estates after prospering from their support of the Lancastrian Hungerfords, as mentioned by Henry VIII's antiquary Leland when he wrote : 'One long Thomas, a stoute felaw, was sette up by one of the old lord Hungerfordes, and after by cause this Thomas was called Long Thomas, Long was usurped as the name of the family'. The family badge was the fetter-lock, a crude padlock device used for shackling horses by the leg. Representations of fetter-locks were often carved on buildings built by the Longs and appear on the gatehouse of South Wraxall Manor and on the tomb chest surmounted by a recumbant effigy in the Long chapel of South Wraxall Church where a window contains multi representations of fetter-locks in stained glass.

The first Long recorded at South Wraxall was Robert, a Wiltshire MP in 1433 who probably built the original manor house about half a mile north of the village. At the time in the early-15th century when this house was built England was becoming more pacified and country houses were developing from being fortified houses into more comfortable dwellings and with glass then becoming more available

South Wraxall Manor House

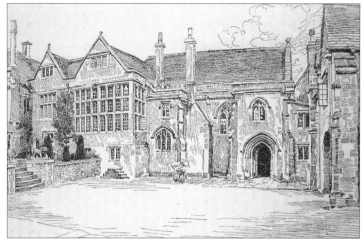

houses were beginning to be built with larger windows for comfort more than for defence. South Wraxall Manor House is stone-built with a stone-slated roof and a south-west front with many gables, large bay windows, a variety of chimneys, pointed door openings with drip-moulds, some Gothic pointed windows also with drip-moulds, and large square-headed multi-light windows divided up by stone mullions and transomes. In the 16th century Sir Thomas Long added the gatehouse with its fine oriel window that lights the first floor porter's room, and the adjacent buildings that link the gatehouse to the original house. More alterations were added in the late-16th and early-17th centuries by Sir Walter Long (died 1610) who created within the house an extraordinary bombastic Elizabethan style drawing room that Professer Pevsner suggested 'can hardly be matched anywhere in lavishness'. The overall impression created by this house is of constant adaptation and extension that have fortunately not degraded it in any respect and South Wraxall Manor House is regarded as one of the finest examples of 15th century domestic architecture in Wiltshire. It was described by Edward Hutton in 1917 as 'noble and beautiful' and by Pevsner in 1963 as : 'an outstandingly successful mixture of the C15 and the later Elizabethan and Jacobean'. South Wraxall also admirably fulfils most of the criteria listed for the ideal working Wiltshire manor house by John Aubrey when he wrote :

Gateway to South Wraxall Manor House

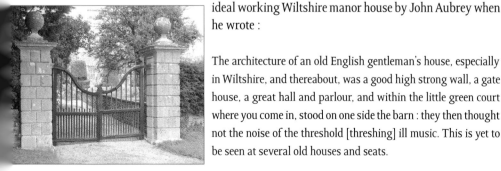

The architecture of an old English gentleman's house, especially in Wiltshire, and thereabout, was a good high strong wall, a gate house, a great hall and parlour, and within the little green court where you come in, stood on one side the barn : they then thought not the noise of the threshold [threshing] ill music. This is yet to be seen at several old houses and seats.

Distant view of South Wraxall Manor House

Its gatehouse, hedges, and planting unfortunately obstruct the view of South Wraxall Manor House from the road, although a good distant view of it may be obtained from the footpath that runs north from South Wraxall church.

In the late-16th century the Long succession at South Wraxall was changed when Sir Walter Long disinherited his eldest son, and in Victorian times the house fell upon evil days. Between 1820 and 1826 it became a boarding school, and it then stood empty until 1900 when the house and its gardens were restored. In 1910 Walter Long announced that because of taxation he would be selling off most of his Wiltshire estates and in 1919 most of the South Wraxall estate was broken up and sold. The family however retained the house until 1966 when it too was sold.

Several legends are told about South Wraxall. Sir Walter Raleigh was a friend and smoking companion of Sir Walter Long and it was here according to local tradition the two Sir Walters, when indulging in the then virtually unknown smoking habit, were drenched by a well-meaning maidservant who unaccustomed to the new habit believed them to be on fire. This story is told of many locations, although its attribution to South Wraxall gains some credence from Aubrey who wrote : 'Sir Walter [Raleigh] was the first that brought Tobacco into England and into fashion. In our part of North Wilts, e.g. Malmesbury hundred, it first came into fashion by Sir Walter Long'.

When Sir Walter Long in 1593 decided to disinherit his eldest son by his first wife in order to make a younger son by his second wife his heir, it was alleged that the clerk drawing up the Will was interrupted by the ghostly delicate 'White Hand' of the deceased first Lady Long looking after the interests of her son. Sir Walter Long was also said to have ben posthumously associated with another supernatural event when, again according to Aubrey

The second lady [Katherine Thynne]of Sir Walter Long (whither voluntarily, or upon Sr Walter's desire I have forgott) did make a Solemn Promise to him, on his Death-bed, that she would not marry after his Decease. But not long after, one Sir Somerset Fox, a very Beautiful young Gentleman, did win her Love : so that notwithstanding her Promise aforesaid, she married him at South-wrax-hall. As he led her by the hand from the Church into the Parlour, the Picture of Sir Walter, that then hung over the Parlour-dore (the String being eaten off with the rust of the naile) fell down upon her Ladyship, and crack'd in the fall : (it was painted on wood as was the fashion in those days). This made her Ladyship reflect on her Promise, and drew some Tears from her Eyes.

Aubrey's account was in some respects incorrect as the registers of St Mary-le-Bow in London reveal that the marriage took place at that church in 1611, rather than at 'South-wrax-hall'.

South Wraxall manor was in AD 1001 granted with Bradford on Avon to the Abbey of Shaftesbury. Later some now undefined part of the manor was conveyed to the Priory of Monkton Farleigh and after the Dissolution was associated with a number of national figures. At the Dissolution in 1537 it went to Sir Edward Seymour, Queen Jane Seymour's brother who as a direct result of his sister's marriage to Henry VIII became Duke of Somerset and Protector Somerset to the young Edward VI. It remained with the Seymours until 1610 when they sold it. Documentary evidence also reveals that South Wraxall was associated with two important Elizabethan poets, the first being the poet-laureate Samuel Daniel (1562-1619) who after retiring from James I's court in about 1606 lived at Beckington near Frome in Somerset where he is buried. In his retirement Daniel became the bailiff for the lands in South Wraxall that had in 1582 been confirmed to the Protector's son Edward, Earl of Hertford. The other Elizabethan poet associated with South Wraxall was Sir Philip Sidney's friend Fulke Greville, the First Lord Brooke (1554-1628), who at the time when he was murdered by an irate servant in Warwick Castle in 1628 was the owner of part of South Wraxall manor. The Longs then acquired Fulke Greville's holding and merged it with the rest of their South Wraxall manor.

Embedded in a farmhouse a short distance north-east of South Wraxall Manor House are the ruins of the hospice of St Auden (834655) that belonged to Glastonbury Abbey and provided, as did Chapel Plaister three miles to its north (see pages 199-200) and the hospice of St Mary at Bradford on Avon (see page 254) three miles to its south, hospitality and accommodation for pilgrims travelling to Glastonbury. After being abandoned at the Reformation the South Wraxall hospice was incorporated into the Manor Farmhouse. A plan reproduced in Volume 14 of the *Wiltshire Archaeological Magazine* (facing page 100) shows it containing a hall that must have served as both a dormitory and a chapel, with a tiny dwelling attached that would have housed a warden. Pevsner described the 14th century parts of the farmhouse as being 'T-shaped' and the chapel as having : 'a N. window with cusps, a S. window similar to that of the hall, and inside, against the E wall, the remains of a tripartite reredos'. At the

South Wraxall Church

Dissolution this hospice went with Monkton Farleigh Priory and South Wraxall manor to the Earl of Hertford, and it was later owned by Hertford's steward Sir John Thynne of Longleat, having been presumably passed on to him by Hertford. It too was in 1629 purchased by John Long.

Pevsner described South Wraxall village (833643) as containing an 'attractive group' of fine stone buildings around its rather quirky church. Massingham drew attention to : 'the saddle-back mannerism of the limestone church cluster in north-west Wiltshire', about which I commented earlier at North Wraxall, and South Wraxall church has stone-slabbed saddleback roofs on its tower and its stair turret. Apart from its tower and the south chapel of the Longs, the church was almost entirely rebuilt at various times in the 19th century. Its Long monuments include a grandiose example consisting of a huge urn under a classical pediment supported by corinthian columns to Thomas Long (d.1759) and his wife who predeceased him in 1733.

The Lost Mansion of Great Cumberwell

WITHIN A RADIUS of about a mile are three fine surviving houses in Monkton Farleigh and South Wraxall just described, and the nationally important manor house at Great Chalfield that will be described later (pages 222-5), but a little over a mile south-west of South Wraxall and a short distance north of Bradford on Avon (at about 822632) there once existed near the present hotel another important mansion house that has now disappeared almost without trace.

No estate was shown at Great Cumberwell on John Speed's 1610 map, but a house with extensive landscaped grounds was shown there by Andrews and Dury on their 1773 map of Wiltshire. 'Comerwell' was however marked by Robert Norden on his 1695 map, implying that the estate was developed at some time between Speed in 1610 and Norden in 1695. 'Comberwell' was also marked on the first edition of the Ordnance Survey of about 1820, but by then it had become a much less significant site than that shown by Andrews and Dury only about fifty years before. This cartographical evidence suggests that Great Cumberwell existed as an important estate for only about a hundred and fifty years between the approximate dates of 1650 and 1800. The reason for its disappearance so completely that virtually nothing of it now survives is not recorded.

Great Cumberwell estate as shown by Andrews and Dury in 1773

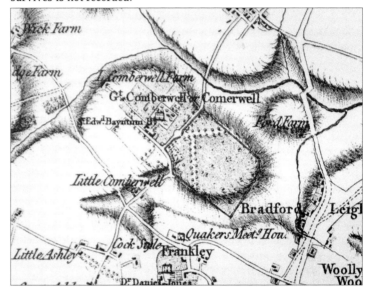

The landscaped grounds shown by Andrews and Dury were roughly rectangular and measured about one mile from north-west to south-east and almost half a mile across in the other direction. They consisted of two equal approximately square areas, the northern area being apparently formal gardens around the house while the southern, more distant from the house, seems to have been landscaped pleasure grounds laid out with two avenues of trees. Tree avenues were popular in England in the early-17th century when many were planted, but in the 18th century landscaping became informal and avenues went out of fashion. The two landscaped areas were separated by a road that ran north-east from 'Little Comberwell' to 'Lower South Wraxhall' with a 'rond-point' where the two avenues met. This road appears to have followed the line a little north-west of the present lane which runs north-east out of the A363 past Great Cumberwell and becomes a lane as it continues to South Wraxall. A transfer of Andrew's and Dury's layout of Great Cumberwell on to the modern map suggests that the mansion house was situated in an open area (at about 822 632) near the site of the present hotel and golf clubhouse which stand at the south-west edge of the former landscaped grounds.

In the 16th or 17th century the Cumberwell estate was acquired by the Button family of Alton Barnes in the Vale of Pewsey. At his death in about 1679 Sir Robert Button left Cumberwell to his nephew Charles Steward (died 1698), the only son of Dr Richard Steward who had married Robert Button's sister Jane and became Dean designate of St Paul's Cathedral but was never installed. He stood in high favour with Charles I, accompanied Charles II into exile during the Interregnum, and died in Paris in 1657. His son Charles Steward described himself in his Will dated 1692 as being of Cumberwell in the parish of Bradford. Photographs (reproduced in *WAM* 93 : 251-54) of an unroofed house at Cumberwell taken shortly before its demolition in 1903 suggest on stylistic grounds that the house was built in the late-17th century, in which case it was probably built by Charles Steward, a man who appears to have suffered from delusions of grandeur presumably arising from his father's associations with the royal house of Stuart. He may have been in exile with his father at Charles II's court, and he appears to have used his name of Steward to imply a relationship to the Stuarts. When he died in 1698 as a result of a fall from his horse he was commemorated by an imposing monument in Bradford church that depicts him full-length dressed in the style of William and Mary with a crown surmounting his monument that is apparently an unjustified assumption. The slightly enigmatic Latin inscription reads :

AB ANNOSA PROSAPIA AC HONESTIS PARENTIBUS
(He had sprung from noble stock and honourable parents)

and in view of Charles II's propensity for fathering bastard children one wonders whether there was any justification for Charles Steward's claims. His widow Jane Button left Cumberwell to the Walkers one of whom had married into the Button family, and in 1723 Heneage Walker sold the estate to the Trowbridge woollen manufacturer John Allen Cooper who died in 1749. A Thomas Cooper of Cumberwell was in 1752 Sheriff of Wiltshire, and on 1 November 1759 the *Gentleman's Magazine* announced the marriage of 'John Cooper of Cumberwelle, Wilts, Esq' (presumably a son of the above) to 'the daughter of Edward Baynton, Esq., member for Chippenham'. Andrews and Dury in 1773 show Great Cumberwell occupied by 'Sr Edwd Bayntun', John Allen Cooper's widow Mary having conveyed Cumberwell to her father Sir Edward Baynton-

Rolf (died 1800) in trust for her children.

In 1786 Cumberwell mansion house with servants' quarters and stables in a 33-acre park described as being 'well stocked with deer' was put up for sale and was bought by a clergyman called Dr Robert Taunton of the Bradford family of Taunton (or Daunton) which had at one time leased the Chantry House at Bradford. Shortly after this a description of the house and a note of pessimism about its future was sounded in a letter by the Misses Jane and Eliza Purbeck after they stayed at 'Cumberwell Park' :

> The prospects round it are beautiful and there appears to be a very pleasant neighbourhood, but the house is old, and too large to be comfortable ; there was something gloomy in the idea of a number of uninhabited rooms, which, large as their family is, you will imagine must be the case, when I tell you there are more than thirty apartments in the house. The Dr [Robert Taunton] is at present undecided what he shall do with the great pile of a building ; he sometimes talks of dividing it, at other times of building a new house in the Park. There is an old Chapel.

Dr Taunton's 'great pile of a building' was in 1790 gutted by a fire said to have been started by a negligant servant drying laundry, although the fact that Dr Taunton died at Cumberwell in 1797 suggests that he continued to live in one wing of the house that seems to have survived the fire. When the Cumberwell estate, including the refurbished house, was put up for auction in London in 1802 it was not sold and the Taunton family retained it until it was sold in 1820 for £15,400 to the clothiers John and Thomas Clarke of Bellefield House in Trowbridge. Possibly due to the state of the house they merely used the grounds of Cumberwell for recreation and family outings. They also kept up the deer in the park, a fact that interests me because in the late-19th century my grandfather Frederick Watts (born at Bradford in 1851) was in return for helping Major Clarke with his charity accounts given haunches of venison that would have come from either Great Cumberwell or from the tiny deer park around Bellefield at Trowbridge. By 1903 Cumberwell House was utterly ruinous and in that year Mrs Dorcan Clarke sold the estate to Captain Pinckney who demolished the ruins and built cottages from its materials, probably at Pinckney Green (801644) a short distance north-west of Cumberwell.

At the time when Volume VII of the *Victoria County History* was written 'the whole area was enveloped in woodland', foundations were traceable 'in places and dressed and moulded stones were scattered over a considerable area', and there were 'some standing portions of boundary walls, some of stone, and others of red brick faced with stone, and revetment walls forming a ha-ha'. For a time a fine pair of tall gateless gate piers stood isolated at Cumberwell in the middle of a field until they were bought by Colonel Jenner of Avebury Manor and transported the eighteen miles to Avebury where they stand today, re-erected as the gate-piers to the north drive that runs from the A4361 road to Avebury Manor. The fine quality of these gate piers implies a similar quality in the architecture of the house.

The disappearance of Cumberwell House is apparently attributable to its having become a white elephant to Dr Taunton who towards the end of the 18th century contemplated demolishing his vast house after most of it was gutted by fire, and in 1802 unsuccessfully tried to sell it. The the question arises what had prompted him to buy it? He may have wanted the house for its fine site and allowed it to become ruinous intending to replace it with a new one, a dream that was never realised. The grounds were then used by the Clarke family of Trowbridge as a recreational estate for the family and friends to visit, to eat *al fresco*, and maintain the deer for ornamental and perhaps culinary use. The ruins of the house were then demolished and cleared away by Captain Pinckney early in the 20th century, and by 1950 the estate was owned by Lord Halifax. Today the site of Great Cumberwell is occupied by a hotel and a golf course.

Great Chalfield

O F THE MANY fine stone-built manor houses of this region Great Chalfield is undoubtedly the finest. Now in the care of the National Trust, it is of national importance as an example of a pure late-Gothic building that despite being built as late as 1480 was utterly

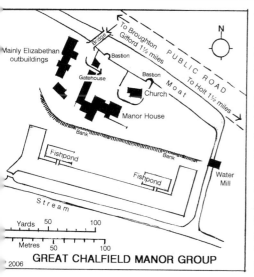

GREAT CHALFIELD MANOR GROUP

uninfluenced by any classical influences. It is approached from both its north and its south along roads that appear to be private drives than public roads.

When the normally restrained H. J. Massingham discovered Great Chalfield while undertaking his explorations for his *Cotswold Country* (1937) he described it in uncharacteristically emotive terms :

In a very remote part of the country between Bradford and Lacock is a manorial grouping of farm, church, manor, barns, mill and outbuildings, self-contained and surrounded by a moat and outside by a ha-ha hedge. These I mention as parts of a singularly precise dream I had while I was wandering about this eastern fringe [of *Cotswold Country*] ... In my dream, as I stood staring across the flags and lichened wall of the moat with my mouth open in astonishment at this hardly credible grace there came to my ears the the murmuration of a psalm from the crazily beautiful little church. Thereupon it all vanished under the dusky wing of a January day's end.

Great Chalfield resembles South Wraxall in having few defensive provisions although it is built around a courtyard with a slight moat that has south of the house been formed into rectangular fishponds but has north of the house along its inner edge the base of a curtain wall and the remains of two small round bastions that were presumably once formidable and may date from the time of its de Perci Medieval first owners. In the Civil War Great Chalfield was from mid-1644 until the autumn of 1646 garrisoned for parliament as an outpost from Malmesbury, and in April 1645 it withstood what must surely have been a half-hearted siege of a not very defensible house by a royalist force under the notorious Lord Goring. The ancillary buildings at Great Chalfield are mostly Elizabethan in date, but they probably replaced earlier buildings.

Long before the present house was built Great Chalfield was mentioned in 1191 as *Chaldefelde* in the records of the Knights Templar, suggesting that they had an interest in the estate that was by 1199 held by William de Perci (c.1183-1245) who may have been descended from William de Perci who accompanied the Conqueror to England. When William was only fifteen in 1196 his father Henry de Perci died and his uncle after managing his estates during his minority for a time refused to relinquish them although William ultimately secured his inheritance. According to the *Tropenell Cartulary* he 'hadde and okyppyed ye offyce

it Chalfield Manor
'se Group

of ye Constabilship of ye said castell of Trobrigge', and he joined the baronial party in rebellion against King John.

Manor House from churchyard

Ownership of Great Chalfield was in dispute after the death of the last male Perci owner in 1356 until Thomas Tropenell (c. 1405-1488), to whom we owe Great Chalfield substantially as we see it today, established his right to it. Tropenell was a Wiltshire lawyer whose election in 1429 as the MP for Bedwyn in Wiltshire seems to have launched him upon his dual careers as a lawyer and substantial landowner. From about 1438 he was associated with the Hungerfords and when Robert, the 3rd Baron Hungerford (1431-64), was held prisoner until 1460 after the English defeat of Castillon (1453) that terminated the Hundred Years War with France, Tropenell was entrusted with arranging the heavy mortgages on the Hungerford estates needed to raise his ransom. By his own account after much legal wrangling he in 1467 finally obtained possession of Great Chalfield manor by claiming descent from its de

Manor House from garden side

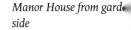

Perci former owners. His claim was probably weak but he was rich, he had the support of the powerful Hungerfords, and he seems to have been an extremely shrewd man as he demonstrated during the Wars of the Roses when, despite almost certainly sympathising with the Lancastrians, he contrived to keep such a low profile that his name was included in the general pardons issued by the Yorkist monarchs Edward IV and Richard III. He died in 1488 three years

after the Lancastrian triumph at Bosworth, and is commemorated by an elaborate monument in Corsham church.

After Giles, the last Tropenell owner of Great Chalfield, was killed in a freak hunting accident, his sister took Chalfield by marriage to the Eyres of Wedhampton in Pewsey Vale. By 1630 the estate was held by Sir Richard Gurney who was in 1642 Lord Mayor of London. He died in the Tower in 1647 after claiming that he had lost £2000 as a result of damage sustained by Great Chalfield during the parliamentary occupation and the royalist siege.

Great Chalfield Church

In 1673 Great Chalfield was acquired by the rich Bradford clothier John Hall and from him it passed to his granddaughter Rachel Bayntun who took it by marriage to the First Duke of Kingston whose son the 2nd Duke was posthumously involved in the notorious bigamy scandal of 1776 (see page 260-4). In 1795 the estate went by marriage to Admiral Sir Harry Burnard (d.1840) who assumed the name of Neale, its previous owners. Shortly before his death Admiral Burnard employed a pupil of the Gothick Revivalist architect A. W. Pugin (1812-52) called T. L. Walker to prepare drawings for reconstructing Great Chalfield. Pugin wrote of Great Chalfield in Volume 3 of his *Examples of Gothic Architecture*: 'The north front is nearly perfect, with its porch and groined roof, the hall at its centre flanked by a gabled building at each end, each with an oriel. The whole front is one of the finest and most elaborate we have'.

The proposed reconstruction was not immediately undertaken and the house was let to a farmer until 1878 when it was bought by the Fullers who in 1905-12 appointed Sir Harold Brakspear to reconstruct the house using Walker's drawings to ensure the autheticity of his reconstruction. The Fullers then retained Great Chalfield until 1943 when Major Fuller gave it to the National Trust retaining occupancy for his family.

Thomas Tropenell also reconstructed the 'crazily beautiful little church' (Massingham) that stands beside the house and has at its west end a bellcote with a small crocketed spire. Inside the church Tropenell added in about 1480 a family chapel in the Gothic style with a stone screen and much heraldry. The pulpit is a 17th century three-decker, and the Neale family in about 1775 added a chapel of their own.

Church interior

Garden of The Courts at Holt

Holt

A MINOR HEDGELESS ROAD that runs south-west from Great Chalfield reaches after little more than a mile the village of Holt which has at its centre the attractive Ham Green surrounded by 'nice houses' (Pevsner). This road crosses a park-like area around Holt Manor (856626) that, since the 1316 *Calendar of Patent Rolls* record the carrying away of deer and a foal from 'Holte' Park, may have once been a Medieval deer park owned by John de Holt, the Sheriff of Wiltshire in 1314-15, who in 1346 transferred Holt to William of Edington, the Wiltshire-born ecclesiastic who became Bishop of Winchester and Edward III's chancellor and treasurer. By the late-14th century the manorial rights were held by John, the 6th Baron Lisle (d. 1429), who emanated from a Hampshire family. The Lisles retained Holt for hundreds of years and William Lisle, who was knighted in 1606 and died 1646, married a daughter of Sir John Hungerford of Down Ampney near Cricklade. Their eldest son Sir William Lisle (d.1665) was an ardent royalist who accompanied Charles II into exile, and during his absence abroad Holt was taken over by his parliamentarian younger brother John Lisle who, after graduating as a lawyer from Oxford, became in 1640 MP for Winchester and is said to have married two heiresses in order to offset the extravagances of his father. In parliament John Lisle expressed strong anti-royalist feelings and later drafted the ordinances for the creation of the New Model Army which secured the final defeat of the king. He also took part in the trial of Charles I sitting next to the president of the court as his adviser, and was one of the sub-committee of seven that drew up the death sentence on the king. During the Interregnum he was elevated to the peerage by Cromwell, and at the Restoration of the monarchy he fled to Switzerland where in 1664 he was stabbed to death on his way to church at Lausanne by an Irish royalist called Thomas Macdonnell. His royalist brother Sir William meanwhile retained Holt manor.

Twenty-one years after John Lisle was assassinated his elderly widow Dame Alice Lisle (c.1614-85), then living at Moyle Court in Hampshire, was in 1685 tried for sheltering two rebels after Sedgemoor. At her trial in Winchester she was brutally bullied by Judge Jeffreys who sentenced her to be burnt at the stake. Her treatment in court and the severity of her sentence may have been because her husband had been a parliamentarian and a regicide. A public outcry against the savagery of her sentence failed to save her, although it was amended to a more merciful public beheading which she suffered in Winchester market place with immense courage and dignity.

The success of Bath inspired a fashion for health spas at which patients drank and sometimes bathed in waters that were alleged to be naturally mineralised before they emerged from the ground. Such a spa was opened at Holt which then became known as Holt Spa. Here the waters from a well sunk in 1688 were first used medecinally in 1713, and at least four wells called The Old, The New, The Great Nose, and Harrises, were opened, all located at The Midlands on the site of the later John Sawtell's bedding factory (863620) that now contains remains of the spa consisting of the former classical portal of the well-house with an urn in relief and an inscription indicating that the Lady Lisle and the Rev. James Lewis : 'patronised this spring and rendered it famous in the year 1720'. It seems that the Lisles were then still at Holt and were involved in the spa enterprise. William Cobbett vehemently described spas as places :

> to which East India plunderers, West India floggers, English tax-gorgers, together with gluttons, drunkards, and bebauchees of all descriptions, female as well as male, resort, at the suggestion of silently laughing quacks, in the hope of getting rid of the bodily consequences of their manifold sins and iniquities

but the Holt waters were believed to be beneficial in the treatment of the tubercular disease called scrofula or the King's Evil, and Holt attained sufficient celebrity as a spa for its waters to be bottled and sent to London for sale. They were promoted by a succession of pamphlets which appeared as late as 1776, although by that date the spa at Holt was becoming unfashionable. However it still survived in 1817 when the Melksham Guide was disparaging about its waters, and some time later John Britton described Holt as being 'more famous for its medicinal waters than for any other peculiarity', but by 1850 the spa was defunct.

A number of village industries that had developed at Holt created employment that compensated for the closure of the spa. In the 17th century there were many weavers in Holt and a cloth factory that was owned from 1842 to 1875 by a Mr J. E. Davis continued in business until about 1890, latterly under different ownership. Although their records date back to only 1783 the leatherworking firm of J. and T. Beavan, makers of leggings and gloves, claimed to have originated at Holt in the 17th century. In 1758 this firm acquired some cottages and converted them into offices, and a three-storied factory followed at The Midlands. In 1924 about 150 hands were employed in this factory, as well as several hundred women home-workers who worked for the firm in their cottages.

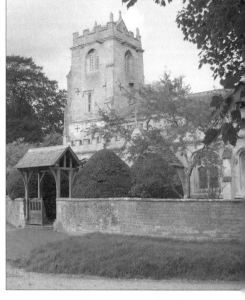

Holt Church

Although no longer a spa and with much of its industry now gone, Holt still contains something of historic interest towards the south end of the village in the early-18th century house known as The Courts (861616) that is so-named because local weavers brought to it their disputes to be resolved. This may explain why the first known Chartist meeting in Wiltshire was held at Holt in July 1838. Pevsner disliked the exuberant five-bay baroque facade of The Courts which he criticised as being : 'wildly overdone in all its details' and as 'an instructive example of what a vulgar mind can do with promising elements'. As for myself, I must confess to a liking for the house, as obviously did the National Trust when in 1943 they accepted it as a gift from Major T. C. E. Goff, a great-grandson of William IV. Its fine garden (but not the house) is regularly open to the public.

Down a turning from Ham Green and nicely situated at the south edge of the village stands Holt Church that has been restored but is, unlike so many Victorian restorations, well done in a style described by Pevsner as æ°free-Gothic'. Its principal features are its Perpendicular saddle-backed tower and its original south porch.

Broughton Gifford

A FTER BEING HELD from 1160 until 1260 by the Dunstanvilles the manor of Broughton, about two miles south-west of Melksham and almost two miles north-east of Holt, passed to John, the

*Broughton Gifford Comm
looking n*

*Gifford Hall on The
Common*

First Baron Giffard, from the important Norman family of Gloucestershire-based Marcher Lords. The Giffards, as did most of the great Marcher Lords, sometimes supported and at other times defied the throne by force of arms. After appending his name to Broughton John Giffard died in 1299 and the manor was forfeited when his son, another John Gifford known as 'le Rych' because of his immense wealth, was beheaded by Edward II in 1322 at Gloucester for supporting the barons in their civil war against that monarch's Despenser favourites.

Broughton Gifford (879635) is an attractive extended linear stone-built village. The houses at its northern end are loosely spread around the huge Broughton Common that may have originated as a squatter development in the 16th and 17th centuries when many weavers were operating independently on hand looms in the cottages, a practice that would have died out when the factory system drew them into the local manufacturing towns. Broughton Common was then more formally redeveloped in the 18th and 19th centuries when substantial houses including the fine Queen Anne Cotswold-style Gifford Hall at its northern end replaced the squatter dwellings.

Many cloth workers were for political reasons non-conformists and their chapels at Broughton Gifford are noticably situated at this north end of the village, away from the largely Early English parish church of St Mary at its opposite end. In the west wall of Broughton Gifford churchyard is a typically Cotswold-pattern stone-slabbed step-over style, and an interesting brass memorial in the church dated 1620 commemorating 'Robert Longe' was I believe engraved by Richard Haydocke, a Salisbury physician who learnt engraving in order to illustrate his medical publications and later engraved funerary monuments on brass. Aubrey described how this man in 1618 medically examined Sir Walter Raleigh when he passed through Salisbury on his way to London for execution :

Stile into Broughton Giffc Churchyard

When [in 1618] Sir Walter Raleigh was carried prisoner from the West to London, he lay at Salisbury, where, by his great skill in Chimistry, he made himself like a Leper : by which meanes he thought he might retard his journey to a Prison : and study his escape. Dr Heydock was sent for to give his opinion, if the Prisoner might be carried to London without danger of his life. The Dr feeles Sir Walter's Pulses, and found they did beat well : and so detected the imposture.

Haydocke was an eccentric who claimed to be able to preach in his sleep, and Aubrey also amusingly related how James I exposed him as a cheat :

Richard Heydock, M.C., quondam Fellow of New College in Oxford, an Ingenious, and a learned Person, but much against the Hierarchie of the Church of England. He had this Device to gaine Prophelytes by preaching in his Dream : which was much noised abroad, and taled of as a Miracle. But King James 1st. being at Salisbury went to heare him : He observed that this Harangue was very methodicall &c. that he did but couterfeit a Sleep. He surprized the Doctor by drawing his sword, and swearing by Gods

waunes I will cutt-off his head : at which the Dr started, and pretended to
awake. So the Cheat was detected.

Lord Byron's writer-politician friend John Cam Hobhouse (1786-
1869) in 1831 took his title as 'First Baron Broughton of Broughton
Gyfford' from Broughton Gifford with which the Hobhouse family were
associated when they lived at the old manor of Cottles (850655), now
Stonar School, nearly three miles to its north-west. Hobhouse was the
closest of Byron's several friends with Wiltshire associations who
included the poet Tom Moore and Dr Polidori, and he remained his close
friend until Byron died. His father Sir Benjamin Hobhouse (1757-1831)
was the son of a Bristol merchant who became a politician and an MP,
and married as his first wife John Cam's mother Charlotte Cam (c. 1760-
91), a daughter of a prosperous woollen clothier of the Chantry House
at Bradford (see page 253). By this marriage Sir Benjamin Hobhouse
acquired at Bradford Barton Farm and Chantry House where the
Hobhouses lived. They then became the town bankers and after
embarking on a campaign of land purchase in west Wiltshire Sir
Benjamin in 1789 acquired Broughton Gifford from the Horton family
when the Rev. W. H. Roberts, a nephew of Thomas Horton, sold the
manor to Sir Benjamin who was then living at Cottles. His father's
marriage to Miss Cam and his inheritance of Broughton Gifford from
his father explain the middle name of John Cam Hobhouse and his title
'of Broughton Gyfford'.

John Cam Hobhouse was diminutive in size and pugnacious by
nature and it may have been the latter characteristic that attracted Byron
who practised pugilism. After becoming at Cambridge a friend of the
poet — who called him 'Hobby' — Hobhouse accompanied him in the dual
role of manager and friend on his extensive travels around the
Mediterranean when Byron fled abroad to avoid a scandal. In 1815 he
was best man at Byron's wedding to Annabella Millbanke, and Byron
after being finally driven out of England in 1816 dedicated to him Canto
IV of *Childe Harold* (1817) and in his *Lines to Mr Hodgson* wrote of :

> Hobhouse muttering fearful curses,
> As the hatchway down he rolls,
> Now his breakfast, now his verses,
> Vomits forth and d***s our souls.

Back in England Hobhouse was in 1819 imprisoned for publishing
a satyrical pamphlet, and the following year he entered parliament as a
radical MP. He succeeded to the baronetcy in 1831, held several cabinet
offices from 1832 until 1852, and is believed to have originated the

Broughton Gifford Manor House

expression 'His Majesty's Opposition'. His memoirs are entitled *Recollections of a Long Life, 1834-1852*, and at his death in 1869 he was succeeded in the barony by Sir Charles Parry Hobhouse.

Early in the 19th century Broughton Gifford became a meeting place for writers and artists when the fine 17th century Cotswold-style manor house (879635) east of the road junction towards the south end of the village was the home of the playwright and author Clifford Bax (1886-1962), the brother of the composer Sir Arnold Bax (1883-1953) who was also often at Broughton Gifford. From 1911 to the outbreak of the Great War Clifford Bax organised from Broughton Gifford his Old Broughtonian cricket team of artists and writers who during late summer annually assembled at the Manor House and played friendly matches against local village teams. In *Inland Far* (1925) Clifford Bax wrote a brief evocation of England prior to the Great War that :

Broughton Gifford Manoi House

> It may be that we who lived in the country, a dozen or fifteen years ago, were seeing the very last of that unsophisticated England which has been pictured for all time by Thomas Hardy . . . If our cricket eleven was to play against a neighbouring team, we jogged along the lanes in a horsewagonette : and if I had to buy goods in the nearest town [Melksham], I went there on a bicycle.

In notes that he wrote for a visit of the Bath Group of the Somerset Archaeological Society to Broughton Gifford Manor House Clifford Bax indicated that in the 19th century the house was divided into two cottages, and that in about 1908 an architect called Schmidt restored it intending to live in it, but died just as the work was completed. Bax also described the manor house in *Inland Far* (1925) :

The Manor House had been built, in the reign of King Charles the First, by a gentleman called Sir John Horton. He had made for himself a modest home, three-storeyed, three-gabled, and with one wing only, so that the ground floor formed an L. He had topped each gable with a stone, and on the flat of each stone, so that it faced the sky, he had grooved a cross ; in order, as I was told, that the angels in passing might not hesitate to bless the house. The roof – now a many wrinkled surface – was tiled with stone. The casement windows were mullioned. A gabled porch, with wooden seats inside it, led to a broad nail-studded door of oak. Coming up to the house by the flagged path of the front garden, between two little square lawns, any one would have recognised that it had an air antique and gracious . . . His [Sir John's] bedroom, I think, must have been on the first floor, in the wing : for the villagers told me that, a few years earlier, when the floor had been taken up, the builder had collected a sufficient number of Caroline coins, both gold and silver, 'to fill a pint pot'. From year to year, I suppose, they had slipped through a crack as he donned his hose or his coat of broad-cloth.

Anyone viewing the manor house should not fail to notice the tiny mice carved on the inscribed ball-finials of its gatepiers.

Monkton House

ABOUT A MILE south of Broughton Gifford is Monkton (883623) that was formerly known as Little Broughton and only became Monkton after being in the 12th century granted to Monkton Farleigh Priory (pages 212-13). It was 'Mountain Farm' on Andrew's and Dury's 1773 map. At the Dissolution of the monasteries Monkton went to Sir Edward Seymour, the future Protector Somerset, and after his execution in 1552 his son the Earl of Hertford managed to retain it and is said to have built a house at Monkton. The present gabled house however dates from 1647 and was subsequently owned by the Longs, the Thynnes of Longleat, and the Duke of Kingston. It then became a farmhouse standing in rich grazing land beside the River Avon.

When the Duke of Kingston bigamously married Elizabeth Chudleigh (as described later on pages 260-4) he is said to have on the advice of his agent sold his Monkton estate without ever having seen it. When subsequently hunting in the area he expressed his admiration for Monkton and enquired about its ownership. When told that he had once owned it the Duke vowed to never again sell a property that he had not seen.

Coins found at some earthworks (at 878623) towards Holt a short distance west of Monkton House indicate that this site was a Romano-British riverside settlement.

Semington and Isaac Gulliver the Smuggler

A S IT STANDS ON THE A350 mainly south of the Kennet and Avon Canal Semington (897606) lies geographically strictly outside the remit of this book, but as it adjoins and has a wharf on the the canal I am including it here.

The smuggling of contraband goods is generally associated with the coastal trade but smuggled goods had to be distributed inland and the small village of Semington, three miles south of Melksham, was the birthplace of a celebrated smuggler called Isaac Gulliver (1745-1822). Although apparently accepted as a son of Isaac and Elizabeth Gulliver, his nominal father described him as: 'my son or reputed son, otherwise Matravers', suggesting that young Isaac's father may have been the son of a member of the local family of Matravers or that he was adopted into that family. A James Matravers who could have been young Isaac Gulliver's grandfather is commemorated by a 1799 monument in St George's church at Semington that is a small mainly Victorian church with a bell-cote copied from Biddestone, as was another similar one at nearby Whaddon.

Young Isaac somehow became involved in the coastal and inland smuggling trade and was according to a customs officer: 'one of the greatest and most notorious smugglers in the West of England and particularly in the spirits and tea trade'. Described also as a man of: 'great speculating genius', he became known as 'the gentleman smuggler' because he was said to have never harmed an exciseman. In 1768 he married Elizabeth Beale, the daughter of William Beale the publican-blacksmith at the Blacksmith's Arms that is now Thorney Down Farm a mile south of Sixpenny Handley beside the A354 in Cranborne Chase. This inn, that was ideally situated for organising the distribution of smuggled goods northwards across the Chase into Wiltshire, became one of Gulliver's regular depots for his contraband. We cannot be sure how far Gulliver carried his smuggled goods into Wiltshire, but as much of the south coast trade was directed at Bath where most of London society spent the season it is likely that some of his contraband was carried across his native county. This suggestion seems to be confirmed by the fact that even after he had prospered and acquired several other Dorset properties he retained the Blacksmith's Arms near the southern boundary of Wiltshire.

Excise duty on luxury goods was in the 18th century regarded as an imposition by all classes of society in England who were sympathetic to the smugglers who supplied them free of duty. Even the authorities seem to have turned a 'blind eye' upon Isaac Gulliver's activities as in

Isaac Gulliver and his gang

1782 he was granted a 'free' pardon under an amnesty, and in return paid for two men to serve in the Royal Navy. As smugglers often carried information across the Channel Gulliver may have earned his pardon by in his lugger the *Dolphin* bringing information from France that was useful to the government. The Dorset historian George Roberts described how: 'A smuggler named Gulliver kept 40 or 50 men constantly employed who wore a kind of livery, powdered hair and smock frocks, from which they attained the name of 'White Wigs'. The scale of Gulliver's operations is indicated by the occasion when his pack train was described as extending over two miles. He is said to have been a large man as seems to be confirmed by an 18th century engraving believed to represent him with his gang in which he is a big bald-headed man seated among his 'White Wigs' on a beach surrounded with small barrels of contraband spirits.

In his book *In the Country* (1972) Kenneth Allsopp relates how Gulliver: 'once escaped a custom officers' raid by chalking his face white and posing as a corpse'. When by his illegal activities he had amassed a fortune Gulliver attained respectability by entering the legitimate wine trade at Poole and becoming a churchwarden at Wimborne Minster where his fine Georgian house in the High Street, now called Gulliver House, bears a plaque commemorating his occupancy. His new-found respectability enabled one of Gulliver's daughters to marry a Blandford doctor and another a member of the Fryer banking family of Wimborne.

Gulliver died at Wimborne in 1822 leaving the then substantial sum of twenty thousand pounds and property in four counties. He was buried in Wimborne Minster under a ledger stone with an inscription beginning: 'Isaac Gulliver, Esquire, Aged 77'. How he would have appreciated that 'Esquire' with its implied respectability. This stone was originally set in the floor of the central aisle of the nave but when its lettering became worn it was moved to the inside of the north wall of the west tower where it may be seen today, its inscription now illegible except for his name.

Isaac Gulliver is also commemorated indirectly by the name of a now built-up district between Poole and Bournemouth. This was in his time a remote coastal heath at the mouth of the Bourne and a favourite landing-place for smugglers and as there Gulliver landed much of his contraband it became known by a play on words as Lilliput, this being the name of the legendary island in Swift's *Gulliver's Travels*. Although now built-up it remains Lilliput to this day.

Packhorse Bridge near Monkton House

The Lower Bristol Avon

AFTER LEAVING THE LIMESTONE COUNTRYSIDE around Malmesbury and flowing south through the claylands around Great Somerford, past Christian Malford, and through Chippenham, the Bristol Avon re-enters the district covered by this book when as the Lower Bristol Avon it flows under the A350 at the west end of Melksham (900638). The existence of a 1765 'Plan for Extending Navigation from Bath to Chippenham' suggests that these lower reaches of the river were at one time navigable, and the Lower Bristol Avon from Melksham over the remainder of its course through Wiltshire differs much from the Upper Bristol Avon around Malmesbury. West of Melksham it flows through the flat pasture land known as Challimead (896635) and this stretch of the river, that is from Melksham to Monkton House roughly followed by the B3107 to its north-west and by a footpath to its south-east, was admired by the poet Edward Thomas who considered 'the broad meadow called Challimead' to be 'beautiful . . . with its towered [Melksham] church lying along the summit of the gentle rise in which it ends'. In his book *In Pursuit of Spring* (1914) Thomas also admired the way in which 'the Avon serpentined along the meadow without disturbing the level three furlongs of its perfect green', and suggested that 'For this meadow at least there should be a place in any Elysium'.

John Aubrey described the Lower Bristol Avon as 'inriching the meadows as it runnes to Chippenham, Lacock, Bradford, Bath [etc]', and its lush low-lying pastures have for centuries been recognised to be excellent grazing land. When a dispute over stolen cattle came before the Court of Star Chamber in 1623 a yeoman from Whaddon called William Brouncker (presumably from the Melksham family of that name which provided in Lord Brouncker the first President of the Royal Society) stated that he was a grazier who frequently used to: 'repayre to certain Fayres in Shropshire and the county of Radnor to buy Rother beasts [cattle] there to stock his grounds [at Whaddon] as the Grasiers dwelling near your subject in the said county of Wilts use to doe'. Melksham derives its name from milk, and a further testament to the quality of the

*The Avon north of
Whaddon*

*Packhorse Bridge at Barton
Farm, Bradford on Avon*

grazing in this area was provided by the 1875 *Wiltshire Post Office Directory* when it noted: 'it is said that some of the best land in the county for grazing purposes is the pasture at Monkton, by the side of the River Avon'.

A very good walk may be taken west from Semington, initially along the canal and then along Semington Brook, through Whaddon and along the River Avon to Staverton. From Whaddon a diversion may be made north to visit the the little stone-built packhorse bridge (882621) that stands a little south-west of Monkton House (see above page 233). This, the only bridge across the Avon in its four-mile reach between Melksham and Staverton, was built in 1725 to provide a crossing for packhorses carrying bales of wool from the weavers at Broughton Gifford to Whaddon. Consequently its parapets are kept low to allow unimpeded passage of packhorses carrying low-slung bulky bales of wool, and another interesting feature of this bridge is that its raised central arch seems to confirm that the Lower Bristol Avon was used for inland navigation prior to the building of the Kennet and Avon Canal. The return walk to Semington may be along the canal towpath.

The Avon west of Avoncliff looking east

After being joined by Semington Brook a short distance north-east of Whaddon church, the Avon turns west and flows south-east of Holt to Staverton (856608). From Whaddon a public footpath that is in my experience extremely muddy in wet weather roughly follows the south bank of the river west as far as Staverton where at the flood plain of Forewoods Common the roads are despite being raised on causeways often flooded in wet winters. In his *In Pursuit of Spring* (1914) Edward Thomas described the Avon at Staverton as 'a beautiful willowy river', and mentioned 'Staverton's little church which the trees half conceal'. This church incorporates one of the several saddleback roofs of the Wiltshire Cotswolds and is associated with a number of three-storeyed former weaver's cottages.

After passing through Staverton the river swings south and flows down the east edge of Great Bradford Wood with its long-established heronry and then, just before reaching the Kennet and Avon Canal at Ladydown (846596), it turns sharply west. From Staverton to Ladydown at the north-west edge of Trowbridge no footpath approaches the river, but from Ladydown a footpath runs west between the river and the canal and where these diverge (at 845596) the path approximately follows the Avon at some distance from its bank as the river resumes its course north-west to Bradford where, towards the south edge of the town it flows first under the Town Bridge and then under the Medieval packhorse bridge (823604) at Barton Farm. As it accompanies the Kennet and Avon Canal west through Barton Farm Country Park and past on its north bank a new hedged maze planted in 2005 (at 814603) the river becomes embowered by trees until at Avoncliff it passes under the canal that crosses the river over the elegant Avoncliff Aqueduct (804600). Although it is here a substantial river the reach of the Avon from Avoncliff to near Freshford was designated 'Belcomb Brook' on Andrew's and Dury's 1773 map.

The Avon south of Dundas Aqueduct

Towards the county boundary at Freshford the banks of the river, still followed by a public path, become more open with intermittent trees along its banks, although the valley remains wooded away from the river. Near the railway bridge a little east of Freshford the river is joined by the River Frome and it then turns north and passes under the railway. For a short distance it forms the Somerset–Wiltshire boundary and after flowing north-west under Murhill it opposite Limpley Stoke bends and after flowing for a mile north between the railway and the canal under Conkwell Wood it passes under the Dundas Aqueduct (784626) and leaves Wiltshire.

A. E. Trueman in *Geology and Scenery in England and Wales* (1949) describes how after leaving Bradford on Avon 'by a deep gorge the river winds its way through the oolite uplands to Bath' and then flows through Bristol to enter the Severn estruary at Avonmouth.

From Limpley Stoke to beyond Dundas Aqueduct the river is accompanied along the Limpley Stoke Valley by the the canal, the A36 trunk road, and the former Great Western Railway, three comparatively modern introductions that in no way mar the beauty of the valley. When surveying the line for the Great Western Railway line Brunel rode up this valley beneath Claverton and Limpley Stoke in April 1833 and noted: 'The side of the hill is a rotten description of oolite laying over clay', an unflattering description of this beautiful wooded valley that was so much admired by the Victorians that they knew it as the Nightingale Valley.

The Avon Valley from Brassknocker Hill.

Whaddon and the Longs

A LITTLE SOUTH of the point where the River Avon is joined by
Summerham Brook stands the remote hamlet of Whaddon
(880614) that is reached by driving a mile and a half down a minor road
north from the village of Hilperton near Trowbridge and across the
Kennet and Avon Canal. Whaddon is by no means the most remote
village in Wiltshire but as it is situated at the end of a cul-de-sac road it
must be one of the least-visited. Its remoteness must explain the scant
attention afforded to it by the early-20th century topographical writers
and more recently by Pamela Street who makes no mention at all of this
Whaddon in *The Illustrated Portrait of Wiltshire* (1971), her passing
reference to Whaddon being to its namesake in south-east Wiltshire, as
was Ralph Whitlock's in his Batsford *Wiltshire* (undated). Sir Nikolaus
Pevsner however took the trouble to visit Whaddon for his Wiltshire
volume of *The Buildings of England* (1963) and was suitably appreciative
of its little church dedicated to St Mary. Today Whaddon consists of this
church, a farm, a few cottages, and some modern dwellings standing
around the north end of its access road. The now redundant railway line
from Devizes that joined the main line near Holt once crossed this area
a little north of the River Avon opposite Whaddon church.

Whaddon may also be reached along a number of public rights-
of-way, from Staverton to its west, from Semington and Melksham to its
east, and from Broughton Gifford to its north. The path from the latter
runs south by fieldpaths from Broughton Gifford church across the B3107
Bradford to Melksham road (at 881626). It then crosses a Cotswold style
stone-slabbed stile, the railway by a pedestrian crossing, and the River
Avon by the hump-backed packhorse bridge (882621) west of Monkton
House described above (page 237). From this bridge Whaddon is then
reached across a nice little modern iron footbridge (882616) which crosses

Iron footbridge at Whad·
with church in backgrou·

Summerham Brook near its confluence with the Avon a short distance
north-east of Whaddon church.

The old parish of Whaddon now forms the north-west corner of
the modern parish of Semington. Despite its small size the parish was
an ancient one mentioned in Domesday as *Wadone* meaning 'woad hill'.
It then amounted to three hides and was held by Alvric of Melksham,
but by 1249 Henry de Whaddon (died 1254) held Whaddon under the
Earl of Salisbury. The village remained in his family until 1342 when it
was acquired by Thomas Gore. Soon after this the parish was with
neighbouring Trowbridge acquired by the Duchy of Lancaster. Whaddon
it is traditionally said to have been deserted as a result of the Black Death
in the 14th century but in the 16th century it was acquired by the
Beauchamps from whom it passed to the Bayntuns of Bromham who held
it only until 1555 when it was acquired by Henry Long. From that date
the history of Whaddon is inextricably linked with that of the Longs.

The Longs of Whaddon were landowning gentleman-clothiers who
manufactured cloth at both Trowbridge and Whaddon. Sir Walter Long
of Whaddon was in 1627 MP for Bath and Charles I's Sheriff of Wiltshire.
Because he strenuously opposed the royal party in parliament Clarendon
called him one of the chiefs of the Presbyterian party and in 1628 he was
one of the MPs prosecuted in the Court of Star Chamber by which
Charles I tried to control his 'over mighty subjects'. His fine of 2000
marks did not persuade him to change his politics and he became a
supporter of the ardent parliamentarian Sir John Eliot. After being at
constant loggerheads with the king Sir Walter was imprisoned in the
Tower which made him even more ardently anti-royalist. At the start of
the Civil War he raised a troop of horse for parliament and fought at Edge
Hill where his horse was shot under him. In 1646 parliament voted him
an indemnity of £5000 but, disliking Cromwell's rule as much as he had
that of the king, he expressed his views so forcibly that the army brought
serious charges against him. He fled to France and at the Restoration
returned to England and was created a baronet in 1661. His will is dated
1672 and he is buried in the Long mortuary vault beneath Whaddon
church.

Whaddon is shown on Andrew's and Dury's 1773 map of Wiltshire
as a substantial place associated with Whaddon House that until it was
destroyed by fire in 1835 stood on the site of the present Whaddon Grove
Farm (885615). A water colour drawing by Buckler in 1808 of old
Whaddon House, now in the collection of the Wiltshire Archaeological
and Natural History Society at Devizes, was reproduced in Volume 7 of
the *Wiltshire Victoria County History* (facing page 173) and reveals that
the house was a probably Elizabethan stone-gabled building in a
vernacular Cotswold-style with mullioned windows.

Whaddon Church (881614), that stands on a bank above the river,
was greatly altered in the 14th century and again in 1879. Its nave walls

are however Norman, and it has re-used Norman doorways, that in the south porch consisting of an assemblage of elements including Norman chevron mouldings and capitals, octagonal engaged columns, and a probably pseudo-Norman low-relief carved tympanum in the arch that was criticised by Pevsner as being: 'alas reconstructed and evidently not quite correctly'. In the 1879 restoration a new chancel was built, the Norman south porch was rebuilt as just described, and a tiny bellcote modelled on

WhaddonChurch from t south

that at Biddestone near Castle Combe was added to replace a derelict timber one. The north chapel with round-headed windows and Y-tracery that was added as the Long memorial chapel in the 19th century contains memorials to two members of the family who attained great age, Walter Long who lived to be ninety-five and his sister Katherine who died aged ninety-seven in 1814. Katherine is commemorated by a fine marble monument by Westmacott with an extended inscription reciting her many virtues, while Walter Long, who died in 1807, has a massive standing marble monument by King of Bath. There is also a brass with a shield to Henry Long who died much earlier in 1612. Beneath the Long Chapel is a tunnel-vaulted mortuary vault of the Longs that was formerly approached from outside down a flight of steps but is now inaccessible. It has a datestone inscribed '1778'. This charming little church is now scheduled as a Grade II building of special interest.

One of the rectors of Whaddon was Dr Edward Cooper (born 1728),

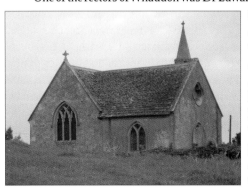

an uncle of Jane Austen (1775-1817) who had married Jane's mother's sister Jane Leigh. I do not know precisely when Dr Cooper left Whaddon but it is possible that Jane Austen, who travelled widely and often

WhaddonChurch from t river

visited her relatives, came to Whaddon to see her Uncle Edward, although he would have been seventy-one when Jane Austen first visited Bath in 1799. Jane's favourite author was the Rev. George Crabbe (1754-1832) who was the rector of Trowbridge a couple of miles from Whaddon from 1814 until his death, and the fact that Jane said that if she had any inclination to marry she could imagine herself as Mrs Crabbe suggests that she may have met Crabbe socially.

Bradford Hill from the River

Bradford on Avon

THE BEST WAY TO APPROACH BRADFORD is from the south because from this direction its dramatic situation on a steep hillside at the edge of a limestone plateau that here plunges about 300 feet (91 metres) down to the River Avon is best appreciated. Bradford is historically and architecturally almost on a par with Malmesbury, a town that it resembles in that both towns flourished by cloth-making and are partly built on steep hills. A glance at the map however reveals that Bradford is geographically larger because it has expanded over the flat ground south of the Avon and also up over its hill, whereas Malmesbury has remained more confined on its hilltop and has extended very little south of its river that is incidentally the same Bristol Avon as Bradford stands upon.

Although cloth-making ceased at Bradford in 1905 the town had prospered from this trade for many centuries. When it was at its peak in 1800 there were thirty-two cloth factories at Bradford, as well as no doubt many home-workers' looms surviving in cottages. In 1834 the town was referred to as 'Great Bradford', although by that date the industry was in decline and the cloth-workers were suffering great hardship because from about 1820 the Bradford clothiers sent work out of the town to obtain cheaper rates that were obtainable elsewhere, which must explain why four Bradford cloth-workers took their own lives on a single day in 1821. The industry struggled on but from the mid-19th century it declined rapidly although the ultimate extent of its deterioration does not seem to have been foreseen as in 1875 the Gane Brothers of Trowbridge, who were specialist factory builders, were commissioned to build beside the Avon in the middle of the town the huge multi-storeyed Abbey Mills that have now been converted into flats. My own family history reflects the decline of cloth-making at Bradford in that my paternal grandfather who was born in 1851, and my other grandparents on both sides of my family, all worked in the woollen industry, although neither my father nor my mother who were born respectively in 1888 and 1896 were employed in the then rapidly declining industry.

As the woollen industry declined diversification took place into the manufacture of alternative products. Because one small factory started making snuff Bradford became for a time derisively known as 'Snuffy Bradford', and in about 1840 the fortress-like Seven Stars Brewery

Abbey Mills

(825610) with its tiny windows in its massive cliff-like stone walls was built in Newtown, but the real salvation for Bradford came in 1842 when an Englishman who had learned rubber manufacturing in America called Stephen Moulton arrived in the town and recognised that Bradford's proximity to Bristol, the ready availability of vacant factory premises, and an agreement by Captain Palairet of Woolley Grange (see later page 256) to invest £5,000 and become a partner in the enterprise, provided the ideal circumstances for introducing the rubber industry to Bradford. The vacant Kingston Mills were acquired, in 1891 Mr Moulton was joined by George Spencer and Company, and the company then expanded under the name Spencer Moulton's. More premises were acquired including the Abbey Mill in 1926. Production initially consisted mainly of rubber components for railways and in the Great War groundsheets were produced for the army. After the war the company made motor tyres, became the Avon India Rubber Company, and then removed its activities to Melksham.

The striking hillside situation of Bradford has prompted some writers to liken it to an Italian hill town, although the town centre occupies the flat ground at the foot of the hill beside the Bristol Avon. As more dwellings were required for an increasing labour force the town expanded up the steep hillside to the north-west of the town that was rapidly developed into a tortuous maze of steep lanes, alleyways, and steps linking the successive terraces of stone-built houses that were built along the contours of the hill. Space for building on the hillside was at such a premium that builders squeezed buildings into the most unpromising spaces, gabled cottages adjoined more imposing clothiers' dwellings, and houses were crammed into corners on the hill that is so steep that the entrances to some houses are into one floor on one side and into a higher floor on the other. The resultant jumble of stone buildings created the picturesque backcloth to the town that induced H. J. Massingham to describe Bradford as a 'terraced town of the clothiers who made urban England without deserting their countrysides'.

In 1889 the great poet, artist, designer and latterly socialist William Morris (1834-96) visited Wiltshire on his 'anti-scrape' activities that were intended to discourage the then prevalent ruination by restoration of so many fine historic buildings. He came during this visit to Bradford and recorded his generally favourable impressions of the town in a letter to Mrs Burne-Jones dated 13 May 1889:

> Quite a pretty town and as gay as gay; away from the downs in a steep little valley built all up the southern-looking slope ; all up and down with steps and queer nooks: of stone every house, most of them old, a good many mediæval. The bridge fifteenth-century, with a queer little toll-house on it. The church a very big and fine one, but scraped to death by G. Scott, the

(happily) dead dog. Close by the Saxon chapel, a very beautiful little building, but shamefully vulgarised by restoration, cast iron railings, and sixpence a head. Out in the meadow, awkwardly near the Railway Station, Barton Farm with old house and farm buildings, the big fourteenth-century barn one of them. It is very fine, but I think Great Coxwell is bigger, and I like it better.

Bradford possesses a long and interesting history. A circular earthwork (821615) at Budbury on the hill west of the town probably dates from the Iron Age, and a Roman presence at Budbury was long ago established by the discovery of several Roman stone coffins and many coins. No coins of very early date have to my knowledge been recorded, although a few of Antonius Pius dating from about AD 150 have been found. More recently a large Roman villa was excavated in the 1990s beneath a school playing field also at Budbury.

When Saxon invaders were expanding westward out of the open Wiltshire chalklands towards Bath the *Anglo-Saxon Chronicle* for AD 652 recorded: 'In this year Cenwalh fought at Bradford on Avon'. Cenwalh was the Saxon king of Wessex who was constantly at war with the Britons as the Saxons extended their territories. The *Chronicle* does

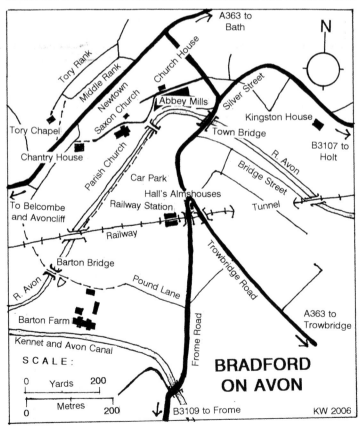

not identify his opponents at Bradford but as one account indicates that this was a civil war his enemies may on this occasion rival Saxons and not Britons. A settlement then seems to have developed at Bradford after Aldhelm (c. 640-709) of Malmesbury founded a small monastery here.

My family connections with Bradford do not I believe unduly influence my opinion that Bradford provides the best historic town walk in this district. I say this because it is larger than Malmesbury, its river runs through the centre rather than around the town, and it also has the canal. The extremely beautiful Castle Combe is only a large village, and Bradford's other rival Corsham has neither a river nor a canal.

Bradford Tithe Barn

One of the finest of Bradford's many architectural attractions is the magnificent Barton Farm (823603) that stands on level ground beside the Avon a short distance south of the town centre. Twenty-three years after the boy Ethelred's attendants made him king of Wessex by treacherously murdering his elder half-brother Edward the Martyr at Corfe in Dorset, in a belated act of contrition Ethelred II in 1001 AD granted Bradford to the Abbey of Shaftesbury and here the abbess later built as her abbey grange Barton Farm that is now considered to be one of the finest surviving Medieval farm groups in the England. Its buildings include a large early-14th century timber-framed tithe-barn, a timber-framed granary on staddle stones, and an ancient but re-modelled farmhouse, all built of the local stone and roofed with the stone slates that are so redolent of the Cotswolds. Near the farm is Barton Bridge (823605), a Medieval packhorse bridge beside a former ford across the Avon.

The barn is generally open and it is a truly memorable experience to enter its dimly-lighted interior and see the daylight pouring through the cruciform opening in its west gable. This cruciform aperture generates in this monastic barn an ecclesiastical feeling far greater than exists in many churches and it was presumably this feature that persuaded Pevsner to describe this barn as being: 'as monumental as a monumental church'. On each of its long sides the barn has a pair of cart porches, large ones on its north side to allow heavily-laden wagons to enter, and on its south smaller porches that are sufficiently large to allow the unladen wagons to leave after their loads had been spread on the stone-paved threshing floors that link the porches across the barn. The barn is truly immense in scale and I can recollect in the early 1960s passing it daily and watching with interest the apparently interminable progress on the task of re-slating its huge roof.

Packhorse Bridge, Barton Farm

Between the Tithe Barn and the farmhouse stands the West Barn, an award-winning rebuilding that was undertaken after this little barn had been destroyed by fire. An 1877 watercolour in the V and A Museum by G. P. Boyce shows the West Barn roofed with stone slates, and it is a pity that for reasons of economy it had to be re-roofed with red clay tiles. Dendrochronology has established that this West Barn dates from the late-13th century and is therefore older than the Tithe Barn. Barton Farm stands towards the east end of Barton Farm Country Park and from it an excellent three-mile waterside walk may be taken west to Avoncliff

Looking through the Tithe Barn north to south (below left)

Interior of south porch of Tithe Barn (below)

Recostructed West Barn of Barton Farm

(see later, pages 277-8), along the River Avon one way and the canal towpath the other.

From Barton Farm the town centre may be reached either down Pound Lane, through the large station car park past the railway bridge over the river, or best of all along the pleasant riverside walk. All three alternatives eventually take you to the Town Bridge over the River Avon.

On the Frome Road near the station approach on the Barton Farm side of Bradford stands a small building that would grace any Cotswold town. John Hall's Almshouses for old men consists of a range of stone-built cottages with a hipped stone-slated roof. It was built by the Bradford clothier John Hall and a cartouche over the door bears his arms ('Sable with three battleaxes'), the date 1700, and the motto *Deo et pauperibus*. Wrought iron battle axes adorn the gates which are flanked with stone piers with ball finials. Although built nineteen years later, these Bradford almshouses are reminiscent of the Hungerford Almshouses at Corsham (see earlier, pages 205-6). The Bradford gatepiers resemble those at Corsham, and both buildings have a heraldic display of their sponsors carved above their doors, but the Halliday arms at Corsham are much more exuberant than are the Hall arms at Bradford and the architectural style of the Bradford almshouses is also more restrained than at Corsham. This reflects the change in architectural taste that had taken place in the two decades that separate the two buildings, away from undigested classical baroque style of Charles II's reign at Corsham to the more correct classicism of the Queen Anne period at Bradford. The spherical stone ball-finials at both of these buildings, that so often appear on gatepiers in the Wiltshire Cotswolds, are traditionally said to be recollections of the times when victors in battle set the heads of their

Hall's Almshouses

defeated enemies on their gates, just as in Tudor times the heads of executed traitors were displayed on spikes above gateways.

Bradford grew up around the 'broad ford' over the river, from which it derives its name. The Town Bridge was originally built beside this ford in the 13th century as a narrow bridge, and original work may be seen on its east side where the two southernmost arches are ribbed and pointed while the other seven date from the 15th century. The west side of the bridge consists entirely of semi-circular arches dating from the 17th century when the bridge was widened. As it now stands the Town Bridge is a fine nine-arched stone bridge with perched on one of its cutwaters a small square stone building with a chimney and a corbelled stone roof that has served as a toll-house, a prison, and as an ammunition store, although it was probably built as a chapel. This structure has generally been assumed to be a 17th century reconstruction of an earlier predecessor, although the fact that Leland omitted to mention it when he wrote in the 16th century: 'Bradeford bridge hath nine fair arches of stone' raises the question did it exist in his time? About a hundred years later John Aubrey mentioned it when he wrote: 'here is a strong and handsome bridge in the middest of which is

Entance to Hall's Almshouses

a little chapelle as at Bathe for masse'. This little building has probably been periodically reconstructed, although John Buckler's 1808 water colour of the Town Bridge shows it as it is today with its corbelled base, chimney, stone roof, and stone finial. The 19th century drying house behind the Old Court at Avoncliff (see later, page 267) appears to have been very closely modelled on this little structure, but at Avoncliff with a central chimney instead of a finial. The ford beside the Town Bridge continued to be used as an alternative river crossing until the 19th century when its north end was blocked by the erection of a quay.

Town Bridge & Chapel

Near the north end of the Town Bridge is The Shambles (826610), an ancient pedestrian shopping passage with on the post office a datestone inscribed 'E VIII R, 1936' that is unusual as Edward VIII reigned for less than a year. The name of The Shambles arises from the fact that here was formerly held a meat market, and in The Shambles a protestant martyr called Traywell was burnt at the stake in the reign of Queen Mary.

Down a lane that runs east out of Mason's Lane, the continuation north-east (right) at a Tee-junction uphill out of Market Street, is all that survives of a former circular tower mill (828612) whose Bath stone ashlar tower has been reduced in height and capped with a conical stone-slated roof with wide eaves. This building was in the 1860s known locally as Old Mill and we know that it was a corn mill because a windmiller was sought at Bradford in 1809. As early as 1817 it was advertised as 'formerly used as a Wind Mill but now converted to Tenements' and it is now converted into a dwelling. This windmill would once have been a prominent feature in the Bradford scene as its tower, now reduced in height and devoid of its sails, is still very visible from the Town Bridge.

Saxon Church

Church Street contains a number of buildings of interest. Opposite the splendid late-19th century multi-storey Abbey Mills stands the 16th century Church House that was built for church functions and was mentioned by Leland. The Saxon Church of St Lawrence (824609) is the oldest and architecturally probably the most important building in Bradford, being a pure Anglo-Saxon building that was was re-discovered when the rector Canon Jones spotted it in the mid-19th century from the hill above embedded among other buildings and being used as a cottage. It was however prominent only a few years earlier in an engraving in John Britton's *The Beauties of England and Wales* (1814). William Morris campaigned to prevent excessive restoration of this ancient church that is sometimes thought to be the church that St. Aldhelm built at Bradford in the late-7th century AD, although its superstructure with its low-relief round-headed blind arcading is distinctly Romanesque in feeling and is almost certainly of the 10th century when Norman influence was already becoming strong in England. The church may however occupy the site and possibly the foundations of St Aldhelm's church.

Opposite the Saxon church stands its successor the large Parish Church of the Holy Trinity that was originally Norman but is much

altered, and was obviously built to accommodate a growing population.
It should be seen for its many interesting features that are too numerous
to be mentioned here other than the monument to General Henry
Shrapnel (1761-1842), a local man who expended much of his family
fortune inventing the shrapnel shell that was decisive in many Napoleonic
battles including Waterloo, the Steward monument (see page 220), and
the multi-panelled Millennium tapestry that is beautifully displayed and
depicts many events from Bradford's history.

North of the west end of the parish church is the Jacobean house
(823608) of Edward Orpin (d.1781), the parish clerk whose portrait in the
Tate Gallery was for more than a hundred years as the plaque on Orpin's
House indicates attributed to Thomas Gainsborough (1727-88) during
the time that he lived at Bath from 1760 to 1784. However, when 'The
Parish Clerk' was exhibited among other Gainsboroughs at an exhibition
at the Tate in 1953 its provenance was questioned by the experts and
subsequent detailed research indicated that it was not by Gainsborough.
'The Parish Clerk' was therefore omitted from Ellis Waterhouse's 1958
catalogue of the painter's work and Orpin's portrait is now generally
attributed to William Hoare (d.1792), the Bath painter whose style of
portraiture often closely resembled that of Gainsborough. One wonders
in what circumstances the humble parish clerk, who is buried in an easily

Orpin's house

Chantry House

Gazebo at west end of Barton Orchard

identified marked tomb under the churchyard wall only a few yards from his front door, came to be painted by an eminent society painter.

Facing east from the west end of the parish churchyard is the Chantry House. Sometimes known as the Little Chantry, it was built in the 16th century by the clothier Thomas Horton of nearby Iford on land that had belonged to a chantry founded in the parish church in 1524 by the then vicar William Birde. Chantry chapels were added to churches on the understanding that perpetual prayers and sung masses – hence the name chantry – would be offered for the repose of the soul of the sponsor. This one failed when Birde was in 1540 with Walter Lord Hungerford of Heytesbury and Farleigh accused of having supported the Pilgrimage of Grace (1536-7), the northern rebellion that attracted widespread support in protest against Henry VIII's Dissolution of the smaller monasteries. Birde was said to have remarked to a friend going off to join the rebels: 'Seest thou not how the King plucketh down images and abbeys every day? . . . the great master of all is a heretic and such a one as there is not his like in the world'. As this rising posed the greatest challenge to Henry VIII's position during his reign it was ferociously suppressed and Birde and Lord Hungerford were attainted on charges of treason and heresy. The former was fortunate to lose merely his living as Hungerford was beheaded with Thomas Cromwell on Tower Hill. Birde's chantry was then dissolved and its lands fell into the hands of Thomas Horton who built his Chantry House on the chantry lands. The house was refronted early in the 17th century and some time later it was given an elegant early-18th century facade overlooking the churchyard. It later became the home of the Hobhouse family (see Broughton Gifford, pages 231-2).

Slightly uphill from Chantry House is Barton Orchard with at its west end a nice little early-Georgian gazebo that faces south across the River Avon. From Chantry House a climb is recommended past the east end of Barton Orchard and up footpaths and many steps through the terraces successively named Newtown, Middle Rank, and Tory Rank to enjoy splendid panoramic views across the town. The name Tory is derived from 'tor' meaning hill and at the west end of Tory Rank on the high promontory at the top of Wellpath Hill is the 15th century Chapel of St Mary that Aubrey considered: 'the finest hermitage I have seen in England, several rooms and a very neat chapel of freestone'. It is shown as 'The Hermitage' on a 1743 map of Methuen property but when workspace in Bradford was at a premium in the 18th century it became a cloth factory. By the 19th century it was 'in ruins', but in 1870 it was sensitively restored. The district is called Ladywell as the spring that once supplied Bradford with running water issues from a cave below St Mary's Chapel that is, in my experience over many years usually left open.

Tory Chapel from Newtown

Non-conformity flourished among the Bradford cloth-workers as a radical reaction against the established religion and its popularity is demonstrated by the many non-conformist chapels that exist throughout the town. From about 1780 until 1884 Bradford was the centre of Methodism in north Wiltshire and after John Wesley first visited the town in 1739 he was subsequently often here but was usually obliged to preach at Bearfield and on at least one occasion out of doors near the Town Bridge. A Methodist preacher called William Hitchens described in a letter to Wesley dated 28 February 1757 how he had been pressed for a soldier and imprisoned for a night in the prison on Bradford bridge. The Methodist chapel in Market Street at Bradford was opened in 1756 thirty-four years before Wesley's last visit to Bradford in August 1790, the year

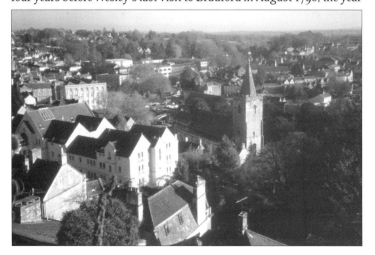

Bradford from its Hill

Bearfield Church

Selina, Countess of Huntingdon

in which another Methodist chapel was opened at the top of Coppice Hill. The following year Wesley died.

Possibly Bradford's most charming chapel is the tiny Bearfield Church (824614) near the top of the hill on the east side of Huntingdon Street. This was built in the 1780s by Selina Shirley (1707-91), a daughter of the Earl Ferrars who by her marriage in 1728 to the 9th Earl of Huntingdon became the Countess of Huntingdon. After the death of her husband in 1747 she devoted her considerable wealth to religion and sided with George Whitfield in his dispute with John Wesley. She financed the building of sixty-four chapels but autocratically insisted on exercising complete control by training and appointing her own ministers while still remaining in the Anglican church. In 1783 the bishops understandably ruled that her rank and wealth did not entitle her to appoint Anglican chaplains and she then seceded from the Church of England and declared her chapels dissenting places of worship. In 1790 she formed them into an association known as the Countess of Huntingdon's Connexion. For attempting to recruit members of the aristocracy she was derided by many members of the upper classes as 'Pope Joan of Methodism', although George III made it known that he wished there was a Lady Huntingdon in every diocese. Soon after her death in 1791 her 'Connexion' failed and Bearfield Church together with most of the Countess of Huntingdon's chapels became Congregational.

As I approach the end of this account of the history and topography of the Wiltshire Cotswolds I am aware that the majority of the secular

Woolley Grange

buildings that I have described are either small vernacular Cotswold cottages or medium-sized Tudor-Jacobean manor houses. There are however at Bradford but a little away from the town centre and consequently not seen by the majority of visitors, three important medium-sized houses of various architectural styles and periods that are of considerable interest and worthy of description. These are Woolley Grange, Belcombe Court, and Kingston House.

Woolley Grange (837616) is practically unknown because it is in summer half-concealed behind foliage and a high wall west of the minor road that runs north-east out of Bradford to Woolley Green. The house was built in the plague year of 1665, the year in which Wren visited Paris to study its architecture, and it illustrates how the vernacular Elizabethan style of architecture continued to be employed in this region after it had become practically extinct elsewhere. The only concessions that this Carolean-period stone-slated house with its gabled front and traditional drip-moulded casement windows makes to the by then fashionable mild baroque classicism are the balustrades to its bay windows and its two-storeyed porch, and even these may date from the 1860s when its then owner Captain Palairet reconstructed the house and had the road from Bradford to Woolley Green diverted away from his house that subsequently became for a time a nursing home and is now a hotel.

Belcombe Court

Seventy years after the building of Woolley Grange, Belcombe Court (816606) was built on the north side of the Avoncliff road (Belcombe Road) to the west of Bradford. It occupies a 65-acre south-facing site consisting of mixed woodland and landscaped grounds, with a grotto and a small lake beside the house near the road. It is an important house in the revived Palladian style that from about 1715 was promoted for political reasons by the new royal House of Hanover as a reaction against the mild English baroque style that had been

Belcombe Court

practised by the elderly Wren and his followers in the preceding reign of the Stuart Queen Anne. In the early-18th century the Yerburys had become very prosperous woollen manufacturers in Bradford and when young Francis Yerbury (1706-78) decided in the 1730s to update his 15th century house house at Belcombe he appointed as his architect John Wood the Elder of Bath (1704-54). Wood designed for him a pure Palladian house that was completed in 1734, only about ten years later than Stourhead House in south-west Wiltshire that was one of the seminal buildings of the 18th century English Palladian revival. The commission to design Belcombe came early in Wood's local career as he had only started to work in his native Bath in about 1726 and Queen Square, his initial major town-planning contribution towards his plan for the new city of Bath, was not completed until 1736.

The Yerburys had according to John Wood used Belcombe as 'offices and Workhouses'. For them he refronted the existing range of mainly 15th century buildings and added a new wing with a pedimented three-bay south front in the pure Palladian style that he was then employing in his redevelopment of Bath. This prompted Pevsner to suggest that Belcombe really 'belongs to Bath' and that it 'ought really to be across the border in Somerset'. Wood's Palladian wing is in fine Bath stone ashlar and its principal windows are dressed with moulded surrounds, pediments, and with balusters that are echoed in the low curved stone balustrades capped with urns which sweep forward from either side of the frontage. Belcombe is stylistically utterly different from Woolley Grange that was built only seventy years earlier, and it demonstrates how rapidly the new Palladian ideal could be disseminated into the provinces, although Belcombe was a rather special case in that Wood was at the time Palladianising Bath only eight miles away. Here at Belcombe he showed none of the fear of exterior decoration that had so often inhibited English Palladian architects in their sometimes over-bleak reaction against the exuberances of the Continental baroque. Wood was particularly proud of his 'work at Belcombe' which he rather immodestly decribed as: 'the best tetrastyle [four-columned] frontispiece in square pillars [they are actually pilasters] of the Ionic order yet executed in or about Bath'. Inside Belcombe he was similarly exuberant, for example in the charming little room described by Sacheverell Sitwell in his *British Architects and Craftsmen* (1945) as: 'an enchanting little octagonal ante-room by the elder Wood with corner cupboards, swags of flowers upon the walls, an octagon cornice, and a ceiling of cupids holding wreaths of flowers'. Sitwell considered that 'In this little room Wood shows a delicate fantasy and imagination of a high order', and as he is known to have sometimes undertaken landscape design John Wood may also have laid out the extensive grounds around Belcombe where much of the 18th century landscaping survives, including a small lake, a rotunda, an ornamental cottage in the picturesque style, a gazebo with wide-ranging views, and a grotto of tufa stone decorated with shells. Because this house of national importance has escaped the attention of most topographical writers and architectural historians, Belcombe has been described in some detail, but it stands in private grounds and as it is screened by a balustrade-capped wall and large trees it is only visible from the road in winter.

Readers may however like to visualise the scene in 1787 when a huge crowd of angry weavers stormed up to Belcombe determined to wring concessions from their employers. The event was described in a contemporary account quoted by Canon Jones in his *Bradford on Avon: A History and Description* (1907):

> Some 1500 or more weavers from Bradford and Trowbridge having compelled their masters to acquiesce in certain regulations, were so flushed with success that they marched in triumph from Trowbridge to Bradford, but were repelled at the entrance of the latter place by the principal inhabitants. At Belcomb Brook they also met with a stout resistance, for Mr Yerbury had planted two patereroes [small guns] at his windows, which swept the lawn. Supported by many armed friends, he addressed the rioters in so able a manner as to induce them to retire without causing any disturbance. The military arrived the next day and the combination was at an end.

The use of the name 'Belcomb Brook' for this house in the above account is worthy of comment as this was the name given to the reach of the River Avon around Avoncliff on Andrews and Dury's 1773 map, and evidently the house became known by that name.

The third of these three important Bradford houses is Kingston House (831608) that predates the other two and also stands behind a high wall south of the B3107 Holt Road at the eastern edge of Bradford. As it

Kingston House

was the manor house of the Hall family of Bradford clothiers Kingston House is also known as The Hall or Hall's House after its builder John Hall, or sometimes as the Duke's House after its later owner the Duke of Kingston. The house is in an exuberant Elizabethan-Jacobean style with a profusion of gables, stone mullioned and transomed bay windows, a multitude of chimneys, much Flemish-style strapwork cresting its bays, and balustraded terraces. Despite its many elaborate features it emulates the local vernacular style by having stone-slated roofs and rubble-stone minor elevations. Pevsner described this house as 'the one nationally major mansion of Bradford, not a town house but a country house in character'. With its classical detail grafted on to its symmetrical gabled front, Kingston House dates from the time in the late-16th century that was quaintly described by Horace Walpole as being: 'not Gothic, but of that betweenity that intervened when Gothic declined and Palladian was creeping in'. It was chosen to be the model for English domestic architecture at the British Pavilion at the 1900 Paris Exhibition, and it stands like Belcombe in its own private grounds. It is however distantly visible among its trees from the east end of Tory Rank above Newtown at the bottom of Conigre Hill (823610), or obliquely over its high garden wall from the bottom of Mill Lane (827607).

After the Dukedom of Kingston became extinct Kingston House was in the early-19th century made into apartments for workmen and was even for a time a woolstore until the 1830s when it was occupied by Samuel Pitman, the clothier father of the inventor of Pitman's shorthand. In about 1850 the Moulton family of rubber manufacturers acquired and restored the house and still occupy it.

*Kingston House (centre)
from Bradford Hill*

Having indicated that these three fine Bradford houses are not easily seen from the public roads that pass them, I should mention the grounds of both Belcombe Court and Kingston House have sometimes been opened for charity under the national gardens scheme. Woolley Grange is now a hotel and can be seen from the road in winter.

Kingston House is associated with a notorious scandal that attracted national interest in the late-18th century.

A Bradford on Avon Bigamist

THE SCANDAL in connection with Kingston House at Bradford was a case of bigamy in high society that attracted national interest in 1776. It concerned Elizabeth Chudleigh (1720-88), a notorious society beauty who was described by Horace Walpole in a letter to Sir Horace Mann (10 July 1774) as 'a beautiful but weak-minded and illiterate woman'. After becoming a maid-of-honour to Augusta, Princess of Wales, Elizabeth bigamously married Evelyn Pierrepont, the 2nd Duke of Kingston (1711-1773), who was descended from the Hall family of Bradford clothiers. The Duke died in 1776 and an enquiry into the marriage was then instigated by the Pierrepont family in an attempt to prevent Elizabeth from inheriting the ducal estates including Kingston House where she is said to have sometimes lived. The so-called marriage became the subject of a parliamentary enquiry by the House of Lords which declared it to be bigamous on her part.

Elizabeth was the only child of Colonel Thomas Chudleigh, the lieutenant-governor of Chelsea Hospital. At his death in 1726 the six-year-old Elizabeth and her mother were left poorly provided for but some years later Sir William Pulteney, the heir to the Earl of Bath, took an interest in Elizabeth after meeting her out shooting and arranged for her to become a maid-of-honour to the Princess of Wales. When Elizabeth was twenty-three in 1743 the nineteen-year-old James, 6th Duke of Hamilton, proposed to marry her but her aunt intercepted and kept their letters and Elizabeth understandably believed that he had lost interest in her. Then, on a visit in 1744 with her aunt to Lainston House a short distance north-west of Winchester, Elizabeth met at Winchester races Lieutenant the Hon. Augustus John Hervey, the naval officer heir to the Earldom of Bristol, and they were married in the chapel of Lainston House on 4 August 1744, clandestinely but significantly in the presence of witnesses. In 1747 Elizabeth had a son by Lieutenant Hervey but after the child died young the couple separated and Miss Chudleigh as she had continued to be known remained a maid-of-honour by keeping her marriage secret, although some years later she for some reason persuaded Mr Amis, the dying rector of Lainston, to enter the marriage in his parish register.

Elizabeth now acquired a reputation for indelicate conduct by appearing as Iphigenia at the Venetian ambassador's masquerade wearing little more than a smirke. A contemporary drawing of Elizabeth in her costume reveals that her dress that was so diaphanous that the bluestocking Lady Mary Wortley Montagu – a Pierrepont from West Dean in south Wiltshire and so related to Elizabeth's second 'husband' – commented that Elizabeth 'was so naked that the high priest might easily inspect her entrails', and Horace Walpole reported in a letter that Miss Chudleigh: 'was so naked that you could have taken her for Andromeda'. George II was so enthralled that he momentarily forgot his notorious meanness and presented Elizabeth with a thirty-five guinea watch. She is said to have reciprocated by in 1754 encouraging the Prince of Wales (later George III) in his love affair with the Quakeress Hannah Lightfoot whom he was rumoured to have married, a circumstance that if true would have rendered his later marriage to Queen Charlotte bigamous. In 1760 Elizabeth became the mistress of the Duke of Kingston and with her husband threatening divorce she denied their marriage and in March 1770 bigamously married the Duke of Kingston at St George's Hanover Square.

Evelyn Pierrepont, the 2nd Duke of Kingston (1712-1773), was the only son of William, Earl of Kingston, by his wife Rachel, the daughter of Thomas Bayntun of Little Chalfield two miles north-east of Bradford on Avon. When Evelyn was only one his father died aged only twenty-one of smallpox in 1713 and Evelyn was subsequently innoculated against the disease by Lady Mary Wortley Montagu who was a pioneer practitioner of innoculation. From 1726 to 1736 he went on the Grand Tour to the Continent and as the young owner of immense properties he gained a dubious reputation as a gambler and was described by Walpole as: 'a very weak man of the greatest beauty'. Among the estates that he had inherited in and around Bradford was Kingston House, then known as

Elizabeth Chudleigh at the Venetian Ambassador's Ball

The Hall, that had been built by John Hall who died in 1631 in the very early-17th century. The last of the male Halls, another John Hall, at his death in 1711 surprisingly left his estates to Rachel, the daughter of Elizabeth Bayntun who was the wife of Thomas Bayntun of Little Chalfield two miles north-east of Bradford. This unexpected bequest has been explained by a suggestion that is supported by some evidence that Rachel was the child of a relationship between John Hall and Elizabeth Bayntun. If this were the case it explains John Hall's bequest and also provides a link between the Halls and the Pierrepont Dukes of Kingston, Elizabeth Bayntun's daughter Rachel, the possible daughter of John Hall, having married William Pierrepont the son and heir of Evelyn Pierrepont (1665?-1726) who became the First Duke of Kingston and married Elizabeth, the daughter and heiress of Sir John Evelyn of West Dean in south-east Wiltshire. The Dukes of Kingston also owned extensive properties in Bath where their name is commemorated in Duke Street and Pierrepont Street.

Evelyn Pierrepont, 2nd Duke of Kingston

After being Deputy Lieutenant of Wiltshire in 1701, Evelyn Pierrepont was in 1715 created the First Duke of Kingston-upon-Humber. He then became a member of George I's privy council and the father of the celebrated Lady Wortley Montagu. His son William Pierrepont died in 1713, as did his wife Rachel in 1722 aged only thirty-seven, and in due course their grandson another Evelyn Pierrepont (d.1773) succeeded his grandfather as 2nd Duke of Kingston and assumed his seat in the House of Lords where he seems never to have made a speech or raised a protest. This man 'married' Elizabeth Chudleigh, presumably unaware that she was the Countess of Bristol and had a surviving husband.

The Pierreponts had long been connected with Nottingham. A Pierrepont from that town fought for Richard III at Bosworth in 1485 and during the 1745 Jacobite rebellion the 2nd Duke was charged with preparing Nottingham for a siege. He also contributed a thousand pounds towards raising a volunteer regiment of cavalry which was named Kingston's Light Horse. After Culloden in 1746 this regiment disgraced itself by brutally massacreing helpless fugitives but Cumberland was so pleased with their exploits at Culloden that he proposed to re-muster Kingston's Horse as a regular cavalry regiment under his own name and this may have persuaded the Duke of Kingston to take up his military career during which he was gazetted colonel in 1755, lieutenant-general in 1759, and in 1772 at the age of sixty-one full general.

At his death in 1773 the Duke left his properties to Elizabeth as his apparent wife for life on condition that she did not remarry. Under this constraint she travelled extensively abroad and for a time lived scandalously in Rome where she as usual attracted much attention, not least that of Pope Clement XIV. Rumours that her marriage was bigamous were now circulating and the Duke's outraged family challenged its validity and her inheritance of the Kingston estates. In 1774 the 'Duchess' returned to England, but fled abroad a few hours before law officers arrived to arrest her. In November 1774 the ecclesiatical courts declared her to be Mrs Hervey, and in December 1774 she was indicted for feloniously bigamously marrying the Duke of Kingston. In January 1775 she was again in Rome but in May of that year she surrendered herself to the King's Bench and was bailed. Things then for a time remained quiet and by late 1775 her case was almost forgotten, until Samuel Foote (1720-77) parodied Elizabeth as Kitty Crocodile in his play *A Trip to Calais* that although not licenced for performance was printed.

In November 1775 Elizabeth petitioned the House of Lords for trial, the following month she fainted in church at the Chapel Royal, and in March 1776 the House of Lords decided that a trial should take place. Tickets for the trial were in great demand and at her trial in Westminster Hall on 15 April 1776 she put on a dramatic performance as the Dowager Duchess of Kingston, dressed in mourning for her 'husband' in a black hood and, being then fifty-six, displaying 'but small remains of that beauty of which kings and princes were once so enamoured'. Despite having contrived to destroy much evidence of her first marriage, on the evidence of her marriage entry in the Lainton register all the peers who voted declared her 'Guilty, upon my honour' except for the Duke of Newcastle who declared her 'Guilty erroneously, but not intentionally'. With the trial was going against her Elizabeth feigned illness, and when found guilty she escaped being branded in the hand as a bigamist by claiming the exemption allowed to nobles. A former lover Lord Camden said that he felt it would have been ungallant for him to vote for branding, but also said that he would have acceded to Elizabeth being burned in the hand, but with a cold iron! As her marriage was not formally annulled the 'Duchess' contrived to hold on to the Kingston estates, including Kingston House at Bradford, until her death in 1789.

Elizabeth was now the butt of innumerable coarse society jokes. Her ability to down two bottles of wine had attracted the admiration of Frederick II, and her notorious enjoyment of everything in pairs – which was jokingly said of both bottles and husbands! – prompted Horace Walpole to suggest that a two-headed calf born in Essex must surely be hers. Sir Robert Keith declared that he would be prepared to marry her provided that a grenadier joined him in the nuptials, and when Elizabeth indignantly told Lord Chesterfield of a rumour circulating that she had given birth to twins his lordship offered her scant comfort by wittily replying: 'Madam, I make a point of never believing more than half of what I hear'.

To escape her notoriety Elizabeth ultimately fled to Russia where she met and was befriended by Catherine the Great (1729-1796), who was surely a congenial friend. She then moved to France where she purchased a palace. She died suddenly in Paris in 1788, aged sixty-eight, having enjoyed several love affairs and turned down a proposal of marriage from a Prince Radzivil.

At her death the Duke's estates in accordance with his Will passed to his nephew Charles Medows (1737-1816), the younger son of his sister Francis Medows. His elder brother Evelyn Philip Medows unsuccessfully challenged the inheritance but Charles assumed the name Pierrepont and was in 1806 created the First Earl Manvers.

Avoncliff and the Old Court

ABOUT A MILE AND A HALF south-west of Bradford is Avoncliff (804598) that prior to the construction of the Kennet and Avon Canal and the Great Western Railway was merely a tiny cloth-manufacturing settlement, as is confirmed by its lack of any religious establishment and the fact that it was merely 'Avon Cliff Mill' on Andrew's and Dury's 1773 map. This now tranquil place stands on the Bristol Avon at a point where the steepness of the valley is reflected in the 'cliff' element of its name and its beauty is indicated by its old name of Belcombe meaning beautiful valley. Here at some unknown date a substantial weir was constructed across the river to secure a sufficient head of water to drive the water-wheels of the mills that have for centuries existed on both banks of the river. Daniel Mill on the south or Westwood side of the river started life as a corn mill. became a fulling mill in 1763, and when owned by the Yerbury family of clothiers of Bradford it in 1791 became the first recorded Wiltshire mill to be equipped with water-

Avoncliff from below Turleigh

Avoncliff weir from aqueduct

powered machinery for cloth-making. By 1867 it had become a flock mill that it continued to be until the Second World War. Its chimney indicates that it at some time became steam driven. Old Mill at the opposite north end of the weir was a fulling mill in 1763 and before 1791 it too was in the hands of Francis Yerbury (1707-78) who let it to tenants. In 1860 it was converted forn corn-milling by Barretts of Twerton at Bath who added a large breast wheel under a metal extension that is now a rusty corrugated iron-clad ruin on the point of collapse.

When enjoying the tranquility of Avoncliff today it is difficult to imagine the times in the early and mid-19th century when it suffered from successive prolongued visitations of two armies of 'navvies' engaged in building first the canal and then the railway. These were gangs of the notoriously rough men who were described by one of Robert Stephenson's railway engineers as:

generally the terror of the surrounding country . . . completely a class by themselves as Gipsies . . . Possessed of all the daring and recklessness as the Smuggler without any of the redeeming qualities . . . their ferocious behaviour can only be equalled by the brutality of their language. It may be truly said, their hand is against every man, and before they have been long located, every man's hand is against them: and woe befall any woman, with the slightest share of modesty, whose ears they can assail . . . they put at defiance any local constabulary force; consequently crimes of the most atrocious character are common, and robbery without any attempt at concealment, has been an everyday occurrance, wherever they have been congregated in large numbers.

Derelict Mill and Weir at Avoncliff

One of the oldest buildings at Avoncliff is the Cross Guns Inn that was formerly the Carpenter's Arms and probably acquired its present name when military firing ranges existed at Avoncliff during the Boer and First World Wars. The deeds of the inn that go back to 1712 refer to a previous inn on the site a hundred years earlier, but the principal building of interest at Avoncliff is a mystery building that is of such great interest that I propose to describe its past in detail, and suggest why it was built.

This building, that was for long known as Old Court but is now known as Ankley Square, stands at the extreme west end of Avoncliff (at 803599) and may be seen by walking from the canal down the vehicular ramp towards the Cross Guns public house and then doubling back left under the aqueduct and walking for a short distance west along the footpath towards Freshford. Old Court is the large building that looms up to the left of the path, U-shaped in plan and apparently of late-

Old Court at Avoncliff

18th or early-19th century date. Unlike many of the buildings of this area Old Court is not built in the Cotswold style as its walls are rendered and colour washed, and although it has stone-slated roofs on its entrance side that faces north, its seldom-seen rear roof slopes are clay-tiled. The bluff and rather bleak Georgian front of the building faces across the river, the canal, and the railway, and at its rear are a number of ancillary buildings. It is obviously an institutional building and we can approximately date its construction from the fact that it is absent from Andrews and Dury's 1773 map of Wiltshire which marked the area that it now occupies 'Hanckley', and it was also absent from a 1792 parish map of Westwood. It was however shown on the first Ordnance Survey of about 1820 and these facts seem to establish that Old Court was built after 1792 and before about 1820, which would make it approximately contemporary with the construction of the canal.

The mystery over the purpose for which Old Court was built was mentioned by Kenneth Ponting, a historian of the West of England woollen industry who after suggesting that it must be connected with the woollen industry admitted that the building was 'most puzzling'. Sir Nikolaus Pevsner was similarly mystified when he wrote in the Wiltshire volume of his *The Buildings of England* (1963) of: 'The big, blank building with three ranges round a courtyard, and no redeeming feature save a heavy debased Grecian doorway'. After also mentioning that he had been told that it 'was built as a weaving establishment in the C17' Pevsner, who was seldom non-plussed by a building, speculated:

Buildings to the rear of Old Court

How is one to understand that? The most likely thing is that they were weavers' cottages, built at one go, and even then they would be extremely interesting. At the back the CHAPEL, also early C19, and behind this the domed weavers' DRYING HOUSE, with a top chimney.

The buildings to the rear of Old Court, which may be viewed from the public footpath that runs up the hill towards Westwood along the west edge of the building, include a former chapel in the Regency Gothick style and the building described by Pevsner as 'the domed weavers' drying house' has an interesting stone-slabbed (that is as opposed to a stone slated) roof that closely resembles in size and construction that of the town bridge chapel at Bradford. Pevsner was as he suspected misinformed when told that the Old Court dated from the 17th century as is shown by the cartographical evidence mentioned above, but the question remains: For what purpose was Old Court built?

Drying House behind Old Court

The building's date of construction between 1792 and about 1820 makes it approximately coeval with the construction of the canal, but it seems unlikely to have been connected with that undertaking, and documentary evidence indicating that it was built by a John Moggeridge on land bought in 1791 by two clothiers, himself and a man called Joyce, implies a connection with the woollen industry.

An 1816 committee report reveals that at about the time in the 1790s when Old Court was probably built clothiers were procuring pauper and orphan children, many of them from London. The authorities were only too willing to send them away into the provinces where, from the age of eleven to twenty-one, they were often bound as 'apprentices' in the cloth industry and as such became virtual slave labour in the factories. Having contracted to house, clothe and feed these children, the clothiers built for them establishments known as 'prentice houses' near their mills and it seems likely that Old Court was built to be one of these establishments. It is relevant to note that John Moggeridge was the brother-in-law of the Bradford on Avon clothier John William Yerbury, that Queen Elizabeth's Apprentice Act was not repealed until 1814, and that the importation from afar of pauper children as virtual slave labour had by 1816 become so scandalous that an Act was passed limiting to forty miles the distance over which a child could be removed to be apprenticed. In the context of young children being employed as slave labour in factories it is also a matter of interest that the family of Lord Ashley (1801-1885), who as the 7th Earl of Shaftesbury saw through parliament much of the legislation regulating the employment of child labour in factories, emanated from a family that had lived at Ashley less than two miles north of Avoncliff, and from that tiny hamlet took his title of Lord Ashley.

When in the mid-19th century Old Court became the local workhouse the timing of its sale and change of use also lends some support to the 'prentice' house theory. In 1832 a Commission of Enquiry into the Working of the Poor Law drew attention to the cost of 'outdoor relief' of the poor in their homes, and in 1834 the Poor Law Amendment Act stipulated that Unions of parishes should be formed administered by boards of guardians of the poor elected by ratepayers. The parishes of Bradford, Broughton Gifford, Chalfield, Freshford, Monkton Farleigh, Westwood and Wingfield were combined as the Bradford Union that in 1836 exercised its option under the Act of acquiring Old Court for £3000 as their workhouse and spending almost £2000 adapting it to accommodate 250 inmates.

The timing of the sale in 1836 of Old Court to the Bradford workhouse guardians three years after Lord Ashley's 1833 Factory Act provides extremely interesting evidence to support the suggestion that Old Court had been a 'prentice house', particularly as the 1833 Act was the first really effective Factory Act, and it made the employment of young child apprentices very much less attractive to the clothiers by imposing onerous requirements for their welfare, including a requirement that they must be provided with schooling. These expensive requirements must have shocked the owners of 'prentice' houses who may already have been uneasy about an Act of 1824 that had made slavery a capital punishment, and these factors may have precipitated the sale of Old Court in 1836.

Old people of past generations dreaded being taken into the 'the house' as they called the workhouse, and after Old Court became the local workhouse on 10 January 1880 the *Wiltshire Times* printed a piece headed 'The Entertainment at the [Avoncliff] Workhouse' describing: 'the annual fete and entertainment when all the inmates of the "house" from the child able to toddle to the aged pauper who has seen more of the "downs" than the "ups" of this life, participated in the general enjoyment'. The reporter mentioned that this establishment was sarcastically known by the local people as the 'Avoncliff Paradise', but re-assured his readers that : 'It might with fitness be remarked that the children's quarters at this workhouse are entirely removed from the adult wards, so that the young may in no way be contaminated by the impure stream of tramps and "roadsters" continually flowing through the "house"', this being a reference to the rule that demanded that vagrants could stay at any one workhouse for a restricted time and so were obliged to circulate around a succession of workhouses. The rule requiring that pauper husbands and wives should be accommodated separately was intended to inflict unhappiness and indignity, although the *Wiltshire Times* in 1888 reported the case of an elderly couple in the Avoncliff workhouse whose attainment of their golden wedding prompted the Guardians with the best of intentions to offer them shared accommodation, which both politely refused!

When Old Court was converted to a workhouse large wards and workrooms were formed, the women being housed in the east wing and the men in the west, with a house at its centre reserved for the master. The Guardians also added a kitchen, a dining room and a chapel at the back of the building, and at some time a schoolroom was built at the south end of the workhouse garden, probably to satisfy the requirement of the 1833 Factory Act that required schooling to be provided for child apprentices. A gatehouse at the north side of the square was demolished in the early-20th century.

After the 1911 National Insurance Act rendered workhouses largely redundant the inmates of Avoncliff workhouse were in 1917 removed to Warminster workhouse and the Bradford Guardians then let their building to the British Red Cross Society as a hospital for war wounded soldiers. After the First World War the building was sold in 1923 to Walter Morres who converted it into a hotel which he called Old Court, and during the Second World War the building was used by the British Museum as its evacuated headquarters, but after this war it fell into disrepair. It was perhaps due to local awareness of its dismal past as successively 'prentice house', workhouse, and hospital for war-wounded soldiers from the Western Front that Old Court was on the point of being demolished when it was in the 1990s rescued and reconstructed as housing, ten houses being constructed within the main building and two more in the former chapel. A little later in 1996-7 an underground house called Ancliff Down was built in its former reservoir.

Avoncliff is a former place of industry that is now beautiful and it should on no account be missed, even if visiting it necessitates walking along the riverside public footpath or the canal towpath from Bradford to avoid the problem of finding at Avoncliff a parking place for a car.

The Winsley Plateau

To the immediate north and north-west of Avoncliff in the extreme south-west of the region covered by this book is a limestone plateau which has at its centre Winsley (799609) and to its west a wedge-shaped salient of Wiltshire that reaches west from Winsley between the Dundas Aqueduct (784626) and Freshford (790801) across the Avon almost to Midford (761607). In the north of this area the county boundary reaches the River Avon at a point about 400 yards north of Dundas Aqueduct that carries the Kennet and Avon Canal over the Avon into

Somerset, and about 400 yards south of this aqueduct the boundary turns west away from the river and for a mile and a half follows Midford Brook south-west to near Midford from where it turns back across the railway and returns east, passing west of Limpley Stoke (781607) and north of Freshford in Somerset, to rejoin the Avon opposite Murhill (at 794604). This promontory of Wiltshire into Somerset is in common with the other fringes of north-west Wiltshire described earlier in this book an essentially rural district that contains a number of interesting villages. From near Conkwell (792626) and Murhill (795607) signs may still be traced of two tramways that carried stone from quarries down to the canal, and half a mile south of Conkwell is a stone-built hip-roofed house

Dry-stone walls above Winsley

called Conkwell Grange (790616) that was designed in 1907 by Guy Dawber in a kind of William and Mary style.

My decision to extend the bounds of my Wiltshire Cotswolds as far south as Bradford is vindicated by the pronounced Cotswold character of the countryside in this area, particularly around the village of Winsley on its wold-like limestone plateau that stands about 300 feet (91 metres) above a beautiful wooded bend of the Bristol Avon and is criss-crossed by many dry-stone field walls. The old Ward Lock & Co. guide to Bath refers to 'the picturesque Limpley Stoke Valley, extending northwards along the course of the Avon for three miles', and describes it as being 'among the most romantic and beautiful in the west of England'.

In the neck of this promontory of Wiltshire into Somerset is Winsley (799609) that has a Victorian church with a Perpendicular tower described by Pevsner as 'lively' and 'quite unusual in its composition'. When the old church was demolished and rebuilt in 1841 its original tower, surmounted by the last of the several quirkily attractive saddleback roofs that we shall meet in the Wiltshire Cotswolds, was retained and linked by a passage to the new church. Winsley has had two particular 20th century associations with health care.

Turleigh Manor House

nsley Church

West of the village, between the B3109 Bath road and Murhill, was the now-demolished Winsley Chest Hospital (793609) that was built in 1903 to the design of Silcock and Reay as a sanatorium for the treatment of tuberculosis patients. The other association of Winsley with health care is the former Sutcliffe private school (798608) in the village that has now become a Dorothy House hospice.

Adjoining Winsley downhill to its south-east is Turleigh (805606) with its fine seven-bay early-Georgian manor house with good gatepiers at a bend in the road next to an early-19th century coach house that appears once to have been a tiny chapel. Another house worth noting in Turleigh is Uplands, up the hill south of the manor house and dating from about 1700.

In remote upland situations on the limestone plateau about a mile north-east of Winsley the two tiny places known as Great Ashley (813620) and Little Ashley (813624) are all that remain of the once substantial manor of *Ashelegh juxta Bradford* (1357) that belonged with Bradford on Avon to the great Abbey of Shaftesbury. The Ashley hamlets have another Shaftesbury connection in that from at least 1280 until about 1571 its tenants were the Ashley family, and Hutchins tells us in his *History of Dorset* that Henry de Ashley (d.1549) was an ancestor of the great Dorset dynasty of Ashley Cooper Earls of Shaftesbury who became nationally influential in politics and the arts. After being an MP for Wiltshire and one of Charles II's ministers, the First Earl of Shaftesbury, Sir Anthony Ashley Cooper (1621-1683), for religious reasons led the campaign to exclude the catholic James II from the throne in favour of the protestant Duke of Monmouth. Accused of treason he fled to Holland where he died in 1683, two years before Monmouth invaded. Two later

Winsley Hill from south-east of Limpley Stoke.

Earls of Shaftesbury attained eminence in other fields of activity. The 3rd Earl, Anthony Ashley Cooper (1671-1713) became after being driven by ill-health out of politics immensely influential upon the 18th century English landscape movement that is arguably the greatest English contribution to world art. By in the early-18th century suggesting, at the time when strict formality was the order of the day, that the sublime was the highest order of scenery he led the Georgian informal landscape movement and prophetically wrote: 'I shall no longer resist the passion growing in me for Things of a natural kind'. Much later the 7th Earl of Shaftesbury (1801-65) was the great Victorian philanthropist who devoted his life to promoting the welfare of working children. He forced through parliament the successive Factory Acts (1833-50) (as described earlier on page 267) and the Mines Act of 1842, and he also collaborated with Florence Nightingale in reforming nursing and army welfare. Andrew's and Dury's depiction on their 1773 map of a tree avenue running south-east from Little Ashley towards Bradford suggests that here was the site of a large house that was probably the home of the Ashley family, and the former existence of a chapel at Ashley is indicated by the field name Chapel Field where some burials were found in 1859.

The Winsley plateau offers much scope for wandering over its stone-walled landscape north-east of Winsley and centred on the two Ashley hamlets as in addition to being criss-crossed by dry-stone walls and by a network of narrow minor roads and public footpaths, the plateau is crossed by The Macmillan Way long distance path that passes a little east of the Ashleys on its way from South Wraxall and Great Cumberwell to Bradford and then along the valley of the Bristol Avon to Avoncliff.

About half a mile west of Winsley the delightful linear hillside village of Limpley Stoke (781607) extends for about half a mile along two parallel roads which run along the steep hill between the A36 Warminster to Bath road and the River Avon. The village enjoys fine views both down and across the valley of the Avon at a point where the river, the Kennet and Avon Canal, and the Great Western Railway all run along the valley bottom with Winsley Hill rising steeply to its east. Between the lower road and the river towards the north end of the village is a 17th century manor house with a Georgian front facing east across the river and a 17th century front to the road with stone mullioned and transomed cross-windows somewhat incongruously framed by classical stone bolection surrounds.

A fine grade of Bath freestone known as Stoke Ground was quarried at Limpley Stoke whose early name was Hanging Stoke from the hanging woods around this village. The word 'hanging' is not much used in Wiltshire place-names but is more common in Hampshire for a wood apparently 'hanging' on a steep slope, but the derivation of the first element of Limpley Stoke's unusual current name is obscure. The *Geological Survey of England and Wales* (1859) also shows a band of the Fuller's Earth that is often associated with limestone running across the Limpley Stoke parish. This material resembles clay, and its name arises from its being extensively used in the cloth industry by fullers for cleaning cloth and wool of grease and oil. Fuller's Earth occurs in only a few places in England and was regarded as so valuable that exporting it was prohibited.

Beside a footpath north of Chatleigh House (781614) in Limpley Stoke Wood is an ancient holy well known as Shingle Bell Well (779616), and further north of Limpley Stoke the A36 trunk road is carried over the valley of the Midford Brook by an eleven-arched brick-built viaduct (781619) over a hundred yards long and just within Wiltshire at the foot of Brassknocker Hill. This viaduct was disliked by the local people when it was built by a Mr David Aust in 1834, although like so much Victorian engineering it is in my view handsome and it dramatically enhances the the landscape.

Limpley Stoke's ancient little church of St Mary (783603) stands a little away from the village to its south-east towards Freshford, a fine stone-built former cloth-manufacturing village that is well worth straying the few yards over the county boundary into Somerset to visit. Upon entering Limpley Stoke church a tall narrow Saxon arch that has been incorporated into a much later nave arcade opposite the porch immediately reveals its extreme age. Professor Baldwin Brown considered this church to be basically Saxon and dating from the beginning of the 10th century, although its tower is later. Some huge stones, such as those in the west jamb of its door and the north-west corner of the tower, were used in the construction of this church that stands in a beautiful position and is well worth seeing for its unrestored

Saxon Arch in Limpley Stoke Church

beauty, its massive masonry, its stubby west tower surmounted by its short stone spire, and for the Saxon-Norman work in its interior.

At the east end of Limpley Stoke churchyard an elaborate stone monument surmounted by an urn commemorates the Daniell family of local clothiers one of whom, Mr J. C. Daniell (1783-1862), was an inventor who lived in the village and patented many textile and agricultural innovations and also took out a patent for 'Certain improvements applicable to stone-masonry'. From 'Winsley near Bradford, December 9, 1842' he wrote *An Address to the Agriculturalists of the United Kingdom* in which he described his experiments and promoted his patent manure and cattle-food.

The now largely lost Roman road from Bath (*Aquae Sulis*) to Poole ran through the salient of Wiltshire that extends west from the Winsley plateau towards Midford. This road crossed the west end of Limpley Stoke parish and probably diverged from its known line between near Tucking Mill (764617) and Midford Hill to cross Midford Brook near the

mill (762607). A little east of this diversion and a short distance south of the modern road from Midford to Limpley Stoke there was at Cleeve Rocks (at 772612) a Roman settlement. It was merely three miles from the centre of Roman Bath, and here were found Romano-British potsherds, a rotary quern, some Samian ware, and several Roman coins.

The 1940 Defensive Line along the River Avon

I N 1940 HITLER'S ARMY in a panzer 'blitzkrieg' drove through Belgium, overran northern France, and drove the British army to the Channel coast from where after suffering heavy losses of men and materials many of its personnel were successfully evacuated back to England from Dunkirk. In the retreat the British army lost most of its guns in France and in England the Chief of the Imperial General Staff General William Edmund ('Tiny') Ironside (1880-1959), faced with the prospect of imminent invasion, ordered the hurried construction of an

Limpley Stoke Church with Daniel Monument in foreground

inland anti-tank defensive line across southern England that was intended to defend London and the manufacturing areas of the Midlands. Ironside's plan was to hold mobile columns in reserve behind his defensive line while eight infantry divisions and the bulk of the available eight hundred field guns were deployed south of a line from Dorset to The Wash to oppose German landings on the beaches. Part of that inland defensive line that was constructed to be a second line of defence behind the fortified south coast beaches, ran along the River Avon from Freshford through Bradford to Semington.

General Ironside was in 1940 an elderly man who had served as a secret agent in German SW Africa during the Boer War. In the First World War he had displayed generalship of a high order but by 1940 he was rather old fashioned in his outlook and he had no experience of mobile tank warfare. Later in that year he was promoted to field-marshal and retired with a peerage as Baron Ironside. His defensive line included overall over seventy-five miles of anti-tank ditch, more than fifteen hundred pillboxes, and many road blocks formed of a combination of the large concrete cones known as 'dragons' teeth' and metal obstructions made from redundant tram lines. These augmented existing obstacles such as rivers, canals, and railway embankments. Some of the defensive pillboxes built along this line still exist. Although it is now often associated with the Home Guard this defensive line was intended to be held by the regular army,

These defences were completed within a few months during the summer of 1940. They extended across Somerset from near Burnham-on-Sea, entered Wiltshire at Freshford, and continued eastwards along the River Avon through Bradford on Avon and north of Trowbridge. From Staverton east of Bradford the Avon was followed as far as its junction with Semington Brook at Whaddon (882615), and from there the line was continued along Semington Brook to its junction with the Kennet and

Ironside's Defensive Line: the Avon west of Avoncliff, with pillbox left centre

Avon Canal (897609). The line then left the area covered by this book by following the canal for most of its course across Wiltshire and on to Reading where its total length amounted to about sixty miles. About a hundred and thirty of its pillboxes still survive, forty being the anti-tank type and ninety infantry pattern. These numbers reflect the current shortage of light artillery arising from the fact that the British Expeditionary Force had been obliged to abandon many of its guns and vehicles in France. Examples of the infantry pillboxes, that were designed to be manned by riflemen and Bren gunners, may be seen at various places along the Avon including one between Freshford and Avoncliff, a semi-concealed one beside Barton Bridge at Bradford, and an isolated one in an open field (at 883623) beside the river south of Monkton House near Broughton Gifford.

Pillbox west of Avoncliff

Only a few months after its construction the principle of the defensive line was dismissed as obsolete by General Alanbrooke (1883-1963) when he replaced Ironside as Commander-in-Chief Home Forces on 19 July 1940. Although he was only three years younger than his predecessor Alanbrooke had obtained first-hand experience of tank warfare when commanding the 2nd Corps of the British Expeditionary Force against the German panzer divisions in France. Because of his acute shortage of guns he believed that any attempt to be strong at every point could only result in weakness everywhere, and that any attempt to hold a thin extended line against a panzer 'blitzkrieg' would be a disastrous reversion to the obsolete static First World War philosophy of trench warfare. Convinced that mobile counter-attack was the only effective way to resist the panzers Alanbrooke wrote in his diary on 22 July 1940 three days after his appointment:

> I also discovered that much work and energy was being expended on an extensive system of rear defence comprising an anti-tank ditch and pill-boxes, running roughly parallel to the coast and situated well inland. This static rear line did not fall in with my conception . . . To start with, we had not got sufficient forces to man this line, even if we had wanted to do so. To my mind our defence should be of a far more mobile and offensive nature.

At a time of extreme national emergency immense expense and effort had been expended on a defensive measure that was regarded by the new commander-in-chief useless, but it was never put to the test because on 12 October 1940 all threat of invasion was in great secrecy postponed by the Germans.

The postponement was attributed by Churchill and by British public at the time to the success of the Royal Air Force in winning the Battle of Britain and preventing Goering's Luftwaffe from achieving aerial superiority. This was to a large extent true, but without wishing to in any way belittle the immense success and sacrifice of the young pilots of the greatly outnumbered fighter command, another factor influenced Hitler's decision not to invade. This was the threat that was posed to a cross-channel sea-born invasion force by the superiority of the traditionally all-powerful Royal Navy.

Napoleon had feared to embark the invasion force that he assembled across the Channel because of the looming presence of the British navy, and in 1940 the German navy had recently suffered heavy losses in the invasion of Norway. Documentary evidence confirms Hitler's anxiety about the threat that the Royal Navy posed to an invasion of England. On 11 July 1940 he told Admiral Raedar: 'The invasion of Britain is an exceptionally daring undertaking, because even if the way is short this is not just a river crossing, but the crossing of a sea that is dominated by the enemy'. He obviously feared that his invasion barges would have suffered grievously from the attentions of the undefeated allied navies, and contemporary German military opinion is also known to have held that view. Some modern military analysts believe that had the German army succeeded in landing on the south coast of England it could not have succeeded in reaching the inland defensive line along the Avon because the Royal Navy and the Royal Air Force would between them have so disrupted its cross-Channel supply lines that the German army would have been starved of vital ammunition and supplies. Hitler was also aware of this possibility as we know from him also telling Admiral Raedar: 'We cannot count on supplies of any kind being available to us in England'. Many Germans in authority at that time believed that Hitler never seriously intended to invade England and that he had had bluffed all along hoping to persuade Britain, a country that he greatly admired, into entering into a negotiated settlement with him.

The anti-tank ditches of Ironside's defensive line have now been filled in and its obstructive elements have now generally been removed, but its surviving pillboxes and conical tank obstructions known as 'dragons' teeth' are now justifiably recognised by the Council for British Archaeology to be historic monuments of the Second World War.

Suggested Walks in the Southern Wiltshire Cotswolds

Note: refer to General Notes relevant to all of the Suggested Walks in the General Introduction.

A: Bradford on Avon, Avoncliff, Winsley, and Great Ashley (5 miles)

This walks offers considerable variety being from a Medieval farm along a stretch of the Kennet and Avon Canal [186-90] to the interesting canalside hamlet of Avoncliff [264-9]. It then passes through

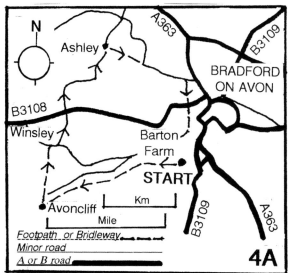

Turleigh [271] and the edge of Winsley, rises on to the limestone plateau NW of Bradford on Avon, and ends by descending through the historic town of Bradford on Avon [243-64]. It is largely over hard surfaces and is therefore particularly suitable after wet weather, but there are some hills including a short steep one from Avonclff to Turleigh a long uphill slope on to the plateau from Turleigh, and a descent through Bradford.
– Note: there are public houses on this wall at Bradford, Avoncliff, Winsley, and Uppe Bearfield.

PARK at the signposted Barton Farm Country Park (823604) [247-9] at the SW edge of Bradford.

1: Walk W for a mile along the Kennet and Avon Canal passing above a modern hedged maze planted beside the river in 2005 (at 814603) to Avoncliff [264-5].

2: Here the Old Court former workhouse [265-9] may be seen by taking a short diversion down the ram towards the public house and W under the aqueduct .

3: Return and walk N across the viaduct and at the small private car park above the railway halt a 804601 enter ahead the signed footpath through a small copse and follow a slight ridge diagonally N uphill towards a gap in a hedgerow. Ignore the gap and with the hedge on your right follow the hedgerow up the hill and at the end of a wall at 804604 turn right through a gate and follow a narrow lane a shor distance NE to a cluster of houses at a road at the S end of Turleigh (805604) [271].

4: Here turn left and walk N up this road for ¼ mile and at its end in Turleigh turn right, walk E for short distance through Turleigh, and at a tall narrow building on your left (806606) turn left and wal uphill up Ashley Lane for ½ mile skirting the edge of Winsley and crossing a minor road to the B3108 807614.

5: Cross the B3108 and take the right fork up the minor road to Great Ashley for a mile, first bearin right round a bend and then left around a corner.

6: At the cluster of houses at Great Ashley (813620) cross a stone slab stile on your right and walk S for ¼-mile along field footpaths along a hedgerow on your left and as you near its end at a large tre veer away right to a metal farm gate in a stone wall at the far corner of the field, pass through this ga to a bend in the road at 818619 and continue ESE past the Dog and Fox public house at 818617 along th road for about ¼ mile to Bearfield on the outskirts of Bradford.

7: Opposite an open space behind a wall on your left turn right through a narrow gap marked Huntingdc Street between cottages with rounded walls marked, walk S down the pedestrian lane between cast iro bollards, cross the B3108 Winsley Road (at 823613) and continue straight on down the lane marke Conigre Hill.

8: At a fork in the lane at the east end of Tory Rank turn right and proceed along Tory Rank to visit t Chapel of St Mary at its W end [254].

9: After returning a short distance E along Tory Rank turn right and descend Wellpath Hill to La Well [254], at the road at the bottom of the hill turn left and walk a very short distance E along Newtow then turn right and continue downhill to Barton Orchard [254].

10: From Barton Orchard there is a short option back to the start point by walking SW along Barton Orchard and then S across a railway crossing to Barton Farm, but in order to return through Bradford from the E end of Barton Orchard continue E downhill past Chantry House [253-4] and Orpin's House and grave [252-3] at the N edge of the churchyard, the Parish Church [251-2], and the Saxon Church [251], and along Church Street past the Church House to the bottom of Market Street.

11: There carefully cross the busy Market Street by the pedestrian crossing, turn left through The Shambles [251] and at its E end carefully cross the road, turn right past the roundabout and follow Silver Street SW across the Town Bridge [250] into St Margaret's Street.

12: Immediately after the traffic lights where the A363 swings left turn right behind Westbury House into the car park with its public toilets.

13: Walk diagonally left across the car park and at it far corner turn right at the W end of St Margaret's Hall and follow the riverside path [251] SW along the river, under the railway bridge, and so past Barton Bridge to Barton Farm [247-9].

4B: Broughton Gifford, Whaddon and Great Chalfield (6 miles)

This varied rural walk starts from Broughton Gifford [228-33], visits the remote hamlet of Whaddon [240-2], follows a stretch of the River Avon [236-9], and passes through Holt village [227-8] and N of the exquisite manor house group at Great Chalfield [222-5]. It should be noted that after rain the stretch from Whaddon to Staverton beside the Avon can be muddy after periods of heavy rain. If so it may be by-passed by following the canal towpath that runs a little to its south from S of Whaddon and joins the B3105 ½ mile from Staverton at 861602. Forewoods Common at Staverton is occasionally flooded after periods of heavy rainfall.

– Note: This walk is flat with no steep hills and there are public houses on it in Broughton Gifford, Staverton, and Holt.

PARK opposite the church at the south end of Broughton Gifford (878632) [228-33].

1: Follow the field footpath S across the B3107 at 881626 and the railway at 881624 and pass W of Monkton House [233].

2: Cross the River Avon [236-8] by the packhorse bridge at 882621 [237] and from the bridge turn right and follow the River Avon S passing a redundant railway line and crossing Semington Brook by a metal footbridge at 883616.

3: Walk SW up a slight slope to Whaddon Church [241-2] and there turn right and follow the footpath W for 1¼ miles, at first through the S edge of a farmyard, along the south bank of the Avon ultimately passing under the railway and along the the fence to a factory complex to the B3105 at Staverton.

4: Carefully follow the busy road for a short distance N and W across the road bridge over the Avon.

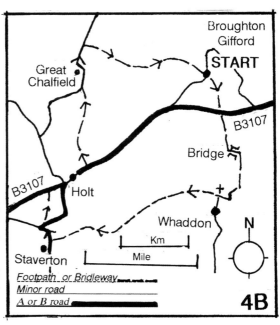

5: Because the B3106 road from this point to Holt is narrow, winding, hedge-lined, and lacks a footpath, it is hazardous to walkers and should be avoided. Therefore from the road junction immediately W of the bridge turn right at 855610 and follow the signposted footpath N from the junction across Forewoods Common passing W of Manor Farm to the B3107 at 856615.

6: From this point follow the B3107 E into the centre of Holt village at Ham Green.

7: In Holt [227-8] continue NE along the B3107 for about ¼ mile through the village past The Courts [228] and from 861618 near a church on your right take the lane N (left) that becomes a footpath across fields to Great Chalfield, and from 860628 follow the minor road N and NW past the N front of Great Chalfield manor house group (860633) [222].

8: From the manor house walk N for ¼ mile up the minor road with wide grass verges and at a stream at 861635 take the footpath E (right) and follow it for a mile across the fields, taking care not to depart too far from the stream on your right.

9: Continue E and swing slightly right towards the church tower of Broughton Gifford church which was the start point. Note the Cotswold stone-stile [230] into the churchyard.

4C: South Wraxall and Monkton Farleigh (4½ miles)

Two seldom-visited villages that are remote from A-roads are included on this rural walk, together with a fine manor house at South Wraxall [214-18]. There are no hills on this walk.

 – Note: there are public houses at South Wraxall and Monkton Farleigh.

PARK in South Wraxall village (833647) [214-18].

1: From the church [218] walk ½ mile SW passing right of the Long's Arms down a minor road to a T junction at 828643.

2: There turn right and walk for 1½ miles W along the road past Rushmead Farm and near Monkton Farleigh ignore the 'Kingsdown' turning on your right.

3: Walk clockwise round the village past the church [212] and at the public house on the corner (805654) turn right and walk N up a road to the corner at 806656. Note on your left across a field the conduit house [213] of the former priory (at 803656) [212-14].

4: This conduit house may be approached by taking a diversion W from the corner at 806656.

5: Return to this corner and continue along minor roads first E, then N and W to point 809658.

6: From there walk a short distance S down the road and opposite the manor house [213-14] and beside a cottage at 808655 turn left over a stile and walk for 1¼ miles E along the footpath down a tree avenue to a minor road beside some gates and piers at 829652.

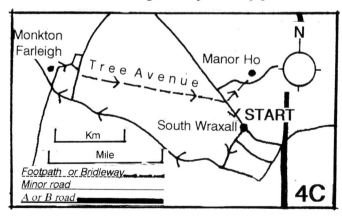

7: Cross the road and follow a footpath NE across fields to a road to view South Wraxall Manor House [214-17].

8: From the manor house it is according to the current definitive map possible to return to South Wraxall by walking S down a footpath, but at the time of writing some of the footpaths, although still officially signposted, have diversion or closure notices posted on them.

9: It may therefore be necessary to return to South Wraxall by returning to the gate piers at 829652 and walking for nearly ½ mile SE down the road back to the village.

4D: Corsham Court and Easton (3½ miles)

Starting from the historic small town of Corsham [201-5], this walk twice crosses Corsham Park [204] along different paths, and also visits two attractive hamlets east of Corsham. There are no hills.
– Note: the only public houses on this walk are at Corsham.

PARK in Corsham at one of the several car parks.

1: Walk E out of the High Street [201] passing S of the gate to Corsham Court [203-4] that is visible through the gateway [204].

2: Continue E along the outside of the S wall of the churchyard of the parish church (874706).

3: At the SE corner of the churchyard wall turn a little left and proceed NE beside a ditch and hedge on your left.

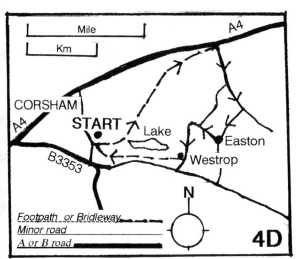

4: After passing left of the circular grove of trees at 882710, continue NE to a gate in a post and wire fence, go through the gate and pass through a linear wood crossing a rock bridge at 882714.

5: After swinging right and emerging from the N edge of the linear wood bear left away from the wood and continue NE to the A4 at 889719 Mynte Farm.

6: Pass through a pedestrian gate in a wall at 889719, turn right and walk S down the minor road past gate piers on your right at 891716.

7: Continue walking S, ignore the first unsigned road on your right, and at the next signposted road (894709) turn right and follow the road SW to Easton [206].

8: After passing between extensive stone farm buildings on either side of the road, at the S end of Easton take care not to miss the minor road on your right at 890706.

9: Follow this road first roughly W and then after bending left S to Westrop, there ignore the private drive by the letter box, and 150 yards S of the letter box at 885703 take the footpath on your right.

10: Follow this footpath W across a field and at 883703 re-enter Corsham Park through a gate.

11: Continue walking W a little S of the lake across Corsham Park back to Corsham Church.

Conclusion

I T IS APPROPRIATE that my account of the history and topography of the Wiltshire Cotswolds should have ended with a description of a feature that was constructed within the living memory of many people and within my own lifetime.

In this concluding chapter I have described the southern end of the Wiltshire Cotswolds and Bradford on Avon, a traditional limestone-built town containing many gabled houses with stone-mullioned windows and stone-slated roofs, with immediately to its north the wold-like plateau criss-crossed with Cotswold-style dry-stone walls around Winsley, Monkton Farleigh, South Wraxall, and Atworth. The landscape of this district, despite being distant from what is usually recognised as the Cotswolds, has many Cotswold characteristics and many of its places and buildings are practically indistinguishable from those of the Gloucestershire Cotswolds.

To me it is Cotswold – but it is Wiltshire Cotswold or, as Robin Tanner described it, 'a Wiltshire version of Cotswold . . . with a rough, earthy difference'.

Bibliography

THE COMPARATIVE LACK of published information about this region is demonstrated by the limited amount of material about it in the *Wiltshire Archaeological and Natural History Magazine*, and at the time of writing (2006) there is no *Victoria County History* for the much of the region, although the Malmesbury and the Bradford districts have been covered.

Many writers whom I have quoted have, together with the titles of their books and their dates of publication, been mentioned in the text, but the following is a select list of the principal sources consulted in the writing of this book:

Andrews, J. and Dury, A. *Map of Wiltshire 1773* (reprinted 1952).
Aubrey, J. *The Natural History of Wiltshire* (ed. Britton, 1847).
Aubrey, J. *Topographical Collections* (ed. Jackson, 1862).
Badeni, J. *Wiltshire Forefathers* (1959).
Grinsell, L. V. *The Archaeology of Wessex* (1958).
Heath, F. R. *The Little Guide to Wiltshire* (1949).
Hutton, E. *Highways and Byways in Wiltshire* (1917).
Huxley, E. *Gallipot Eyes* (1976).
Margary, I. D. *Roman Roads in Britain* (1955).
Massingham, H. J. *Cotswold Country* (1937).
Ordnance Survey First Edition (about 1820).
Pevsner, N. *The Buildings of England, Wiltshire* (1963).
Phillips, D. *The Great Road to Bath* (1983).
Tanner, R. and H. *Wiltshire Village* (1939).
Tanner, R. *Double Harness* (1987).
Victoria County History for Wiltshire, Volumes 7, Bradford area (1953) and 14, Malmesbury area (1991).
Walters, L. D. O.: *The Complete Guide to Wiltshire* (1920).
Wedlake, W. J. *Excavation of the Temple of Apollo at Nettleton, Wiltshire, 1956-7* (1982).
Wiltshire Archaeological and Natural History Magazine (100 volumes, 1854-2007, in progress).
Wiltshire Notes and Queries (8 volumes, 1893-1916).

Index of Persons and Places

FOR GENERAL SUBJECTS see the list of contents, pages iii-v. Page references in **bold** refer to illustrations. The introduction and the suggested walks appended to Chapters 2, 3 and 4 are not indexed

---

Other Books by Ken Watts

Published by Ex Libris Press

Exploring Historic Wiltshire, volume 1: North To be reprinted 2008, 176 pages paperback, ISBN 0-948578-85-8

Exploring Historic Wiltshire, volume 2: South, Reprinted 2001, 176 pages paperback, £7.95, ISBN 0-948578-92-0

The Marlborough Downs, New edition 2003, 192 pages paperback, £9.95, ISBN 1-903341-15-9

Published by Hobnob Press

Figures in a Wiltshire Scene: historical studies of people connected by birth, residence or particular empathy with Wiltshire, relating them to the places with which they are associated, viii, 280 pages, hardback edition 2002, £20.00, ISBN 0-946418-11-X; paperback edition 2006, £9.95, ISBN 0-94641834-9

To see a full list of titles currently in print published by Hobnob Press and Ex Libris Press visit www.hobnobpress.co.uk, or write to Hobnob Press, PO Box 1838, East Knoyle, Salisbury SP3 6FA